STRIKING BACK
MIDWAY AND GUADALCANAL 1942

American History Archives™

Striking Back
Midway and Guadalcanal 1942

5 6 7 8 9 10 / 17 16 15 14 13 12

ISBN 978 1 58159 298 6

The History Channel Club
c/o North American Membership Group
12301 Whitewater Drive
Minnetonka, MN 55343
www.thehistorychannelclub.com

Published by North American Membership Group under license from
Osprey Publishing, Ltd.

Previously published as Campaign 30: *Midway 1942* and Campaign 18:
Guadalcanal 1942 by Osprey Publishing, Midland House, West Way, Botley,
Oxford OX2 0PH, United Kingdom

OSPREY
PUBLISHING

© 2006 Osprey Publishing Ltd.

Editor: Lee Johnson
Cartography by Micromap
Bird's eye views by Peter Harper and Cilla Eurich
Index by: Alan Thatcher
Printed in China through World Print Ltd.

KEY TO MILITARY SYMBOLS

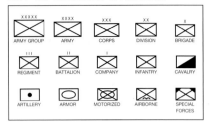

MARK HEALY was born in 1953. He has a Master's degree in
Political Theology from Bristol University. He is by profession
a schoolteacher and is head of the Humanities faculty in a
large school in Somerset. He has written a number of military
history books including *New Kingdom Egypt* and *Kursk 1943*.
He has a great interest in both the ancient and modern
periods, is married with one son and lives in Dorset, UK.

JOSEPH N MUELLER is a Lieutenant Colonel in the USMC
Reserve and the foremost expert on the Guadalcanal campaign.
He has had several articles and books published on the
subject, and maintains a massive collection of photos, written
material and equipment relevant to the battle. In recent years
he has made several trips to Guadalcanal and the surrounding
islands to study the battlefield first hand.

STRIKING BACK
Midway and Guadalcanal 1942

CONTENTS

INTRODUCTION

In early 1942, Japan's military might was at its zenith. The empire's brazen and successful surprise attack on Pearl Harbor on December 7, 1941, galvanized the Japanese appetite for territorial conquest. Little did they know, they had awakened the sleeping giant. In 1942 that giant sprung into action.

There was, of course, the Doolittle Raid. This daring bombing adventure over Tokyo brought respect back to America. It also sent Japan a painful message that the empire was not invincible, a message that became even clearer in the two critical Pacific campaigns of 1942.

Midway was one of the most important naval battles in history. Fought from June 3rd to June 5th, barely six months after Pearl Harbor, the United States dealt a devastating blow to the Imperial Japanese Fleet, sinking four of her most powerful carriers and setting the stage for the beginning of the empire's downfall. The Japanese notion of *Sekai Dai Ichi* ("First in the World") received a deep reality check.

Then, in August, fighting on land began. On what was a virtually unheard-of Pacific island, the U.S. shattered the myth of Japanese invincibility for good when U.S. Marines and Army halted the Japanese advance in its tracks. In five months of bitter fighting, the U.S. emerged victorious … and with a seasoned, battle-trained fighting corps that would go on to sweep the Japanese back across the Pacific, island by island.

In a big and successful way, *Striking Back* was crucial to freedom across the world. *Midway and Guadalcanal 1942* began that glorious march.

PART 1
MIDWAY

In the history of war there have been few military operations in which the trifling material damage inflicted on an enemy has been so totally outweighed by its attendant psychological impact, and the ensuing strategic consequences, as in the Doolittle raid on Japan on 18 April 1942. The audacity of the raid served to demonstrate that, in spite of the remarkable victories that had been achieved by the Imperial Army and Navy in South East Asia since the outbreak of war, the United States remained capable of striking at the heart of the Japanese empire, ridiculing the pretension that territorial conquest had in any way rendered the homeland inviolable.

The Japanese nation's outrage at the raid was compounded by the loss of face experienced by the Imperial Navy. It saw its ability to exercise responsibility for the defence of the seas around Japan, and thereby ensure the safety of the Emperor, impugned. These sentiments were echoed by Admiral Isoroku Yamamoto, Commander in Chief of the Combined Fleet, whose own concern to prevent Tokyo being attacked from the air verged on the obsessional. 'One has the embarrassing feeling of having been caught napping just when one was feeling confident and in charge of things,' he said. 'Even though there wasn't much damage, it is a disgrace that the skies of the Imperial capital should have been defiled without a single enemy plane being shot down.' More significantly, while the Japanese authorities outwardly ridiculed the attack as the 'do-nothing' or 'do-little' raid, the collective disquiet of the Naval General Staff and the planners of the Combined Fleet was sufficient to end their irresolution concerning the detailed timetable appending the decision to launch Operation MI.

On 5 May Admiral Osami Nagano, the Chief of the Naval General Staff, issued Imperial GHQ Naval Order No.18 instructing Yamamoto to 'carry

▶ Lieutenant Colonel James H. Doolittle poses for the camera with Marc Mitscher, captain of USS Hornet, shortly before the famous raid on Japan that bore his name. The raid was to have consequences far beyond the limited damage it inflicted on the targets struck in Japan. (US National Archives)

out the occupation of Midway Islands and key points in the western Aleutians'. One month later the Combined Fleet, convinced of certain victory, had put to sea the largest and most powerful naval force since Jutland. Nevertheless, it was to experience in the Battle of Midway a defeat so decisive as to doom itself and the cause of Imperial Japan to inevitable ruin. That such an outcome was even possible at a time when Japan's military success was at its zenith requires understanding of the strategic context governing decisions pertaining to future operations by the Combined Fleet in the months following Pearl Harbor. This, in turn, draws us to an appreciation of the central role in such planning played by Fleet Admiral Yamamoto, whose strategic perspective was fundamental in the provision of the rationale for, the planning of and execution of Operation MI.

Then What Will Come Next?

On the first day of 1942 Rear Admiral Matome Ugaki penned the following thoughts in his personal diary: 'It has been only twenty-five days since the war started, yet operations have been progressing smoothly and we have enough reason to hope for the completion of the first stage of the war before the end of March. Then what will come next?' That the Chief of Staff of the Combined Fleet could utter

Opposite page, top: The first of the 16 USAAF B-25 Mitchells start their engines as as the crews board their aircraft shortly before launching, 18 April, 1942. (US National Archives)

Opposite page, centre: Having been discovered by a Japanese picket vessel stationed to guard the western sea approaches to Japan, Admiral Halsey was forced to launch the Doolittle force at a range of 824 miles, rather than the intended 650 miles. The unforeseen benefit of this decision was that the

Doolittle force arrived over targets virtually unopposed by Japanese air or ground forces. (US National Archives)

Opposite page, bottom: 'Scratch one flat top'! In the battle of the Coral Sea in May 1942 the US Navy was able to sink the Japanese light carrier Shoho. In this photograph taken by a Yorktown aircraft it is possible to see a TBD that has just launched its torpedo on the extreme right of the picture. (US National Archives)

such a question less than a month after his nation had plunged headlong into war with the United States and Great Britain speaks volumes for the lack of any long-term strategic vision appending that decision. The absence of such was not surprising, given that the motivations governing Imperial Japan's choice of war in December 1941 to resolve its economic problems hardly rested on any rational appraisal of the actual or potential forces she had chosen to oppose. Indeed, the need to secure oil supplies had become so central in driving the formulation of Japan's initial war strategy, and the risks attendant upon its realisation so great, that little thought had been given by her strategists to what would follow, when and if success was achieved.

With a remarkable economy of force comprising 11 divisions, some 1,200 aircraft and most of the navy, in the 100 days following Pearl Harbor Japan proceeded to humble the military forces of the United States, Australia, the Netherlands and Great Britain. By the end of March, as Ugaki had predicted, the Japanese had essentially achieved their initial war aims of securing control over the oil supplies of the Dutch East Indies, and widening the defensive perimeter around the homeland. Furthermore, the material cost of achieving this had been extraordinarily low. Having allowed for fleet losses of at least 25 per cent, the Navy lost only 23 vessels amounting to barely 10 per cent of the anticipated figure. In the four months in which Japan's armed forces had run rampant across the western Pacific and South East Asia, she had shown that her soldiers, sailors, warships and aircraft were equal, if not superior, to those of her despised and supposedly superior enemies. Consequently, few in Japan or in the armed forces would have disputed the view expressed by Ugaki in his diary entry at the onset of the new year: '... the future is filled with brightness... The course of events during this year will determine the fate of the war, so we must work hard, exerting every effort. The main thing is to win, and we surely will win.' Translating these sentiments into reality was the task delegated to Ugaki by Admiral Yamamoto, when told to begin the planning of second-stage strategy immediately.

It was symptomatic of the relative ineffectualness of the Imperial General Headquarters (IGHQ), the body responsible for the formulation of the nation's

Operations AL and MI

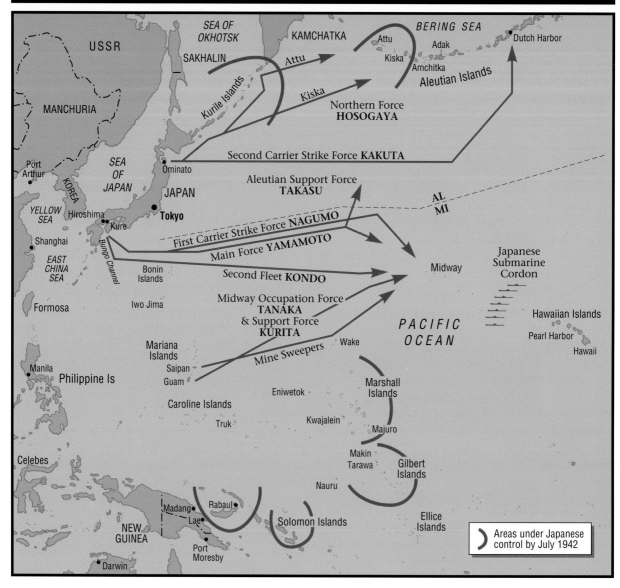

war strategy, that Admiral Yamamoto, as head of the Combined Fleet, could abrogate this major task to himself. However, although the IGHQ comprised the General Staffs of the Army and the Navy under the supreme command of the Emperor, it was rent by a rivalry that never allowed the emergence of a coherent strategy governing the operations of both services. In reality IGHQ presided over two essentially distinct strategy-making bodies. The army, as the senior of the two services, always perceived that its primary focus and Japan's true interests lay in China and the defence of Manchuria against a

greatly feared Soviet threat. This focus meant that its support for the 'southern' strategy, which drove the conflict started on 7 December 1941, was heavily conditional on the degree to which it served the army's interests in its primary theatre of operations in China, and on the limited number of army divisions it was grudgingly prepared to employ in support of essentially 'naval' operations in this new theatre of war. Compounding the army's relative indifference to strategic questions beyond its own sphere of interest was the decline in the influence of the Naval General Staff and its command over the

◄ This map illustrates the maximum expansion of Imperial Japan after Operations MI and AL and the decisive defeat suffered by the Combined Fleet (Rengo Kantai) in the Battle of Midway. As such it shows the only territorial acquisitions made as a consequence of that disastrous enterprise, the two remote Aleutian Islands of Attu and Kiska. Had Midway fallen then it, too, would have been added to the forward Eastern Pacific defence line running from the Aleutians through Midway, Wake Island, the Marshalls and the Gilbert Islands down to Port Moresby in New Guinea. Had the Japanese won the battle, then it is known that Yamamoto would have pressed the Imperial Government to proffer peace proposals to the United States. These would almost certainly have been based on their acquiesence to the territorial conquests made by Japan since December 1941 and in the permanency of the outer defence perimeter.

formulation of naval strategy, which passed in practice from itself to the planning staff of the Combined Fleet under Admiral Yamamoto.

In part, this arose from the dynamic and powerful personality of the Combined Fleet Commander, who held a low opinion of the abilities of his superior, the Chief of the Naval General Staff. Admiral Nagano rarely involved himself in the formulation of Naval Staff strategy. He tended to leave it to the younger officers of the Plans Division of the First Operations Section under the command of Rear Admiral Fukudome. Consequently his role increasingly became that of umpire when the views of Combined Fleet and his own Plans Division conflicted, as in the dispute before the Pearl Harbor Operation, which was strongly opposed by members of his own staff. Nagano had given final approval to Yamamoto's Pearl Harbor plan, even though it was in his domain to reject it, in spite of the latter's threat to resign unless the General Staff accepted it.

While this could be interpreted as acquiescence to blackmail, it was also deference on Nagano's part to one whose abilities he recognised as being indispensable to the Navy. In a most revealing observation it was said: 'Nagano had the utmost confidence in Yamamoto's abilities and judgement. He finally agreed because he knew Yamamoto was not bluffing. If this seems strange it must be remembered that Yamamoto's position and influence in the Japanese Navy were unique. He was in truth a leviathan among men.' Given the success of the Pearl Harbor attack, it is therefore not surprising that his prestige was now such that the formulation of strategy by the Combined Fleet's staff officers under Yamamoto's guidance was tacitly presumed and accepted.

This is not to suggest, however, that the Naval General Staff were simply prepared to acquiesce to Yamamoto designs. There remained in the Plans Division fertile minds who not only advocated their own strategy, but were prepared to fight their corner and, if necessary, oppose the demands of Yamamoto and his planning staff. Even so, as events were to show, it was a forlorn hope to believe that they could deflect the Combined Fleet commander from his chosen course once his mind was made up.

When Ugaki emerged from his cabin on 14 January to present the outcome of his deliberations, he prefaced his recommendations with the crucial observation that Japan could not afford to rest on its laurels by consolidating on its initial conquests. To do so would hand over the initiative for the offensive, allowing the United States to increase its strength while Japan waited passively for the Americans to attack. Under such circumstances the proven effectiveness and technical proficiency of the Imperial Navy would rapidly become a wasting asset. To capitalise on the strategic advantage created by the Combined Fleet in its initial war operations, it behove Japan to resume the offensive. Governed by this rationale, Ugaki evaluated a number of operational possibilities. He finally proposed that Japan should seize the islands of Midway, Johnston and Palmyra with a view to transforming them into advanced air bases before an invasion of Hawaii. He argued that such an operation was likely to precipitate that decisive battle with the US fleet that still lay at the core of Japanese naval strategy. His proposal was rejected by Captain Kuroshima, the Senior Fleet Operations Officer, because he doubted whether the US would risk their fleet to save these islands. He then proffered his own recommendation, shifting the strategic focus of the Combined Fleet westwards towards the Indian Ocean and an operation to seize Ceylon (Sri Lanka). Whilst accepting the critique of his own proposals and approving Kuroshima's, Ugaki insisted on the proviso that an Indian Ocean operation be carried out within the context of a joint Axis undertaking, with the Japanese second-stage offensive 'timed to synchronise with German Offensives in the Near and Middle East'. What might have constituted a major strategic opportunity came to nought, however, when the Germans made no offer of joint operations in the new Tripartite Axis military agreement signed on 19 December. Nevertheless, Combined Fleet continued to explore Kuroshima's proposal as a purely Japanese undertaking. Following war games on the new flagship *Yamato* in February, the western operation was adopted by the Naval General Staff as the official Naval proposal for phase two strategy. It was presented as such to a joint conference at IGHQ in mid March, only to be scuppered by the army when it became obvious that the operation depended upon the supply of more divisions for the amphibious assault on Ceylon.

Remaining committed to the need for offensive action, Combined Fleet cast around for an alternative plan. It returned to Ugaki's initial proposal for action in the eastern Pacific, reworked to exclude the possibility of an army veto. The plan now evolved dropped the ambitious suggestion to invade Hawaii, and required an invasion of the western Aleutians and Midway Island. Not least among the factors shaping Combined Fleet's decision by this time were the decidedly unwelcome, though tactically insignificant, US attacks on the Marshalls, Rabaul, Wake, eastern New Guinea and Marcus Island from February onwards. With the last-named island only 1,000 miles from Tokyo and within the outer ring of Japan's defences, the continued survival of the US carriers allowed the Americans the option of using them for a strike on the homeland. This prospect obsessed the deeply patriotic Yamamoto, and the continued operation of the US carriers threw into sharp focus the need to finish the work begun at Pearl Harbor by ensuring their belated destruction.

This was the rationale for the Midway operation, and it is known that, if it could be achieved, Yamamoto intended to use his undoubted prestige to press Japan's political leaders to make peace overtures to the Allies. Yamamoto believed that victory at Midway would provide him with a strategic edge that would allow Japan to negotiate from a position of strength, and thus force the enemy to come to

terms. He was ever conscious of the latent power of the United States and Japan's relative weakness, and his absolute commitment to the Midway offensive was governed by the overwhelming conviction that, unless victory could be realised quickly and when Japanese power was at its zenith, the alternative for his beloved country was defeat in a long war. There can be little wonder that, when faced with such awesome possibilities, he would brook no criticism or diversion from his chosen path.

The Naval General Staff had also been reviewing options following the army's veto on the Ceylon operation. From within the Plans Division there emerged the view that Combined Fleet and the army should concentrate on a major operation directed at Australia – the *Bei Go Shaden Sakusen*. This proposal was predicated on the assumption that Australia was the logical base for an Allied counteroffensive in the south seas. As such it would become the recipient of vast quantities of Allied and particularly American armaments as their forces built up their strength. To negate this potential threat to Japan's southern flank required either that parts of Australia should be occupied, or, at least, that steps be taken to isolate the subcontinent from the USA. As the former possibility depended on the army stumping up the necessary divisions for the operation, it is not surprising that it, too, went the way of the Ceylon proposal. Even so, the Naval General Staff believed there was sufficient merit in the second proposal for it to proceed to formulate a more limited operation designed to isolate Australia by extending Japanese control over eastern New Guinea and the Solomon Islands. The Naval General Staff proceeded to organise the necessary forces to launch an amphibious operation, code-named MO, to occupy the island of Tulagi in the Solomons and, more importantly, to seize Port Moresby on the southeastern coast of New Guinea. To the naval forces earmarked for this operation Yamamoto added Carrier Division 5, comprising the new fleet carriers *Shokaku* and *Zuikaku*, believing that the Americans would deploy a carrier Task Force to oppose the Japanese. As events were to show, Yamamoto was proffering a hostage to fortune, as the initial planning for the Midway operation presumed that these two vessels would be available to serve with the Nagumo force.

By the end of March the Combined Fleet plan for the Midway campaign was complete and had been presented to the Naval General Staff on 2 April by Yamamoto's loyal and trusted aides, Captains Watanabe and Kuroshima. Over the next three days there was much heated and fervent discussion as these two officers debated the merit of the Midway operation with those in the Plans Division of the General Staff who opposed it. Matters came to a head on 5 April, when Watanabe restated Yamamoto's unambiguous support for the Midway operation by echoing his master's voice: 'In the last analysis, the success or failure of our entire strategy in the Pacific will be determined by whether or not we succeed in destroying the United States Fleet, particularly its aircraft carriers... We believe that by launching the proposed operations against Midway we can succeed in drawing out the enemy's carrier fleet and destroying it in decisive battle. If, on the other hand, the enemy should avoid our challenge, we shall still realise an important gain by advancing our defensive perimeter to Midway and the western Aleutians without obstruction.'

To emphasise his unwillingness to compromise, Yamamoto once again played his resignation gambit. In the face of Yamamoto's resolute stand, Rear Admiral Fukudome expressed the view: 'If the C in C is so set on it, shall we leave it to him?'. Nagano raised no objection, instructing a shift of resources to the Midway operation. Once the plan was adopted by the Naval General Staff the army, given how few troops it would be required to allocate, was more than happy to endorse Operations MI and AL, as the Midway and Aleutian offensives now became known, and thus also passed IGHQ scrutiny on the nod. There now only remained the debate concerning the details of the operation, with Combined Fleet wishing for the earliest practicable date and the Naval General Staff wishing for a delay. So matters continued until 18 April, when Jimmy Doolittle's B-25s roared over Tokyo, bringing further discussion to a rapid conclusion.

Victory Disease

It is apparent that, by this time, Japanese thinking had become afflicted by a canker 'so great that its effects may be found on every level of the planning and execution of the Midway Operation', and which was to have a profound impact on the outcome of

▼ *Sailors aboard one of the heavy cruisers of the screening force of TF-17 observe the evacuation of the crew of the listing and burning carrier USS Lexington in the Coral Sea on 7 May 1942. Hit by bombs and torpedoes, the Lexington was later to founder following a series of massive internal explosions. Nevertheless, the US Navy had realised a strategic victory by halting the Combined Fleet's attempt to capture Port Moresby in New Guinea. It was the first time that a Japanese offensive had been stopped. (via Robert F. Dorr)*

the battle. The emergence of what later became diagnosed as 'victory disease' had its origins in the unique quasi-mythological view the Japanese had of themselves and their nation, which they believed was destined to become *Sekai Dai Ichi*, or 'First in the World'. The Japanese saw in the invulnerability of their sacred homeland evidence of their undisputed military effectiveness. Significantly, this and her successes in conflicts before the outbreak of the Pacific War were explained away in Japan less by reference to material and technical factors than by stressing the moral dimension in war. This engendered a mindset wherein it was believed that the *Nihon Seishin* – the innate Japanese spirit – would allow the nation to triumph over any enemy.

For a Japan imbued with the martial virtues of the Samurai tradition, the denigration of the United States as weak, decadent and effete convinced many that there was little to fear in taking on this great western power. This flawed perception of the United States fostered a profound underestimation of the immense military, industrial and, indeed, moral potential of that nation which in the longer term was to prove fatal for Japan. In the immediate circumstance, however, the remarkable victories of the opening four months of the Pacific War served only to compound the arrogant attitude of the Japanese towards their enemies, and 'by the time of the Midway battle this arrogance had reached a point where it permeated the thinking and actions of officers and men in the fighting services'.

Directly arising from this, and affecting the highest echelons of the Navy, including Yamamoto himself, was the *idée fixe* that the Japanese possessed the undoubted initiative in the forthcoming operation. In consequence it was presumed, to the point that it became an article of faith, that the US Fleet would put to sea only subsequent to the invasion and occupation of Midway. The notion that their carriers might be at sea awaiting the Japanese Fleet, although recognised as a possibility, defied credulity. Indeed, when such a possibility was broached during the Midway war games held on the *Yamato* between 1–4 May to explore the coming battle, the consequences of such an eventuality were dismissed in a remarkably cavalier fashion.

Fuchida and Okumiya related how, when asked to explain how the First Carrier Striking Force would

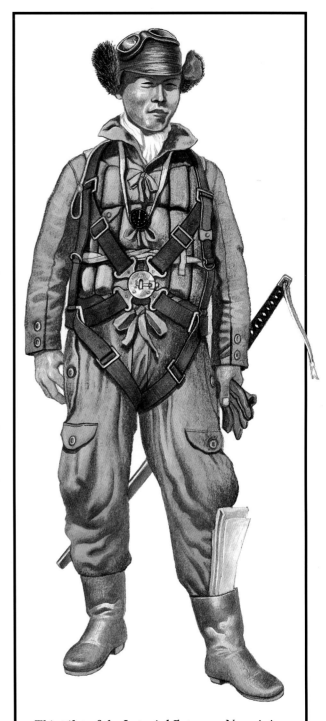

This pilot of the Imperial Japanese Navy is in summer flying gear, wearing a fur-lined leather flying helmet, one-piece green cotton flying suit and leather flying boots. White silk scarves were common among pilots. Officers of the rank of lieutenant commander or higher carried their swords in action. Illustration by Chris Warner.

deal with such an eventuality, Minoru Genda, the normally highly astute and level-headed aviation specialist, replied in such a vague fashion as to imply that there existed no plan to deal with such a contingency. Although Rear Admiral Ugaki remonstrated over the matter, he nevertheless revealed his own inner certainty of victory when, later in the games, he arbitrarily overturned the decision of the umpire who had ruled that the carriers *Kaga* and *Akagi* were sunk, so that only the former was despatched while the latter emerged from battle with only light damage. Furthermore, as the games led on to explore the post-Midway operations, *Kaga* was miraculously resurrected from its watery grave! Other examples of this overweening optimism included the seaplane squadron that sent a remarkably careless signal to the effect that it wished all mail to be forwarded to Midway from mid-June. Possibly the most extreme example of this attitude was evidenced in a statement by a spokesman for the Naval General Staff, who contemptuously stated: 'What we are most concerned about is that the enemy will be loath to meet our fleet and will refuse to come out from his base'.

Final Preparations

Against this backdrop, preparations for the Midway and subsidiary Aleutians operations gained strength as April turned to May. The First Air Fleet had returned to Japan from their Indian Ocean venture on 22 April to hear of the first news of MI and begin refurbishment and training for the operation. They were but four warships in an immense fleet of nearly 200 vessels assembled by Yamamoto for the Midway operation. By the mid-month, however, as the cost of the Battle of the Coral Sea became apparent, Nagumo knew that he would be taking two fewer fleet carriers with him to Midway than originally intended. For, notwithstanding the great victory trumpeted by the Japanese media, the carrier *Shokaku* had been so severely damaged that her repairs would take many months to complete, and her sister ship *Zuikaku* had lost so many of her aircrew that she could not take part in MI because of a lack of replacements.

Although the Japanese regarded the setback of their naval assault on Port Moresby as a short-term

frustration, their compensation lay in the conviction that they had imposed heavy losses on the Allied Task Forces. Certain enemy losses proclaimed by the home media included a Saratoga-class carrier (in reality the *Lexington*) and the USS *Yorktown*. The latter, left sinking and later presumed sunk, was removed from Japan's estimate of the US Navy's order of battle, but was to reappear barely a month later to make a significant contribution to the outcome of the Battle of Midway.

Matters now began to move more quickly as the different elements in the great plan started to move in accordance with the complex timetable. On 21 May Yamamoto led the battleships of his Main Body, Nagumo's four fleet carriers and Kondo's Second Fleet, to sea to begin two days of what would prove to be the final fleet manoeuvres ever staged by the Combined Fleet. Final war games held on the *Yamato* on 24 May, rehearsing both the Midway and the Aleutians offensives, showed that operations would proceed smoothly. On the same day the Midway invasion group of transports carrying the army assault troops of Colonel Kiyonao Ichicki rendezvoused at Saipan with the heavy cruisers of Rear Admiral Kurita's Support Force. The forces earmarked for the AL operation made their way to the Ominato naval base in Northern Honshu before sortieing on 28 May.

All was now ready for the departure of the largest assemblage of vessels ever seen in the Pacific. For those aboard the many ships of the armada there was little doubt of the momentous nature of the occasion. Shortly after 0800 on the morning of 28 May the *Akagi* struck the signal flag ordering the First Air Fleet to up anchor and sortie as planned. To the accompaniment of the cheers and the myriad waving caps of the crews of the battleships of Yamamoto's Main Body, the 21 warships wound their way in line ahead through the Bungo Channel and out into the open sea. No better insight into the sense of invincibility now pervading the Nagumo Force can be offered than the final intelligence assessment which the commanding admiral presented to his crews as they were preparing to close on Midway Island some days later:

'The enemy is unaware of our presence in this area and will remain so until after our initial attacks on the island'.

THE US PREPARATIONS

Yamamoto and Nagumo were sure that they would achieve tactical if not strategic surprise, but they would not have been so sanguine had they known that the Americans had wind of the Midway operation as early as the beginning of April. Although there were suspicions, it was only after the war that the Japanese would discover for certain that Operation MI had been fatally compromised as a consequence of a remarkable American intelligence coup that gave them detailed knowledge of the Japanese plan.

While many other factors were to come into play before victory was delivered to the Americans at Midway, none ranks so high as the breaking of JN25, the Japanese Navy's current operational code. Although this was a remarkable achievement, the code was not understood in its entirety. Nevertheless, sufficient phrases could be read to allow Commander Joseph Rochefort, commander of the Navy Combat Intelligence Office outstation on Hawaii (known as 'Hypo'), to inform Fleet Admiral Chester Nimitz that the Japanese were preparing a very large operation which he was convinced was directed at Midway. Although the intelligence was initially ambiguous enough to allow for other interpretations of Japanese intentions, Nimitz was sufficiently convinced of the case presented by Rochefort to start planning on the basis that Midway was the Japanese target. He had already learned to value Rochefort's judgement, having won his spurs in April, when, on the basis of his existing intelligence, he had forecast the Japanese operation to take Port Moresby. By acting on this and other intelligence sources, Nimitz had despatched Task Forces 11 and 17 which, for the loss of the *Lexington*, stopped the southwards advance of the Combined Fleet.

On 2 May Nimitz made an inspection tour of Midway Island. Although at this juncture he did not enlighten either Lieutenant Commander Shannon and Commander Cyril Simmard, the two senior officers in command there, as to his suspicions, he did ascertain from them what would be needed to hold off a major amphibious assault. On his return to Pearl Harbor he penned them a letter to the effect that the Japanese intended to launch a major attack on Midway Island on or about 28 May. Subsequently manpower and air power on the atoll base was increased to a level that Shannon believed suf-

▲ *Commander Joseph Rochefort was to provide the Americans with an invaluable intelligence coup when he and his SIGINT team on Hawaii cracked the essentials of the Japanese Navy code* *JN25. It was this breakthrough that was to lead the American Naval historian Samuel Morison subsequently to label Midway as 'a victory of intelligence'. (US Navy)*

ficient to hold out against any amphibious assault. Within a few days, however, Nimitz was presented with vital intelligence which established beyond doubt that Midway, and not Hawaii or the eastern coast of the United States, was the objective of the coming Japanese offensive. He was thus able to declare, on 14 May, a state of 'fleet opposed invasion' for the Hawaii area including Midway. Once again it was 'Hypo' and the resourceful Commander Rochefort who provided him with confirming evidence of enemy intentions.

The clinch came as the result of a ruse by Rochefort. In their inter-base communications the Japanese used code letters to designate what were clearly locations, but which code for which location? From other information appended to the code it was inferred that the use of 'AL', for instance, was a reference to the Aleutians, but 'AF' was less certain, although Rochefort was sure it was Midway. To flush out the Japanese, Rochefort secured permission from Nimitz for a message to be sent in plain English from Midway, reporting that there was a water shortage on the island.

As the island lacked any natural water supply, its occupants were dependent upon a water filtration plant that was reported as having blown up. The request for fresh water to be delivered by tanker would thus ring true to Japanese eavesdroppers, for whose benefit the false message was despatched. Two days later, on 12 May, the Hypo team were rewarded by the Japanese broadcasting to their own fleet commanders that 'AF is short of water'. Notwithstanding the niggles that continued to come from Admiral King in Washington concerning the likely target of the Japanese attack, Nimitz was now convinced beyond any doubt that Midway was truly the objective of Yamamoto's massive enterprise. He proceeded to harness his own limited air and naval assets to frustrate Japanese intentions.

On 15 May Vice Admiral William Halsey, commander of Task Force 16 comprising the carriers *Enterprise* and *Hornet*, was recalled by Nimitz to Pearl Harbor from the vicinity of the Solomon Islands, where he had arrived too late to take part in the Coral Sea battle. Nimitz had intended to give command of the Midway Task Force to Halsey, but on the latter's return to Pearl on the 26th it was clear that his very poor physical condition pre-

cluded this. A chronic skin complaint diagnosed as 'general dermatitis' denied a deeply disappointed Halsey the opportunity to take his 'major crack at the Japs'. However, he served Nimitz and his country proud when he unhesitatingly recommended that his replacement be Rear Admiral Raymond A. Spruance. Although he was not an airman, both Halsey and Nimitz held the man in very high regard, and neither had any compunction about placing Task Force 16 in his hands.

In his initial briefing with him, Nimitz told Spruance that he would need to sortie on the 28th, as some days earlier Rochefort and his Hypo team had informed him of the coming Midway offensive and stated that the Japanese had postponed D-Day until 3 June at the earliest. This was only part of a much larger message that Hypo had deciphered just before the Japanese changed the JN25 code, which revealed itself to be nothing more than the principal details of their order of battle for the coming operation. In consequence Nimitz was able to tell Spruance more or less exactly what he was up against, and the general direction from which the Japanese carriers would be approaching Midway. Nimitz was thus in a position to present to Spruance his operational plan for the Task Forces 16 and 17, predicated on the intelligence provided by Hypo.

The following day Nimitz also met with Rear Admiral Frank Fletcher, who had just brought the heavily damaged *Yorktown* limping back into Pearl. Without revealing his sources, Nimitz informed him of the Japanese intention to seize Midway Island and said that they would be employing at least four carriers and many supporting vessels in the operation organised into Nagumo's carrier strike force, a support force and the invasion force. Nimitz then told Fletcher that he would be putting to sea again in the *Yorktown* within a few days to join up with Spruance to the northeast of Midway Island, whereupon he would assume tactical command of Task Forces 16 and 17.

However, this presupposed that the *Yorktown* would be sufficiently repaired to be able to sortie on time. Many who surveyed her damage doubted that it could be done. Estimates of time needed for repairs ranged from a pessimistic three months to Fletcher's own more optimistic prediction of a fortnight. If the latter figure was correct, *Yorktown* would not be available for the coming battle and Spruance would face Nagumo with two, rather than three, carriers – not a wide enough margin to encourage hopes of success.

In a remarkable demonstration of American improvisation the carrier was taken into dry dock, where some 1,400 dockyard workers descended upon the vessel en masse and set to preparing her for for sea, working round the clock. To the sound

▶ *Such was the damage inflicted on the USS* Yorktown *in the Battle of the Coral Sea that the Imperial Navy presumed her sunk. Limping back to Pearl Harbor on 27 May she was placed in Dry Dock No.1 and returned to service within a remarkable 48 hours. Although her many repairs were temporary at best, her presence at Midway was to prove decisive. (via Roger Chesneau)*

This Marine Corps pilot wears the A-4 summer flying suit and A-8 summer helmet. He is also sporting a Navy-issue shoulder holster, worn here slung at the hip. Illustration by Chris Warner.

of pneumatic hammers and by the light of welder's torches the *Yorktown*'s hull was patched up and her damaged compartments strengthened with timbers. Few of the watertight doors worked owing to frames being buckled by Japanese bomb damage, but on Saturday 29 May – the day after Spruance had sailed with Task Force 16 – Fletcher put to sea in the *Yorktown*. Her hastily assembled air group comprised squadrons from no fewer than three carriers.

Along with her escorts, the heavy cruisers *Astoria* and *Portland* and the six destroyers of DesRon 2, the *Yorktown* moved north from Oahu at a stately 27kts, the highest speed her damaged engines could produce, to rendezvous with *Enterprise* and *Hornet*. Barring any unforeseen eventuality, Fletcher felt confident he could satisfy Nimitz's heartfelt exhortation that Task Forces 16 and 17 rendezvous to the northeast of Midway on time.

THE OPPOSING PLANS

The Japanese Plan

The aims governing Operations AL and MI were twofold. First, to establish a new forward defence line running from the Aleutians through Midway, Wake Island, the Marshalls, the Gilbert Islands and the southern Solomons to Port Moresby, and, secondly and more importantly, to effect the destruction of the remaining surface units of the US Fleet in that 'decisive fleet engagement in the Pacific', or *Kassen Kantai*, so dear to the hearts of Japanese Naval strategists. This was to be precipitated by the invasion and occupation of the island of Midway, a base the Japanese believed to be of such strategic importance to the US Navy that it would be forced to sortie from Hawaii with the remaining warships of the Pacific Fleet to challenge Japan's occupation of it. Certain of realising at least tactical surprise and disposing of an overwhelming superiority in warships, Combined Fleet was confident of a decisive victory in the naval battle that would follow.

To achieve this end, Combined Fleet had formulated a complex and critically timed plan involving a two-pronged offensive. The execution of the different phases of both offensives turned on 7 June, designated as N-Day (the Japanese equivalent of the US D-Day). This had been chosen by Combined Fleet as the earliest practicable date that would allow the Nagumo Fleet to recuperate following its return to Japan from its Indian Ocean operation, as well as being last the day in June when there would be sufficient moonlight to allow an amphibious landing on Midway Island at night.

The first and lesser of the two offensives, codenamed AL, was a diversionary operation against the Aleutian islands in the Northern Pacific. The brief given to Vice Admiral Hosogaya for AL required the neutralisation of US air power at Dutch Harbour beginning on 3 June, three days before N-Day, followed by the occupation over a succession of days

of the islands of Adak, Kiska and Attu through to 12 June. Forces allocated to AL included Northern Force Main Body, the Second Carrier Striking Force, the Attu and Kiska Invasion Forces and a submarine unit detached to assist the Aleutians operation. In addition, Combined Fleet had allocated, as a detachment from Yamamoto's Main Body, a screening force of battleships for the Aleutian operation under the command of Vice Admiral Takasu. Whereas the latter would sortie from the main Fleet anchorage in Hashirajima Bay along with the rest of the Main Body under Yamamoto on 29 May, the others would depart from the Ominato Naval Base in northern Honshu a day earlier.

The MI operation fell into two distinct phases, with the participating fleet elements all playing their role according to a very tightly orchestrated timetable. Phase 1 involved the occupation of Midway Island itself on N-Day. Thereafter, it was presumed that the disposition of the Fleet would be such as to place the Japanese in the most advantageous position to effect the destruction of the US Fleet elements that were bound to sortie once news of Midway's fall reached Hawaii. The very large number of vessels employed in this operation, coupled with the need to ensure surprise, led to a wide dispersal of the forces involved.

The plan made provision for the assault on Midway to be initiated by Admiral Nagumo's First Carrier Air Fleet on 5 June, N minus 2. Approaching from the northwest, his four carriers were to launch their aircraft some 250 miles from Midway and then proceed to attack the atoll base, eliminating enemy air power on the island and softening up the defences in readiness for the landings. Having fulfilled this task, Nagumo's carriers would then be free to tackle the US carriers and other vessels it was presumed would sortie from Pearl Harbor following the fall of Midway. Provision of air support for the actual landings on 7 June was to be provided by 'Rufe' floatplane fighters of Rear Admiral Fujita's Seaplane Tender Group who, on N minus 1, would seize the island of Kure barely 60 miles from Midway as a forward operating base. This was but the prelude to the amphibious landings to be made at dawn on 7 June by the Midway Invasion Force, which was coming up on the island from the south and carrying the army's only contribution to the offensive, in the form of the Ichicki detachment. The plan allowed for the discovery by the Americans of Tanaka's invasion force on 6 June (D-1), so that they would be led to believe that the main Japanese attack was coming from the south. The landings on Sand Island and Eastern Island would be given close support by the 8in gun batteries of Vice Admiral Kurita's four heavy cruisers. Lying further to the south and protecting the flank of the invasion force would be Kondo's Main Body.

By N-Day Admiral Yamamoto's Main Body, comprising the Combined Fleet's most powerful battleships and including the flagship *Yamato* (and

of whose presence the US Navy was unaware of until after the battle), would lie some 500 miles to the northwest of the island, along with other fleet elements already mentioned, ready to initiate the most important phase of Operation MI. This would occur when long-range air reconnaissance and the two submarine cordons stationed between Hawaii and Midway, planned to be on station on 2 June, informed Yamamoto that the US Fleet had sortied from Pearl. Rapidly concentrating his widely dispersed forces Yamamoto would then force the 'decisive battle' on the US Fleet, from which the Japanese had no doubt they would emerge victorious, the *coup de grâce* being delivered by the heavy guns of the battleships. There were those among the Japanese, however, who expressed concern over the very tight timetable imposed on Nagumo's carriers. They believed that it placed a potentially dead hand on his freedom of movement by requiring him to reconcile two opposing objectives: destruction of Midway's air power and the defeat of the US carri-

▶ *The flagship of Nagumo's First Air Fleet for Operation MI was the venerable* Akagi *('Red Castle'). Originally designed as an* Amagi-*class battlecruiser she was converted following the Washington Naval Treaty to an aircraft carrier. She was launched in April 1925 with three flight decks forward. (via Roger Chesneau)*

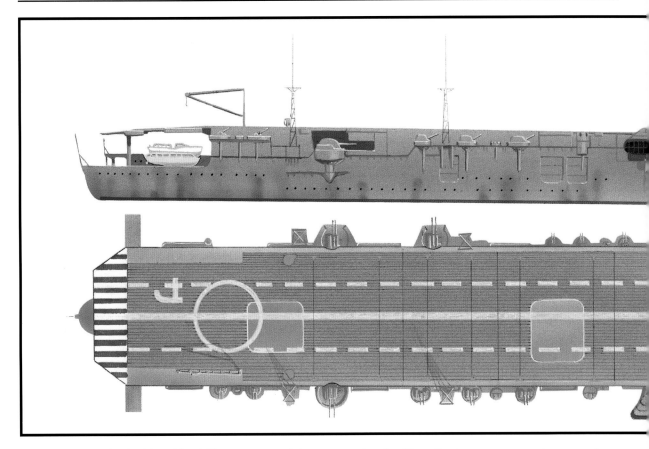

ers, thus severely limiting his ability to respond in the face of an unexpected contingency. However, this was a minority view, and the prevailing sentiment was that all would be well, provided the US Navy responded exactly as the Japanese predicted.

A Profound Failure of Intelligence

Given the poverty of Combined Fleet's knowledge of the whereabouts of the US Pacific Fleet, the presumed certainty of its position and reaction contained within this rigid plan is quite remarkable. In the end it was to prove to be its undoing. Indeed, the last reliable sighting of US warships had occurred as far back as 18 May, when a number were spotted from the air to the east of the Solomon Islands. The estimate of US strength that Yamamoto had issued on 20 May, covering the the Aleutians, Hawaii and Midway, although not accurate, did draw attention to the strength of the Midway defences, reinforcing the necessity for heavy air attacks to be launched on 5 June from Nagumo's carriers. He estimated the strength of US Fleet

assets in the Hawaii area as two or three carriers, two or three escort carriers, four or five heavy cruisers, three or four light cruisers and about 30 destroyers and 25 submarines.

To illustrate the paucity of real knowledge of the position of the US Fleet, the Naval General Staff in Tokyo was of the opinion that a US Carrier Task Force was operating far to the south in the Solomons, providing evidence to their mind that the Americans were unaware of Japanese intentions. Yamamoto's own attempts to acquire more definitive intelligence about the shipping at Pearl came to nought when planned overflights of the Harbor by two Kawanishi H8K 'Emily' flying boats between 31 May and 3 June were cancelled because submarine I-123 reported that US ships were patrolling their designated mid-flight refuelling stop at the French Frigate Shoals. Nor did the submarine cordons have better luck. By the time they came on station, which was two days later than the planned D minus 5, Spruance had already passed by some days before, and *Yorktown* slipped through the cordon without detection.

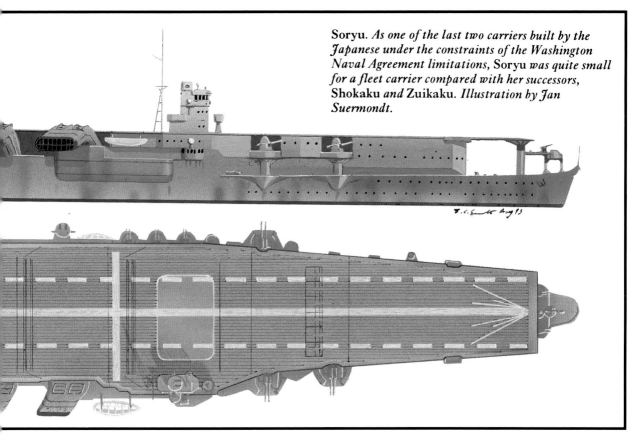

Soryu. *As one of the last two carriers built by the Japanese under the constraints of the Washington Naval Agreement limitations,* Soryu *was quite small for a fleet carrier compared with her successors,* Shokaku *and* Zuikaku. *Illustration by Jan Suermondt.*

Nevertheless, the Japanese did have indications that all might not be as they believed. On 1 June Ugaki observed in his diary: 'Out of 180 radio exchanges observed in the Hawaii district, as many as seventy-two were tagged "urgent". We believe that the enemy are preparing to meet us, after having strongly suspected our movement.' This vital information was denied to Nagumo by the erroneous belief of those on board *Yamato* that this radio traffic must surely have been picked up on *Akagi*, and that Nagumo would, in consequence, take appropriate action. (This position was adhered to in spite of their knowledge that *Akagi*'s radio facilities were deficient. As it was, the American radio traffic was not picked up on the *Akagi*.) On this presumption it was argued there was no need to break the blanket radio silence Yamamoto had imposed upon the operation before the landings. For that same reason an updated and highly revealing message sent by the Naval General Staff on 2 June, speculating about the possible presence of a US carrier force in the eastern Midway area lying in wait to ambush the advancing Japanese, was not passed on to Nagumo. Deprived of the information that could have significantly changed the outcome of the events now about to unfold, Nagumo continued to plunge towards Midway, in possession of an intelligence picture almost as impenetrable as the fog banks through which his carriers were now moving.

The American Plan

The plan that Nimitz presented to Spruance and Fletcher on 27 May had been formulated on the presumed accuracy of the most up-to-date intelligence picture of Japanese intentions and dispositions. Nimitz had already decided that the Aleutian operation was a diversion, but had nevertheless despatched Task Force 8 under Rear Admiral Theobald to the Aleutians with five cruisers and ten destroyers – the most he could spare.

Midway figured prominently in Nimitz's planning by functioning as a fourth, unsinkable, aircraft carrier. While total airpower on the island was raised to 115 aircraft of differing types, by 3 June Nimitz was fully aware that the relative obsolescence of many of

JAPANESE ORDER OF BATTLE FOR OPERATIONS AL AND MI

COMBINED FLEET
Admiral Isoroku Yamamoto in Fleet Flagship *Yamato*.

OPERATION AL

(A) NORTHERN (Aleutians) FORCE (Fifth Fleet):
Vice Admiral Moshiro Hosogaya in CA *Nachi*.
Main Body: Vice Admiral Moshiro Hosogaya in CA *Nachi*.
Screening Force: DD Inazuma: Commander Hajime
Takeuchi DD *Ikazuchi*.
Supply Group: 2 Oilers, 3 Cargo Ships.

(B)SECOND CARRIER STRIKING FORCE:
Rear Admiral Kakuji Kakuta
CARRIER GROUP (CARDIV 4): Rear Admiral Kakuji
Kakuta
CVL *Ryujo*: Captain Tadeo Kato
Air Unit: Lt Masayuki Yamagami
Air Component: 16 Zero A6M2 Type 21: Lt Koboyashi.
21 B5N2: Lt Yamagami.
CV *Junyo*: Captain Shizue Isii
Air Unit: Lt Yoshio Shiga
Air Component: 24 Zero A6M2 Type 21: Lt Shiga.
21 D3A1: Lt Abe.
Support Group: 2nd Section CruDiv 4: Capt Shunsaku
Nabeshima in CA *Maya*.
CA *Takao*.
Screening Group: DesDiv 7: Capt Kaname Konishi
3 DDs: *Akebono, Ushio, Sazanami.*
1 Oiler.

(C)ALEUTIAN SUPPORT FORCE:
Vice Admiral Shiro Takasu in BB *Hyuga* (flagship).
Battleship Group: *Hyuga, Ise, Fuso, Yamashiro*.
Screening Force:CruDiv 9: CL *Kitikami* (flagship), CL *Oi*.
DesDiv 20: 4 DDs: *Asagiri, Yugiri, Shirakumo, Amagiri*.
DesDiv 24: 4 DDs: *Umikaze, Yamakaze, Kawakaze,
Suzukaze*.
DesDiv 27: 4 DDs: *Ariake, Yugure, Shigure, Shiratsuyu*.
Supply Group: 2 Oilers.

(D)ATTU INVASION FORCE:
Rear Admiral Sentaro Omori in CL *Abukuma*.
DesDiv 21: 4 DDs: *Wakaba, Nenohi, Hatsuharu, Hatsushimo*.
1 Minelayer.
1 Transport.

(E)KISKA INVASION FORCE:
Captain Takeji Ono in CL *Kiso*.
CruDiv 21: 2 CLs: *Kiso, Tama*.
1 Auxiliary Cruiser.
Screening Force: DesDiv 6: 3 DDs: *Hibiki, Akatsuki, Hokaze*.
Transports: *Hakusan Maru* (carrying 550 troops), *Kumagawa
Maru*.
Minesweeper Div 13: 3 Minesweepers
Submarine Detachment: 6 Submarines: *I-9, I-15, I-17, I-19,
I-25, I-26*.

OPERATION MI

(F) MAIN FORCE (FIRST FLEET):
Admiral Isoroku Yamamoto in BB *Yamato*.
Main Body: Admiral Yamamoto
Battleship Group: BatDiv 1: Admiral Yamamoto in *Yamato,
Nagato, Mutsu*.
Carrier Group: *Hosho* carrying 8 B5N1 and B5N2.
DD *Yukaze*.
Special Force: *Chiyoda, Nisshin* (although seaplane carriers,
these two vessels carried only midget submarines for this
operation).
Screening Force: DesRon 3: Rear Admiral Shintaro
Hashimoto in CL *Sendai* (Flagship).
DesDiv 11: 4 DDs: *Fubuki, Shirayuki, Hatsuyuki, Murakamo*.
DesDiv 19: 4 DDs: *Isonami, Uranami, Shikinami, Ayanami*.
Supply Group: 2 Oilers.

(G) FIRST CARRIER STRIKING FORCE:
(First Air Fleet) Vice Admiral Nagumo.
Carrier Division (CarDiv 1): Vice Admiral Nagumo in CV
Akagi.
Akagi (CV): Captain Taijiro Aoki.
Air Unit: Commander Mitsuo Fuchida.
Air Component: 21 Zero A6M2 type 21: Lt Commander
Itaya.
21 D3A1: Lt Commander Chihaya.
21 B5N2: Lt Commander Murata.
Kaga (CV): Captain Jisaku Okada.
Air Unit: Lt Commander Tadashi Kusumi
Air Component: 21 Zero A6M2 Type 21: Lt Sato.
21 D3A1: Lt Ogawa.
30 B5N2s: Lt Kitajima.
Carrier Division 2 (Cardiv 2): Rear Admiral Tamon Yama-
guchi in CV *Hiryu*.
Hiryu (CV): Captain Tomeo Kaku.
Air Unit: Lt Joichi Tomonaga.
Air Component: 21 Zero A6M2 Type 21: Lt Mori.
21 D3A1: Lt Kobayashi.
21 B5N2: Lt Kikuchi
Soryu (CV): Captain Ryusaku Yanagimoto
Air Unit: Lt Commander Takashige Egusa.
Air Component: 21 A6M2 Zero Type 21: Lt Suganami.
21 D3A1: Lt Ikeda.
21 B5N2: Lt Abe.
2 D4Y1.
Support Group: Rear Admiral Hiroaki Abe in CA *Tone*.
CRUDIV 8: Rear Admiral Abe.
CA *Tone* and CA *Chikuma*.
2ND SECTION, BATDIV3: BB *Haruna*,
BB *Kirishima*.
Screening Force: DesRon 10: Rear Admiral Kimura in CL
Nagara.
DesDiv 4: 4 DDs: *Nowaki, Arashi, Hagikaze, Maikaze*.

DesDiv 10: 3 DDs: *Kazagumo, Yugumo, Makigumo*.
DesDiv 17: 4 DDs: *Urakaze, Isokaze, Tanikaze, Hamakaze*.
Supply Group: 1 DD: *Akigumo*.
5 Oilers.

MIDWAY INVASION FORCE (SECOND FLEET):
Vice Admiral Nobutake in CA *Atago*.

(H) SECOND FLEET MAIN BODY:
Vice Admiral Kondo.
CRUDIV 4 (less 2nd Section): CA *Atago*, CA *Chokai*.
CRUDIV 5: CA *Myoko*, CA *Haguro*.
BATDIV 3 (less 2nd Section): BB *Kongo*, BB *Hiei*.
Screening Force: DesRon 4: Rear Admiral Nishimura in
CL *Yura*.
DesDiv 2: 4 DDs: *Murusame, Samidare, Harusame, Yudachi*.
DesDiv 9: 3 DDs: *Asagumo, Minegumo,
Natsugumo*.
Carrier Group: Captain Sueo Obayashi
Zuiho: Captain Obayashi.
Air Component: 12 A6M2 Zero Type 21: Lt Hidaka.
12 B5N2: Lt Matsuo.
1 DD: *Mikazuki*.
Supply Group: 4 Oilers
1 Repair ship.

MIDWAY OCCUPATION FORCE:
Rear Admiral Raizo Tanaka
12 Transport vessels,
3 Patrol Boats
(These vessels were carrying approx 5,000 troops. Capt
Ota (Navy) commanded the 2nd Special Naval Landing
Force and the Army detachment under Col Kiyonao Ichiki.)
1 Oiler.
Escort Force: Rear Admiral Tanaka in CL *Jintsu*.
DesDiv 15: 2 DDs: *Kuroshio, Oyashio*.
DesDiv 16: 4 DDs: *Yukikaze, Amatsukaze, Tokitsukaze, Hat-
sukaze*.
DesDiv 18: 4 DDs: *Shiranuhi, Kasumi, Arare, Kagero*.
Seaplane Tender Group: Rear Admiral Ruitaro Fujita in CVS
Chitose.
Seaplane Tender Div 11: CVS *Chitose*.
Air Component: 16 A6M2 -N 'Rufe' floatplane fighters.
4 scout aeroplanes.
AV *Kamikawa Maru*.
8 A6M-2N 'Rufe' floatplane fighters.
4 scout aeroplanes.
1 DD *Hayashio*.
1 Patrol boat.

(J) MIDWAY SUPPORT FORCE:
Vice Admiral Takeo Kurita in CA *Kumano*.
CRUDIV 7: Vice Admiral Kurita.
4 CAs *Kumano, Suzuya, Mogami, Mikuma*.
DesDiv 8: 2 DDs: *Asashio, Arashio*.
1 Oiler.

(K)MINESWEEPER GROUP:
Capt Sadatomo Miyamoto.
4 Minesweepers.
3 Subchasers.
1 Supply ship.
2 Cargo ships.

ADVANCE (Submarine) FORCE (Sixth Fleet):
Vice Admiral Teruhisa Komatsu, in *Katori* at Kwajalein.
SubRon 3: Rear Admiral Chimaki Kono
Rio de Janeiro (flagship at Kwajalein)
(L & M) SUBDIV 19: Capt Ryojiro Ono
I-156, I-157, I-158, I-159.
SUBDIV 30: Capt Maseo Teraoka
I-162, I-165, I-166.
SUBDIV 13: Capt Takeharu Miyazaki
I-121, I-122, I-123.

SHORE BASED AIR FORCE (Eleventh Air Fleet):
Vice Admiral Nishizo Tsukahara (at Tinian)
Midway Expeditionary Force: Capt Morita
36 'Zero' fighters.
10 'Betty' bombers at Wake.
6 flying boats at Jaluit.
24th Air Flotilla: Rear Admiral Maeda
Chitose Air Group at Kwajalein
36 'Zero' fighters.
36 B5N2s.
1st Air Group at Aur and Wotje
36 'Zero' fighters.
36 B5N2s.
14th Air Group
36 H6K Flying boats at Jaluit and Wotje.

these precluded any possibility of preventing repeated raids on the atoll base by Nagumo's aircraft. Under such circumstances he recognised that the only way Midway could maximise the limited capabilities of the airpower it possessed would be to 'inflict prompt and early damage to Jap carrier flight decks', in the hope of catching their aircraft before they took off. He therefore instructed the air commander that the fighters on Midway should be employed to escort the bombers and not to defend the airbase. That task should be left to the anti-aircraft guns. He also expected that the long-range air

US FORCES ORDER OF BATTLE FOR THE MIDWAY CAMPAIGN

US PACIFIC FLEET AND PACIFIC OCEAN AREAS

Admiral Chester W. Nimitz

CARRIER STRIKING FORCE:

Rear Admiral Frank Fletcher

Task Force 17: Rear Admiral Frank Fletcher.
TG 17.5 Carrier Group : Capt Elliot Buckmaster.
Yorktown (CV): Capt. Elliot Buckmaster.
Air Component: VF-3: 25 F4F-4 Wildcat.
VB-3: 18 SBD-3 Dauntless.
VS-3: 19 SBD-3 Dauntless.
VT-3: 13 TBD-1 Devastator.
TG 17.2 Cruiser Group : Rear Admiral William Smith in CA *Astoria*.
CA *Astoria*, CA *Portland*.
TG 17.4 Destroyer Group: Capt Gilbert C. Hoover (ComDesRon 2)

6 DDs: *Hamman, Hughes, Morris, Anderson, Russell, Gwin*.

Task Force 16: Rear Admiral Raymond Spruance.
TG 16.5 Carrier Group : Capt George D. Murray.
Enterprise (CV): Capt George D. Murray.
Air Component : VF-6: 27 F4F-4 Wildcats.
VB-6: 19 SBD-2 & 3 Dauntless.
VS-6: 19 SBD-2 & 3 Dauntless.
VT-6: 14 TBD-1 Devastator.
Hornet (CV) : Captain Marc A. Mitscher.
Air Component : VF-8: 27 F4F-4 Wildcat.
VB-8: 19 SBD-2 & 3 Dauntless.
VS-8: 19 SBD-1, 2 & 3 Dauntless
VT-8: 15 TBD-1 Devastator.
TG 16.2 Cruiser Group : Rear Admiral Thomas C. Kinkaid (ComCruDiv 6).
CA *New Orleans*, CA *Minneapolis*.
TG 16.4 Dest Screen : Capt Alexander R. Early (ComDesRon 1)

patrols flown by PBY-5As from the island, beginning as early as 22 May, would serve as the eyes of Midway and of the Carrier Task Forces, and that first contact with the approaching Japanese forces would be made by them.

However, with the exception of Shannon, Simard and a few other higher ranks, Nimitz had not revealed that the efforts of the defending Midway forces would be supported by the Navy's carriers. There was no attempt to co-ordinate the efforts of

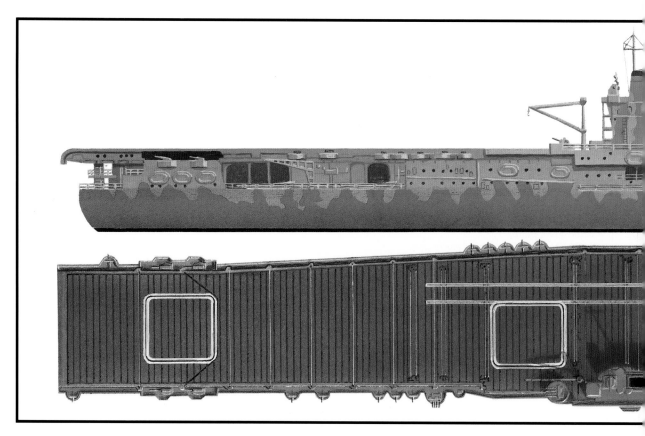

9 DDs: *Phelps, Worden, Monaghan, Aylwin, Balch, Conyngham, Benham, Ellet, Maury.*
Oiler Group : *Cimmarron, Platte.*
2 DDs: *Dewey, Monssen.*

SUBMARINES

Rear Admiral Robert H. English, Comm Sub Force, Pacific Fleet at Pearl Harbor (Operational Control).
TG. 7.1 : Midway Patrol Group 12 subs: *Cachalot,*
Flying Fish, Tambor, Trout, Grayling, Nautilus, Grouper, Dolphin, Gato, Cuttlefish, Gudgeon, Grenadier.
TG. 7.2 : 'Roving Short Stop' Group: 3 subs: *Narwhal, Plunger, Trigger.*
TG 7.3 : North of Oahu Patrol Group: 4 subs: *Tarpon, Pike, Finback, Growler.*

MIDWAY BASED AIR

Capt Cyril T. Simard.
Detachments of Patrol Wings 1 & 2.
38 PBY-5 and PBY-5A Catalina.

VT-8 detachment: 6 TBF-1.
Marine Air Group 22, 2nd Marine Air Wing: Lt Ira L. Kimes.
VMF 221: 20 F2A-3 Buffalo, 7 F4F-3 Wildcat.
VMSB: 11 SB2U-3 Vindicator, 16 SBD Dauntless.
Detachment of 7th USAAF: Major Gen Willis P. Hale
4 B-26, 19 B-17E.

MIDWAY LOCAL DEFENCES

6th Marine Defense Battalion.
Fleet Marine Force: Col Harold D. Shannon.
MTB Squadron 1.
8 PT Boats at Midway: 2 at Kure Island.
4 small patrol craft deployed in area.
2 tenders, 1 DD at French Frigate Shoals.
1 Oiler, 1 converted yacht.
1 minesweeper at Pearl and Hermes reef.
2 converted tuna boats at Lisianski, Gardner Pinnacles, Laysan and Necker.
Midway Relief Fueling Unit: 1 oiler 2 DDs.

Army, Navy and Marine air units on Midway itself, or to co-ordinate them with the Navy forces at sea. Indeed, Navy pilots on the island were told quite specifically that the carriers' first priority was to protect Pearl Harbor, inferring their absence from Midway's defence when the Japanese attacked. Nothing could be permitted that would in any way compromise the absolute secrecy of the presence of the carriers to the northeast of Midway Island, for Nimitz was depending on the aircraft spotted on

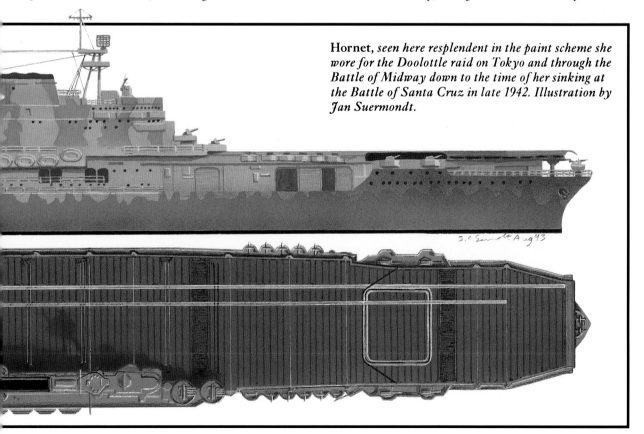

Hornet, *seen here resplendent in the paint scheme she wore for the Doolottle raid on Tokyo and through the Battle of Midway down to the time of her sinking at the Battle of Santa Cruz in late 1942. Illustration by Jan Suermondt.*

Japanese Battleships in Operation MI

Name	Displacement	Armament	Armour	Completed	Fate
Yamato	72,800 tons	9 x 18.1in 12 x 6.1in 12 x 5in AA	400mm belt 500/650mm turrets 200mm decks	Dec 1941	Sunk April 1945
Nagato	34,100 tons	8 x 16in 18 x 5.5in 8 x 5in AA	100/300mm belt	Nov 1920	Expended 1946 in Bikini Atoll bomb tests
Mutsu	34,100 tons	8 x 16in 18 x 5.5in 8 x 5in AA 4 x 533mm torpedo tubes.	356mm turrets Up to 75mm decks	Oct 1921	Accidental internal explosion, 1943
Kirishima	27,500 tons	8 x 14in 14 x 6in 8 x 5in AA	76/203mm belt	Apr 1915	Sunk 1942 off Guadalcanal
Haruna	27,500 tons	8 x 14in 14 x 6in 8 x 5in AA	229mm turrets	Apr 1915	Sunk July 1945

their decks for a successful outcome in the days ahead. For added security Nimitz pulled back some 19 submarines from their offensive duties, and for the duration of the battle allocated 16 of them the defensive task of screening Midway. Another four covered Oahu, leaving three available on call.

The principal target of US action, however, was beyond dispute. It was Nagumo's four carriers, known to be approaching Midway from the northwest. Nimitz pronounced to Fletcher and Spruance that, in seeking their destruction, it was absolutely vital for the US carriers to achieve surprise by hitting them first and from the flank.

The overwhelming Japanese material superiority over the US Navy precluded any option other than a savage and devastating hit-and-run strike. Because surprise and speed were the essence of his plan, Nimitz had consciously eschewed the employment of the slow battleships of Task Force One based in San Francisco.

Given how few were the naval assets now possessed by the US Navy in the Pacific, the option of a drawn-out battle of attrition was not a possibility. If Fletcher and Spruance failed and the US carriers were sunk, the whole of the Pacific and the eastern seaboard of the United States would lay open to the Japanese. Nimitz could not fail to impress upon his subordinates that their actions, in the light of these facts, must be guided by 'the principle of calculated risk'. Fletcher and Spruance were to engage only if they had a good chance of inflicting disproportionate damage on the Japanese. Despite the remarkable intelligence provided by Hypo, Nimitz knew that the operation they had embarked upon was a very great gamble. A great deal could go wrong; certainly the battle was not in the bag. Little wonder, then, that he named the rendezvous point of the three US carriers at 32 degrees north latitude, 173 degrees west longitude and 325 miles to the northeast of Midway 'Point Luck'.

THE OPPOSING COMMANDERS

Japanese Commanders

Admiral Isoroku Yamamoto emerges from any account of the Midway operation as the central and supreme moving force on the Japanese side. It has already been shown how this arose as a consequence of his dominance within the Combined Fleet and over the senior officers of the Naval General Staff. In reality the Midway plan was his, and when it failed and failed totally, he made no attempt to shift the blame to a convenient scapegoat. Post-battle analysis by the Japanese was to reveal a host of shortcomings regarding the operation, but strangely enough these seem never to have coloured their own assessment of Admiral Yamamoto as a military commander of the first order.

Perhaps the key to the failure of Operation MI lies in the temperament of the Combined Fleet Commander. A patriot to his fingertips, he was nevertheless all too aware that Japan's Pacific War was, above all, a reckless gamble. As an inveterate gambler himself, whether at poker or *shogi*, he had perhaps persuaded himself that the only possibility for his homeland's survival lay in an operation in which everything had to be staked on one card. This might

explain not only his almost pathological insistence on the speed with which MI was carried out, but also the reckless commitment of resources to the vast Midway enterprise without a detailed, up-to-the-minute intelligence appraisal of the strength and disposition of the US Fleet. Without doubt, his unwillingness to brook any opposition to Operation MI was driven as much by his own awareness of America's inevitable recovery as it was by his very genuine sense of failure, perhaps even of personal dishonour, in having allowed the Emperor's person to have been threatened by the Doolittle Raid.

► *Admiral Isoroku Yamamoto, Commander in Chief of the Combined Fleet, architect of the Pearl Harbor attack and prime mover behind the calamitous Operation MI. Venerated by the officers and men of the Rengo Kantai, he could trace his career back to service with Admiral Togo at the battle of Tsushima in 1905. After Midway he continued to serve as Fleet Commander until his death on 18 April 1943 when he fell victim to a long-range aerial ambush staged by US P-38 Lightning fighters while undertaking an inspection tour of South Seas bases. He was posthumously promoted to the rank of full Fleet Admiral. (US National Archives)*

His great reputation, particularly in Japan, rests on the claim that he was a pioneer in the development of naval air power. While it is true that he did oversee a major expansion of this arm of the *Rengo Kantai*, there are more than a few pointers in the period between Pearl Harbor and the execution of Operation MI to suggest that, at a more fundamental level, he had not grasped the full implications of the truly radical change that air power had wrought on naval warfare. This can perhaps be inferred from his readiness to comply with the 'breaking up' of the First Air Fleet following the Pearl Harbor attack, as if he were unaware of the revolutionary nature of that unique formation. It is also implicit in the highly convoluted nature of the plan for Operation MI, which turned on the denouement of the US Pacific Fleet in the *Kantai Kessen*, wherein the ruin of American warships would be brought about not by the aircraft of Nagumo's carriers, but by the 16in and 18in guns of Yamamoto's inappropriately named 'Main Body' of battleships. Clearly, the carriers were seen to have a vital role, but as understudies to the battlewagons.

Additionally, the dispersion of the very large number of warships assembled for MI, whilst ostensibly serving the need for surprise and security, actually contributed to the very dissipation of the mass required for the decisive battle. Vital assets like the carriers *Ryujo* and *Junyo* were wasted in the diversionary Aleutians operation which failed totally in its purpose. The dispersion also deprived Nagumo's carriers of the myriad anti-aircraft batteries aboard the many cruisers and battleships that would have greatly assisted the flat-tops in fighting off the US air attacks. Such a proposal, to reorganise the Combined Fleet around three carrier groups in a manner analogous to the US Navy Task Forces, was argued for by Vice Admiral Tamon Yamaguchi in the wake of the Coral Sea Battle, but was not acted upon in time for Midway. To have acceded to this position would have marked the final subservience of the battleship to naval air power in the *Rengo Kantai*. However, it was to take the shattering defeat at Midway for the big-gun capital ship advocates to accept that change. Comment has also often been made on the dead hand placed on MI, once it

Far left: Vice Admiral Chuichi Nagumo commanded the First Air Fleet at Pearl Harbor and at Midway. A man out of place in Naval Aviation, of which he knew virtually nothing, he has been castigated for command failures in both operations. After Midway he continued to command carriers, but was dismissed after the Battle of Santa Cruz in October 1942. As commander of the forces on Saipan he committed suicide when the island was overrun by US forces in 1944. (US National Archives)

Left: Admiral Osami Nagano, who, as Chief of the Naval General Staff, sanctioned Yamamoto's plans for the Pearl Harbor attack and the Midway operation. On both occa-

sions his decision was encouraged by Yamamoto's threat to resign as Fleet Commander unless his plans for both operations were endorsed.

Right: Rear Admiral Tamon Yamaguchi was one of the most air-minded of Japanese admirals. Like Yamamoto, Yamaguchi had served as naval attache in Washington, and had attended Princeton University. Highly regarded by the Fleet Commander he took command of the Second Carrier Division in November 1940 and led it in the attacks on Pearl Harbor and at Midway where he chose to go down with his flagship, the carrier Hiryu at Midway on 5 June.

The Aichi D3A 'Val' equipped the dive-bombing squadrons of the Rengo Kantai from the time of Pearl Harbor through Midway and beyond. However, by 1943/4 excessive losses of experienced aircrew and technical obsolescence made it a declining asset. (Pilot Press copyright drawing)

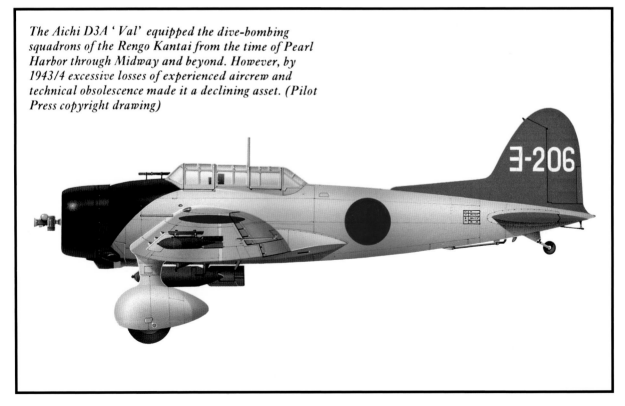

had begun, by Yamamoto's anachronistic decision to go to sea himself. He should have stayed at Hashirajima, as Nimitz did at Oahu, so that he could marshal and command his forces in response to intelligence. Once at sea, as we shall observe shortly, the very radio silence he imposed on the fleet to ensure tactical surprise was also imposed on himself, totally negating any value in his presence at sea.

Much more questionable, particularly when it was within his power to do something about it, was Yamamoto's continued retention of Vice Admiral Chuichi Nagumo as commander of the First Air Fleet. There can be no doubting the excellent service record of this torpedo specialist who had commanded cruisers and battleships, but his appointment to command this formation was a most unlikely choice, given his complete lack of experience with naval air power. Indeed, it was said of him by a close service colleague that he had no real conception of the power or potentialities of the naval air arm. His appointment was not by design, but was the consequence of seniority and protocol which required his filling the post when it fell vacant. Although Yamamoto expressed a degree of unhappiness about Nagumo's performance at Pearl Harbor, he was not prepared to replace him because it is said that he feared Nagumo would take his loss of command as a personal dishonour and commit suicide.

Nonetheless, Nagumo was undoubtedly the most successful carrier admiral in the world at the time of the Midway battle. Besides Pearl Harbor, Nagumo's carriers had rampaged through the south seas and the Indian Ocean, and the sense of invincibility engendered by these victories certainly put Nagumo in a most optimistic state of mind on the eve of Midway. Even so, he was to make a number of major errors in the battle, such as the inadequate air search procedures that, in hindsight, were not insignificant in bringing about the Japanese defeat, even though such decisions appeared both logical and sound at the time.

United States Commanders

There is a real sense in which the main US commanders in the battle revealed a degree of profes-

sional realism and obectivity that sets them apart from their Japanese counterparts. Without doubt the most remarkable was Fleet Admiral Chester Nimitz. Once he had taken on the mantle of Commander in Chief Pacific Fleet, his personable style of man management rapidly raised morale in the wake of Pearl Harbor. The preparation for Midway showed his remarkable gift for trusting colleagues to employ their expertise and then to act upon their ideas when he was convinced they were right. In particular, his willingness to take seriously the views and judgements of Commander Rochefort, and to trust them even when his own superior, Admiral King, did not, was absolutely crucial. His deployment of his own limited naval assets was based on his conviction that Rochefort's intelligence was accurate. Admiral King certainly fretted over Nimitz's judgements concerning Japan's likely

Left: Chester William Nimitz was appointed Commander in Chief of the US Pacific Fleet (CINCPAC) on 31 December 1941, taking over from the dismissed Admiral Kimmel. Within weeks of his appointment he had transformed morale in the fleet. His decision to act on the intelligence provided by Hypo, and in consequence garner his limited naval assets and employ them to defeat Nagumo's carriers, made him the real architect of the American victory. Following Midway he became Commander in Chief Central Pacific Area, wherein he shared responsibility with Douglas MacArthur for prosecution of the Pacific War. In 1944 he was promoted to Fleet Admiral, and in September 1945 he was among the Allied team that accepted the Japanese surrender aboard the USS Missouri *in Tokyo Bay. (US National Archives)*

Above: Rear Admiral Frank 'Blackjack' Fletcher was the commander of the US naval forces at the Coral Sea, and of Task Forces 16 and 17 during the Battle of Midway. Although victor in both battles, he was regarded as an overly cautious carrier commander, illustrated by his handling of the battles around Guadalcanal in August 1942, which was regarded as lacklustre. (US National Archives)

Right: When appointed to replace the unwell Halsey as commander of Task Force 16, Rear Admiral Raymond A. Spruance had no experience as a carrier commander. However, he had a remarkably flexible and adaptable intellect and incisive but balanced judgement, which made his appointment most apposite for the particular conditions of Midway. He was in many senses the 'right man for the right job'. Although unknown to the Japanese before the battle, he was to establish himself from June 1942 onwards as one of the foremost commanders of US Naval forces in the Pacific War. (US National Archives)

intentions before Midway. He was acutely aware that his Pacific admiral was in a position analogous to that of Jellicoe at Jutland, as being the 'only man who could lose the war in an afternoon'. However, the fate of the US Navy could not have been in better hands.

Chester Nimitz never ceased to pay tribute to the crucial role played in the battle by Rear Admiral Raymond Spruance, frequently stating that it was he who was really responsible for the victory at Midway. Given that Spruance was not a carrier admiral and had only been drafted in at the last moment because of 'Bull' Halsey's dermatitis, this is high praise indeed. Some have rated Spruance's appointment as Nimitz's most important command decision of the battle. While he never denigrated Halsey's own particular leadership skills, Nimitz insisted that Spruance's analytical intellect and calm and collective disposition made him absolutely right for the peculiar conditions of the Midway battle. In later years Nimitz, reflecting upon the happy role played by fate in causing Spruance to be appointed to the command of Task Force 16, said: 'It was a great day for the Navy when Bill Halsey had to enter the hospital'. Although he always consciously eschewed the publicity that Halsey loved, Spruance

generated a reputation that, in the end, was totally grounded on his professionalism. However, he was never in any doubt as to where the credit for Midway lay. He laid it firmly at the feet of Nimitz as the one who had the courage to accept the intelligence picture and act upon it.

Although Admiral Frank Fletcher played a crucial part in the victory of Midway, he tends to stand in the shadows of his nominal subordinate Raymond Spruance and his superior Admiral Nimitz. His performance in the Coral Sea exposed him to criticism, but he incorporated his experiences of that battle into his tactics at Midway. Of particular importance was his decision to separate the two Task Groups, so that they would not provide the Japanese with one target had all three carriers operated in close proximity.

The consequences of operating thus was to become abundantly clear to the Japanese before very long. Furthermore, letting Spruance lead off against the Japanese carriers on 4 June inevitably meant that he would acquire the kudos for delivering the first blow. That he knowingly sacrificed this personal prestige for the sake of operational effectiveness has been held by many to be the measure of the man.

The courageous fight put up by US Marine pilots in Brewster F2 Buffaloes – obsolescent by the time of Midway – caused many Japanese flyers bombing the atoll base to misidentify them as Wildcats. (Pilot Press copyright drawing)

THE OPPOSING NAVAL AIR ARMS

The Japanese

The most visible and potent symbol of Japanese military prowess in the first six months of the Pacific War was the Mitsubishi A6M2 'Zero-Sen' carrier fighter. This was a remarkable compromise of a clean lightweight airframe conveying great manoeuvrability allied to very long range and heavy firepower. Ever since Pearl Harbor the 'Zero' had swept Allied airpower from the skies wherever it had been encountered, generating a reputation that, by the time of Midway, verged on the mythical. Only after recovering an almost intact example that had crashed in the Aleutians during Operation AL were the Americans able to divine the Achilles' heel of this outstanding aircraft. Nevertheless, it was the air superiority gained by this fighter, flown by highly skilled and experienced aircrew such as Lieutenant Commander Shigeru Itaya of the *Akagi*, that had enabled the dive bomber and torpedo bomber squadrons of the *Rengo Kantai* to employ their fearful expertise against Allied sea and land targets.

In the Aichi D3A1 'Val' dive bomber the

▼ *Although demonstrating great effectiveness in the Battle of Midway the repeated low level attacks by the TBDs pulled the Zero Combat Air Patrol over Nagumo's fleet down from height to sea level. This left the skies above the Japanese carriers naked and free for the Dauntless dive bombers to deliver their devastating strikes without fear of interception by these potent Japanese fighters. (Philip Jarrett)*

Japanese Aircraft Carriers at Midway

Name	Displacement	Length	Armament
Akagi	36,500 tons	885ft	six 8-inch guns twelve 4.7inch guns 28 25mm AA 63 aircraft
Kaga	38,200 tons	812ft	Ten 20cm MG Eight 12.7cm AA 72 aircraft
Soryu	18,800 tons	746ft	Twelve 12.7cm AA 26 25mm AA guns 63 aircraft.
Hiryu	17,300 tons	746ft	Twelve 12.7cm AA 34 25mm AA 63 aircraft.

Aircraft numbers reflect those actually carried in the Midway attack, rather than total possible number of aeroplanes that could be carried; i.e., *Kaga* could carry maximum of 90 aircraft.

Japanese possessed an effective design which, in the hands of expert pilots, had realised a strike accuracy of 80 per cent against Royal Navy warships during the rampage across the Indian Ocean in April 1942. Although it was a large machine with a fixed spatted undercarriage, the 'Val' had demonstrated a remarkable capacity for dogfighting in the Battle of the Coral Sea. Two examples of the D3A1A's replacement, the Yokosuka D4Y1 'Judy', were present at Midway aboard the carrier *Soryu* for employment as reconnaissance aircraft. The Nakajima B5N2 'Kate', of which 93 equipped the torpedo bombing squadrons of Nagumo's carriers in June 1942, was

▼ *Akagi was extensively rebuilt between 1936 and 1938 and modernised with a full length single flight deck. Her last significant modification was the replacement in the late* 1930s of her 270ft funnel by a large single stack canted downwards to vent the fumes away from the flight deck as illustrated here. She appeared thus at Midway.

US and Japanese Fighter Aircraft at Midway

Country	Type	Armament	Engine	Max Speed	Range	Ceiling	Span	Length
USA	Grumman F4F-4 Wildcat	6 x 0.50in MG	1,200hp R-1830-86	318mph	900 miles	35,000ft	38ft 0in	28ft 9in
USA	Brewster F2A Buffalo	4 x 0.50in MG	1,100hp	300mph	950 miles	30,500ft	35ft 0in	26ft 4in
Japan	Mitsubishi Type 21 A6M-2 Zero	2 x 20mm Type 99 cannon + 2 x 7.7mm Type 97 MG	925hp Sakae 12	316mph	1,940 miles	33,790ft	39ft 4½in	29ft 9in

Japanese Battleships in Operation MI

Name	Displacement	Armament	Armour	Completed	Fate
Yamato	72,800 tons	9 x 18.1in 12 x 6.1in 12 x 5in AA	400mm belt 500/650mm turrets 200mm decks	Dec 1941	Sunk April 1945
Nagato	34,100 tons	8 x 16in 18 x 5.5in 8 x 5in AA	100/300mm belt	Nov 1920	Expended 1946 in Bikini Atoll bomb tests
Mutsu	34,100 tons	8 x 16in 18 x 5.5in 8 x 5in AA 4 x 533mm TT	356mm turrets Up to 75mm decks	Oct 1921	Accidental internal explosion, 1943
Kirishima	27,500 tons	8 x 14in 14 x 6in 8 x 5in AA	76/203mm belt	Apr 1915	Sunk 1942 off Guadalcanal
Haruna	27,500 tons	8 x 14in 14 x 6in 8 x 5in AA	229mm turrets	Apr 1915	Sunk July 1945

the best aircraft of its type in the world, outmatching its American and British equivalents. However, its superior performance was only relative, for like all aircraft of its type its large size, slow speed and poor armament made it vulnerable to fighter attack and anti-aircraft fire. Nevertheless, its achievements during the period to Midway had been remarkable. It was also employed in the level-bombing role in the attack on Midway Island, as well as in its principal role of torpedo bomber in the attacks on the US carriers.

In spite of the technical proficiency of its aircraft, by the time of Midway a major problem had begun to emerge for the Japanese Naval Air Arm which was undoubtedly to have an influence on the outcome of the battle and was to handicap them dramatically throughout the rest of the war. Unlike most of the battleships of the Combined Fleet, which had resided in majestic splendour at the Hashirajima anchorage since the outbreak of war, the carriers of the First Air Fleet had been in almost continual action since Pearl Harbor. As a result, the inevitable attrition had begun to make dangerous inroads into aircrew numbers. The Japanese Navy had entered the war with a fairly small pool of 5,000 pilots, of which some 3,500 were serving front-line flyers. Owing to the policy of retaining the *experten* in front-line squadrons to ensure a qualitative advantage in combat, very few of these veterans survived to pass on their expertise to the new replacement aircrew training in Japan. Thus most, if not all replacement aircrew were rank novices needing a

Grumman F4F-4 flown by Lt.Cdr. John S. Thach, Officer Commanding VF-3, USS Yorktown, Midway, 4 June 1942

US Aircraft Carriers at Midway

As *Hornet*, *Enterprise* and *Yorktown* were of the same class, the following information is generally applicable to all three vessels.

Standard displacement:	19,800 tons
Overall length:	809¹/₂ft
Aircraft complement:	85-100
Armament (1942):	eight 5in 38 cal AA guns (single mounts) sixteen 1.1in MG AA (4 quad mounts) 23 x 20mm MG (single mounts)
Date of completion:	20 October 1941

great deal of time and effort to work up to even minimal combat efficiency.

The fallacy of this policy became apparent after the Coral Sea, when the losses of irreplaceable veteran aircrew such as Lieutenant Commander Takahashi, who had led the dive bombers at Pearl Harbor, resulted in the new fleet carrier *Zuikaku* being withdrawn from Operation MI because of a lack of trained aircrew. Indeed, Nagumo was to comment unfavourably on the poor quality of many of the replacement crews despatched to serve on the carriers. As we shall see, the growing crisis in the supply of aircrew was only compounded for the Japanese by the grievous losses they were to sustain among the remaining veteran aircrew at Midway.

The Americans

In the coming battle, which would be waged by aircraft against each other and by aircraft against warships, the actual number available to the US aboard their carriers and based on Midway Island itself provided them with a small margin of 23 aircraft more than the 325 aboard the Japanese carriers. However, the numbers game counted for little in these circumstances, as every US type employed in the battle was inferior to its Japanese counterpart to a greater or lesser degree.

Whilst the main Navy fighter, the F4F-4 Wildcat, was inferior to the 'Zero', US pilots had learnt through bitter experience the tactics necessary to take on their more manoeuvrable opponent. Whenever possible, the F4F-4s would dive on the 'Zeros', using the fire from their six machine guns to

destroy the lightly loaded and unarmoured airframe of the Japanese fighter. Where dogfighting could not be avoided, the Wildcat had shown itself able to take on the 'Zero'. US Navy pilots were highly trained in deflection shooting, and their reflector gunsights offered accurate gunnery which allowed a high probability of lethal hits. The presence of armour and self-sealing fuel tanks also enabled the portly Wildcat to take the sort of damage that would destroy a 'Zero-Sen' and still return to its carrier. The F4F was the mount of Lt Commander John S. 'Jimmy' Thach, who at Midway commanded the composite fighter squadron composed of the *Saratoga*'s VF-3 and *Yorktown*'s VF-5. His experience fighting the 'Zero-Sen' had led to his formulation of a new tactic that took his name, the 'Thach Weave', which he and VF-3 employed with success in the battle of Midway.

Although the Douglas SBD Dauntless was regarded by the Navy as obsolete by the time of Midway, it was in all probability one of the best dive bombers in the world at the time. Its virtue lay in its great stability and light control responses. At Midway it was to prove to be the real killer of the Japanese carriers when, at the end of its rock-steady dive at an optimum angle of 80 degrees, it was to deposit its 1,000lb bombs deep in the vitals of the enemy vessels. It was, however, the torpedo bomber pilots who flew the most decidedly obsolescent of the major US Navy types employed in the Midway battle. The TBD-1 Devastator had been designed as far back as 1934. In 1937, when it first entered service with the Navy, it was the best of its type in the world, but by 1942 it was totally outmoded. At the time of Midway, however, it was the only torpedo bomber the Navy possessed in any numbers because its replacement, the Grumman TBF-1, was not yet available in sufficient quantities. Indeed, the 21 crews from *Hornet*'s Torpedo Bombing Squadron Eight (VT-8), who had been converting to the new aeroplane in the United States, arrived at Pearl one day after the *Hornet* had departed for Midway. Not only were the torpedo bombing crews thus condemned to fly against the Japanese carriers in a aeroplane that was laboriously slow and had a poor rate of climb, but they were also forearmed with the knowledge that its poor performance in its designated role was compounded by the ignominious reputation of its nominated main weapon, the unreliable Mk.13 torpedo. Its record at Midway was one of glorious failure for, as we shall see, it was the sacrifice of the TBD crews that opened the roof for the dive bombers to destroy the Japanese carriers.

Whereas the Navy at least was flying some modern types, Marine Corps Air Group 22 (MAG 22) on Midway itself was operating decidedly obsolete navy 'hand-me-downs' in the form of Brewster F2A-3 Buffalo fighters, nicknamed 'Flying Coffins', and Vought SB2U-3 Vindicator dive bombers. The latter were disparagingly nicknamed 'vibrators' by their pilots, and had the disconcerting habit of shedding their wing fabric, which was repaired by the liberal application of sticky tape. Some new equipment was available in the form of seven F4F-3s serving alongside the Buffaloes of VMF-221 and some sixteen SBDs operating with the Vindicators of VMSB-241. In the case of the latter, their potential effectiveness was offset by the Marine pilots' virtual lack of flying experience on the type.

To beef up Marine air power on the island, both the Army and the Navy despatched a hotchpotch of types. The Army sent a detachment of its 7th Army Air Force, made up of nineteen B-17 Flying Fortresses and four of the new B-26 Marauder medium bombers, equipped to carry single torpedoes under their fuselages. Much was expected of the former type, but its contribution to the battle was negligible, in spite of the great amount of space it took up on the small Eastern Island air base and the prodigious quantities of fuel used in the B-17 sorties. Offensive Navy air assets on the island were confined to six of the TBFs from VT-8 that had arrived at Pearl on 29 May. From among the crews that had disembarked with the new aeroplanes, six were selected to fly out to Midway, arriving on 1 June.

Most important of all the aircraft types based on Midway were the Navy PBY-5 and -5A Catalina amphibious flying boats of Patrol Wings 1 and 2. They had the vital role of searching out and reporting on the advancing Japanese forces, and by 30 May no fewer than two dozen PBYs were sweeping a huge arc from the NNE to the SSW of Midway out to a distance of 700 miles. Day in and day out the PBYs would lift their overladen airframes into the air to begin the long haul out to the maximum point of their ocean sweep. However, it was only on 3 June, the date identified by Hypo as the earliest feasible for the start of the Japanese offensive, that the imminence of a Japanese invasion of Midway was finally revealed to the aircrews. With the search pattern of the PBYs now covering all likely approaches to Midway, it was only a matter of time before the rapidly closing Japanese forces were seen and the curtain arose on one of the most decisive battles in the history of warfare.

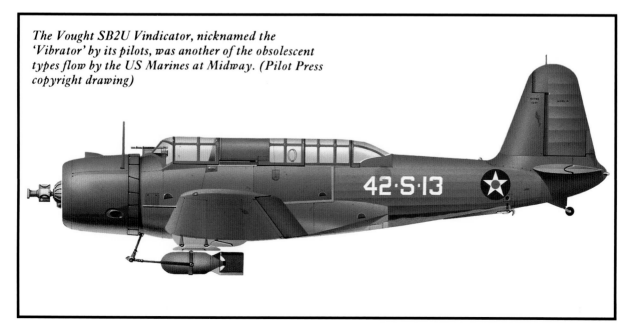

The Vought SB2U Vindicator, nicknamed the 'Vibrator' by its pilots, was another of the obsolescent types flow by the US Marines at Midway. (Pilot Press copyright drawing)

THE BATTLE: 3 JUNE

Combat is Joined

The first act in the great drama now unfolding opened many hundreds of miles from Midway Island when, shortly after 0300, the carriers *Ryujo* and *Junyo* launched their aircraft to attack Dutch Harbor and thus initiate the combat phase of Operation AL. However, owing to the prevalence of the fog and generally bad weather so characteristic of the region, *Junyo*'s attack force of fifteen 'Val' dive bombers and thirteen escorting 'Zeros' was unable to locate the target and returned to the carrier. *Ryujo*'s air group had better luck, and nine of her 'Kate' bombers and three of her 'Zeros' found a break in the cloud which revealed their target

directly below them at about 0808. Radar aboard a seaplane tender in the harbour detected the incoming Japanese strike group, and, although the vessels in the harbour could not make their escape, the anti-aircraft defences were forewarned and were able to put up a heavy barrage. The 'Zeros' also tangled with a number of P-40s that managed to get aloft.

Although damage was inflicted on the base, another raid scheduled for 0945, to attack the naval vessels in the harbour, was launched. The inclement weather hid the target, forcing the aircraft to return to their carriers, but not before they had tangled with some US fighters in the process, losing a 'Zero' fighter. At mid-day, with the aircraft recov-

ered, Admiral Kakuta turned his force to the south-west.

Two days later another strike was made on Dutch Harbor which completed the destruction of the oil farm and further damaged other installations. The Army Air Force responded by launching raids by B-17s and B-26s, but they achieved no hits on the Japanese vessels. By the time his aeroplanes were landing, Kakuta had been told by Yamamoto that, because of events in the Midway battle, Operation AL was suspended and he and his carriers were to stand by for action to the south. Although the invasion of Adak was cancelled, Attu and Kiska were occupied on 5 and 7 June as planned. Nevertheless, the whole AL operation was a pointless exercise, failing totally in its aim. Admiral Nimitz was never in doubt that the attack on the Aleutians was any-

▲ Completed three years after her consort, the **Kaga** *('Increased Joy') shared the common origin as a battlecruiser and was likewise completed with three flight decks forward. In this form she had a maximum capacity of 60 aircraft. (via Roger Chesneau)*

thing more than a diversionary sideshow, and in terms of the wider battle about to begin that is what it remained. Some hours after the first attack on Dutch Harbor, sightings by PBYs on air patrol far to the southwest of Midway Island were to herald the start of the main battle.

Discovery of the Midway Invasion Force

The first contact with the approaching Japanese forces was made by PBY number 6-V-55, whose pilot, Ensign Charles Eaton, reported the sighting of two cargo vessels at 0904. But it was the broadcast some 21min later from another PBY flown by Ensign 'Jack' Reid that electrified the Midway garrison. At the extreme limit of their PBY's patrol search, the crew of 8-V-55 had spotted a group of ships on the horizon. This prompted Reid to despatch the message 'Sighted Main Body', followed a few minutes later by 'Bearing 262, distance 700 miles'. Demanding greater clarification of the

◄ The Kawanishi H8K 'Emily' was the most powerful and formidable long-range flying boat used by any of the combatants in the Second World War. Planned reconnaissances of Pearl Harbor by two of these aircraft between 31 May and 3 June, to provide up-to-date intelli- *gence of US fleet movements before the attack on Midway, had to be abandoned. Additionally, failure of the submarine cordon to do the same left Nagumo totally devoid of any real knowledge of the US fleet's whereabouts. (Philip Jarrett)*

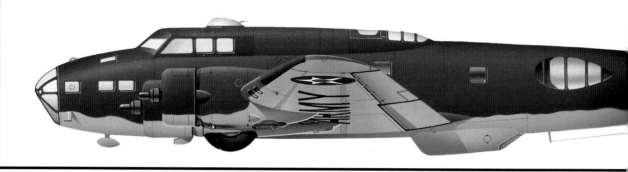

Although a number of raids on elements of the Japanese Fleet were launched by US Army B-17s on Midway, no hits were registered on any warships (Pilot Press copyright drawing)

sighting, for they were not prepared to release their air assets on the strength of such vague reports, Shannon and Simmard then had to wait some hours before they received from the PBY pilot the detailed information they desired.

Hampered by clear skies devoid of any protective cloud cover, Ensign Reid had to change course and altitude frequently to avoid detection and secure the most efficacious position whereby he could obtain accurate information on the makeup of the Japanese force. Approaching from astern, he saw laid out before him Rear Admiral Tanaka's Midway Invasion

Force, cruising at a stately 19kts with the light cruiser *Jintsu* steaming between and at the head of two parallel columns of transport vessels. To their fore in an arc ploughed the ten screening destroyers. The report he now filed was received on Midway at 1125, and in it Reid counted eleven vessels, identifying them as a small carrier, one seaplane carrier, two battleships, several cruisers and several destroyers. The variety of warship types suggests that

▼ **Kaga** *underwent major reconstruction between 1934 and 1935 which saw her displacement raised from 26,900 tons to 38,200 tons. Her triple deck was replaced by a single much length-ened flight deck and her aviation component increased to 90 aircraft. She and Akagi formed the First Carrier Division of the Rengo Kantai. (via roger Chesneau)*

▶ *This shows the approach of the Japanese forces of Operation MI towards Midway up until 0900 of 3 June, when Tanaka's invasion force was spotted by PBY 8-V-55, flown by Ensign 'Jack' Reid. By that time Task Force 16 (A) had been joined by Fletcher's Task Force 17 (B) at Point* *Luck (PL). Both Task Forces had avoided the Japanese submarine cordon put in place by Yamamoto specifically for the purpose of detecting their departure from Pearl Harbor.*

Reid's report was, unbeknown to himself, based upon a composite sighting. In all probability this resulted from his frequent manoeuvring in the intervening hours since his initial message to Midway, in the process of which he not only espied Tanaka's Invasion Force, but also flew across the track of Kondo's 'Main Body', Kurita's Close Support Force and Fujita's Seaplane Tender Group, all of which were operating in close proximity to one another. Despite Reid's inaccurate identification of some of the vessels in Tanaka's convoy, it was clear that a sizable Japanese force was now heading on a direct course for Midway. This knowledge allowed Simmard to give the green light to release the Army pilots for an air strike.

As Reid's PBY turned for home and disappeared over the horizon, a message from *Jintsu* had already flashed through the ether, breaking the blanket Japanese radio silence and conveying the news to the flagship that the Invasion Force had been discovered by American aircraft 600 miles from Midway. Up to this point all was seen to be going well, and accounts indicate that the Commander in Chief and his staff aboard *Yamato* were all in fine fettle. Tanaka's broadcast, however, put an immediate dampener on proceedings with the realisation that

The Fleets Converge

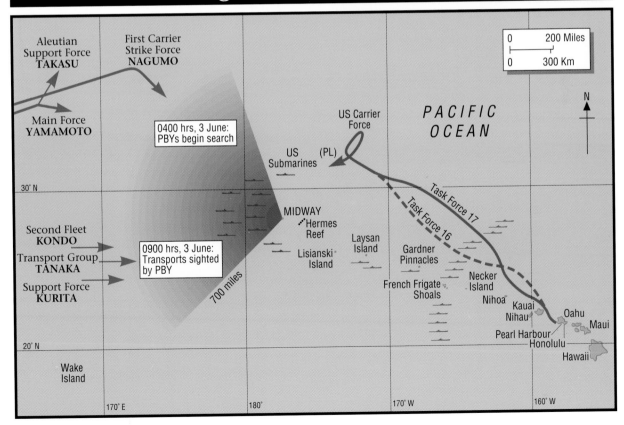

▲ *The carrier* Soryu *('Green Dragon'), seen here under construction at the Kure Naval Yard, was built under the limitations of the Washington Treaty.* *She was formally commissioned into the Combined Fleet on 29 December 1937. (via Roger Chesneau)*

▼ *Although quite small and cramped internally because of the limitations treaty, the* Soryu *still carried a respectable 63 aircraft. She formed the* *other half of Carrier Division 2 of the Rengo Kantai.*

the enemy had established contact with the advancing fleet much earlier than the operational plan had allowed for. As matters now stood, the Commander in Chief and his staff could only reconcile themselves to the premature initiation of combat and the inevitability of early air attacks on Tanaka's Invasion Force.

Of the aircraft on Midway, only the Army B-17s had the range to mount an effective attack on the Japanese force at this distance. Even so, it had been necessary to fit an extra fuel tank in each of their bomb bays, reducing the actual offensive load carried by half, to just four 500lb bombs apiece. Shortly after 1225 nine Flying Fortresses under the command of Lt Colonel Walter Sweeney took off, heading westwards in the general direction of Reid's last sighting fix. It was 1640 before they located the Japanese force and began their high-level bombing runs. Far below, *Jintsu* and her ten screening destroyers opened up at the rapidly moving shapes above them with their anti-aircraft batteries, but the effectiveness of their fire was more apparent than real, for none of the B-17s was hit. In turn, the American bombers failed to hit any of the Japanese ships, although the great waterspouts raised close to

a number of the vessels prompted some totally unjustified claims by the pilots on return to Midway. In their debriefings, pilots and crews spoke of hits on six vessels including two transports, two heavy cruisers and even two battleships. On the presumption that these vessels were now flame-wracked hulks, the submarine USS *Cuttlefish*, which was patrolling in the vicinity, was sent to sink them. Not surprisingly, it was unable to find any trace of the purported wrecks.

Very early the following morning Tanaka's as yet unscathed force was subjected to another, smaller but more successful air attack. Four of the lumbering and vulnerable PBYs had been jury-rigged to carry single torpedoes, and with volunteer crews had taken off from Midway at 2115 late on 3 June with the intention of attacking the Japanese force.

▼*Fitting out at the Yokosuka Naval Yard, next to either the Combined Fleet flagship* Nagato *or her sister ship* Mutsu, *is the* Hiryu. *She was the last carrier built by the Japanese under the restrictions of the Washington Naval Treaty. Commissioned into the Fleet on 5 July 1939 she shared with* Akagi *the unusual distinction of carrying her island on the port side.*

Three reached the convoy, fixing its position with their onboard radar, and, by taking advantage of the bright moonlight which silhouetted the enemy vessels, began their attack at 0130. Only the PBY flown by Ensign Probst registered a hit, his torpedo detonating close to the bow of the oiler *Akebono Maru*. The explosion killed eleven of her crew and wounded a further thirteen, but the damage to the vessel was successfully contained and she was soon able to reposition herself in the convoy. The PBYs succeeded in escaping the hail of anti-aircraft fire sent aloft by the Japanese vessels, and proceeded in their slow plodding fashion to head back to Midway.

▼ **Enterprise** – *the Big 'E' – is regarded by many as the greatest warship to serve with the US Navy. Launched on 3 October* 1936, *she served gallantly throughout the conflict only to be unceremoniously scrapped afterwards. (via Roger Chesneau)*

They arrived back just as the air attack by Nagumo's strike force was beginning.

Task Forces 16 and 17

The tone on board the *Enterprise* and *Hornet* had been set the previous day, when Spruance signalled to the vessels of his Task Force the essence of the plan formulated to deal with the expected Japanese carrier force heading for Midway. A remarkably dispassionate affair, it nevertheless conveyed in its matter-of-factness a subdued confidence. Somewhat later on the the same day the planned and vital rendezvous at Point Luck took place, with Fletcher officially taking over tactical command of both carrier groups, although in practice the two Task Forces were to operate independently. Radio silence was absolute, even the use of the inter-ship communication system, which was believed secure from

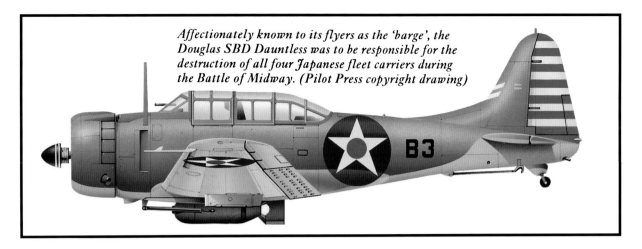

Affectionately known to its flyers as the 'barge', the Douglas SBD Dauntless was to be responsible for the destruction of all four Japanese fleet carriers during the Battle of Midway. (Pilot Press copyright drawing)

signal leakage, being suspended. 3 June saw the three carriers and their escorts ploughing a zig-zag course in and around the vicinity of Point Luck, with Fletcher and Spruance patiently waiting for Nagumo's carriers to show their hand.

The day had not been without its drama, however. Both Nimitz and Fletcher had been party to the news of Ensign Reid's discovery of Tanaka's Invasion Force in the early morning, and the possibility had always existed that his description of the enemy force as the 'Main Body' would be accepted by one or either of them as just that. Nimitz, however, saw nothing, even in the more detailed reports received later in the morning regarding the makeup of the enemy force, to make him doubt the intelligence advice given to him by Hypo that the main Japanese striking force lay in Nagumo's carriers, and that they had yet to make their appearance. Fletcher had also reached this conclusion, receiving confirmation from Nimitz late that afternoon in a coded message flashed to the *Yorktown*: 'That is not repeat not the enemy striking force – stop – That is the landing force. The striking force will hit from the northwest at daylight tomorrow.' With the clock now beginning to run ever faster, Fletcher ordered that *Enterprise* and *Hornet* be flashed a course change, and at 1950 the two Task Forces headed south through the night, aiming for a point approximately 200 miles north of Midway. Assuming that Nagumo would turn up as predicted by intelligence, it was from here that Fletcher intended to launch his aeroplanes against the Japanese carriers early on the following day.

First Air Fleet

3 June was a day of frantic preparations aboard the four carriers of the First Air Fleet. Final refuelling

▲ *Regarded as the half-sister of the Soryu, the* **Hiryu** *('Flying Dragon') was the flagship of Carrier Division 2 and carried the pennant of Vice Admiral Tamon Yamaguchi at Pearl Harbor* *through to her destruction at Midway. Hiryu was the only Japanese carrier to launch a successful strike on the US carriers during the battle. (via Roger Chesneau)*

had been completed, and shortly after 0600 the five oilers of the supply train and their escorting destroyer, the *Akigumo*, fell away. The carriers and their escorts then turned to the southeast and accelerated to 24kts to begin the final run in towards Midway. Deep in the bowels of the carriers, mechanics laboured long and hard on the engines of the aircraft to ensure optimum performance, while the armourers loaded belts of bullets and shells into the machine guns and cannon. Others made ready the bombs and their shackles in preparation for the attack scheduled for the early hours of the following morning. From the bridge of the flagship, Admiral Nagumo observed the scene about him. A tight defensive ring had been formed around the four carriers by the fast battleships *Haruna* and

Kirishima, along with the heavy cruisers *Tone* and *Chikuma*, the light cruiser *Nagara* and the 12 destroyers of the screening force. Symptomatic, perhaps, of the rise in tension was a false sighting of enemy aircraft in the early evening by the watch on the *Tone*, and although three 'Zeros' were launched from the *Akagi* to investigate, nothing was found.

Down below, the pilots detailed for the Midway strike relaxed or slept as the mood took them, while others, perhaps more mindful of their own mortality, took time to visit one of the small Shinto shrines on board, invoking the protection of its *kami* in the trial to come. All through the fleet there was the growing awareness that in a matter of hours the enemy would be engaged, in the greatest battle ever fought by the Combined Fleet. From the lowliest sailor to the most senior officer there exuded the almost tangible expectation of certain victory in the hours and days ahead.

▼ *The dive bombing squadrons of the First Carrier Striking Force at Midway were equipped with the Aichi D3A1 dive* *bomber. Code-named 'Val' by the Allies, the type had notched up many successes since the start of the Pacific War.*

THE BATTLE: 4 JUNE

First Air Fleet Strikes Midway

In the hours before 0245, at which time the aircrew were awoken aboard *Akagi*, *Kaga*, *Hiryu* and *Soryu*, until 0430, when the first aircraft of the Midway attack group were launched, the carriers of the First Air Fleet were hives of intense activity. The regular and persistent metallic clang and associated hum of hydraulic lines reverberated through the carriers as lifts raised the fully fuelled and armed aeroplanes of the first strike wave from the hangar levels below to the flight deck. The whole process of physically manhandling and spotting aircraft in their correct positions on the flight deck was tiring but exacting work. First came the large 'Kate' level bombers, which were positioned at the rear of the flight line, followed in their turn by the dive bombers. The last to be placed were the 'Zero-Sen' fighters, which would be the first to launch, providing the protective umbrella below which their heavier brethren would seek safety. At 0300 engines spluttered then roared into life as mechanics began to warm them up. Below decks, pilots of the first strike wave donned flying suits before moving through the nar-row passageways to the galleys, where breakfast preceded a final briefing. Many were in a state of nervous but excited anticipation, as this was their first combat mission. The employment of the younger replacement pilots in the first attack wave was a deliberate ploy by Nagumo. He was retaining the majority of his veteran flyers aboard the carriers to form a second strike force, and thus ensure against the possibility of American carriers making an appearance.

While this was symptomatic of his natural caution, even Nagumo had no real reason at this stage to suppose that such an eventuality was likely. He perceived the intelligence picture as altogether quite rosy. Having been denied any knowledge of the premature discovery of Tanaka's invasion force on the previous day by Yamamoto's continuing insistence on radio silence, he had no reason to believe that the anticipated element of surprise, deemed so important for this stage of the operation, would not be achieved. Such optimism is implicit in the intelligence appraisal that he circulated to senior commanders shortly before operations commenced:

1. The enemy fleet will probably come to engage

▶ *No photograph survives from Japanese sources showing the air operations of the Nagumo Fleet at Midway. Although this picture dates from just prior to the Pearl Harbor strike in December 1941, nevertheless it conveys very well a scene similar to that experienced aboard the flagship Akagi as it prepared to launch its 'Zero' fighters early on the morning of 4 June 1942.*

when the Midway landing operations are begun.

2. Enemy air patrols from Midway will be heavier to westward and southward, less heavy to the north and north west.

3. The radius of enemy air patrols is estimated to be approximately 500 miles.

4. The enemy is not yet aware of our plan, and he has not yet detected our task force.

5. There is no evidence of an enemy task force in our vicinity.

6. It is possible for us to attack Midway, destroy the land based planes there, and support landing operations. We can then turn around, meet an approaching enemy task force, and destroy it.

7. Possible counterattacks by enemy land-based aircraft can surely be repulsed by our interceptors and anti-aircraft fire.

Apart from point 7, which was shortly to receive dramatic verification, the other observations were hopelessly in error. Such self-deception goes far to explain the tardiness with which the Japanese now approached the whole matter of aerial reconnaissance, on which the security of the carrier force turned.

Mitsuo Fuchida, the designated first strike leader until illness rendered him *hors de combat* shortly after leaving Japan, observed that provision for reconnaissance was made on the basis of a single-phase search, the aeroplanes being despatched only after the launch of the Midway strike force. Assuming that all went according to plan, any American force within the search arc would be located and dealt with by Nagumo's second strike wave. Whilst believing the single-phase search plan adequate (see Map 3), he harboured doubts concerning its efficacy as a result of difficulties experienced in its

employment during the Indian Ocean operation, when enemy surface vessels had been spotted only after air groups from the carriers were already attacking other targets. The limitation of the single-phase search was that it was sufficient only to confirm, as he somewhat pithily observed, what the Japanese already believed – that there was no American force in the area. This failure to instigate a more thorough search procedure, which would of necessity have required the employment of far more aircraft than the few allotted, also stemmed from a great reluctance to employ combat aircraft such as the 'Kate' and 'Val', which possessed the necessary range for such tasks, at the expense of strapping a bomb or torpedo underneath them and using them for offensive purposes. There can be no doubting the impact of inadequate reconnaissance methods on Japanese fortunes in the battle about to commence. Minoru Genda, Air Officer of the Air Fleet, reflecting after the battle, admitted that the search plan was negligent and that in consequence it proved to be 'the initial cause for the Midway defeat'.

Having received their final briefing, the aircrew on the four carriers emerged on to their respective

▶ *It was Minoru Genda, Air Officer of the First Air Fleet and serving with Nagumo's staff on board* **Akagi,** *who was to observe that the slipshod nature of the air search plan illustrated here was the initial cause of the Japanese defeat at Midway. Notwithstanding the failure to instigate a*

much more comprehensive plan, using more aircraft, the delay in launching **Tone** *and* **Chikuma's** *floatplanes was to deny Nagumo the earlier sighting of Task Forces 16 and 17 that would have resulted, had they been launched when originally intended, at 0430.*

Some 1,149 Nakajima B5N 'Kates' were produced. The carriers **Lexington, Yorktown,** *and* **Hornet** *all fell victims mainly to this aircraft. (Pilot Press copyright drawing)*

Air Search Patterns of First Carrier Air Fleet, 0430 onwards, 4 June

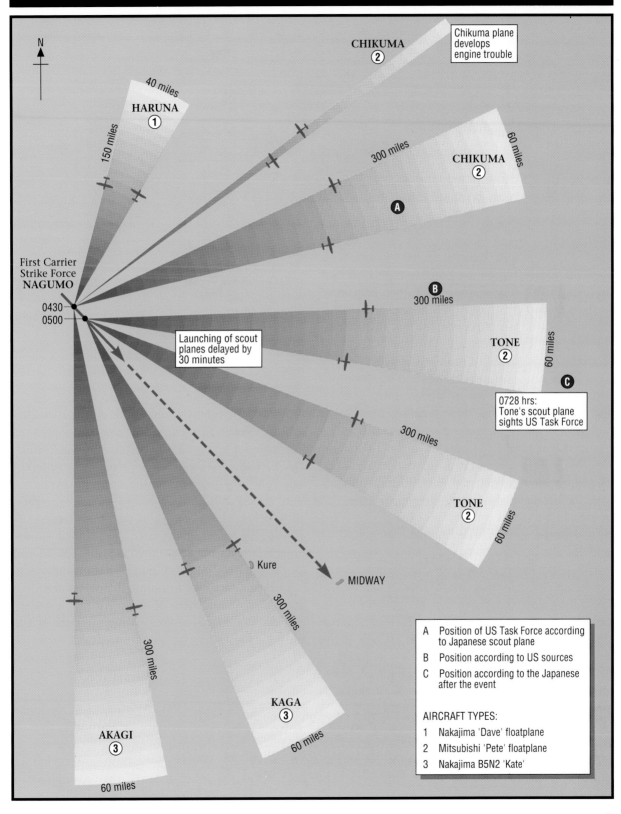

N

CHIKUMA
②

Chikuma plane
develops
engine trouble

40 miles

HARUNA
①

150 miles

300 miles

CHIKUMA
②

60 miles

A

First Carrier
Strike Force
NAGUMO

0430
0500

B

300 miles

TONE
②

60 miles

C

Launching of scout
planes delayed by
30 minutes

0728 hrs:
Tone's scout plane
sights US Task Force

300 miles

TONE
②

60 miles

Kure

MIDWAY

300 miles

300 miles

KAGA
③

AKAGI
③

60 miles

60 miles

A   Position of US Task Force according
    to Japanese scout plane
B   Position according to US sources
C   Position according to the Japanese
    after the event

AIRCRAFT TYPES:
1   Nakajima 'Dave' floatplane
2   Mitsubishi 'Pete' floatplane
3   Nakajima B5N2 'Kate'

decks and proceeded to board their aircraft. Engines were turned over and sprang into life as the 108 aircraft of the first wave warmed up for take-off. With their flight decks illuminated by floodlights, all four carriers turned into the wind. From their respective bridges green lights flashed on, and, as the roar of the engines rose to a crescendo, the first of 36 'Zero' fighters, led by Lieutenant Masuharu Suginami from the *Soryu*, launched promptly at 0430. Against a backdrop of cheering deckhands and waving white caps 36 'Val' dive bombers launched from *Akagi* and *Kaga*, with 36 'Kate' level bombers from *Soryu* and *Hiryu*, under the respective commands of Lt Shoichi Ogawa and raid leader Lt Joicho Tomonaga. One by one the aircraft took up station amid the huge formation circling the fleet. Fifteen minutes after launching had started, Tomonaga gave the order and all 108 aircraft of the First Strike Wave turned to the southeast and headed towards Midway.

No sooner had they departed that the lifts on the carriers were delivering more aircraft on to the decks. Just nine 'Zeros' were sent aloft from *Kaga* to provide a combat air patrol for the 21 vessels of the fleet, with another nine spotted on *Akagi*'s flight deck as a contingency reserve. This was hardly a sufficient strength to suggest expectation of enemy attack, and was no doubt symptomatic of the general air of confidence pervading the fleet.

The next air elements launched comprised the reconnaissance types, all of which were due to take off promptly at 0430. *Haruna*'s floatplane catapulted as planned. *Kaga* and *Akagi* launched their D3A1s to begin their air searches to the south and

▲ The main benefit to the Americans of the Japanese attack on the Aleutians was their recovery of an almost intact example of an A6M2 'Zero' flown by Flight Petty Officer Tadayoshi Koga of the Ryujo. *He had been killed attempting to land the slightly damaged aeroplane on the tundra. By repairing the aircraft the Americans were able to determine its strong and weak points, helping them to develop tactics to combat it as well as influencing the design of the Wildcat's replacement, the Grumman F6 Hellcat.*

southeast of Midway itself. However, the two Mitsubishi 'Pete' floatplanes of the heavy cruiser *Chikuma* did not get aloft until five and eight minutes past the due launch time. Even more unfortunate for the Japanese was the delay on her sister ship, *Tone*. While one her floatplanes was catapulted off at 0442, the second was not finally sent aloft until 0500, some 30min after the planned launch time. Whatever the subsequent explanations offered for these delays, and they ranged from troublesome engines and catapults to simple sloppiness of procedure, the consequences of those lost minutes were very shortly to prove fatal to the fortunes of the First Air Fleet.

Midway Island: 0300–0700

Following reveille at 0300, Midway rapidly became a scene of purposeful activity as the many aircraft squeezed on to the small island base were prepared for the decisive events of the coming day. Half an hour before the Japanese strike wave took off from their carriers, eleven of the amphibious PBYs lumbered down the runway, hauling their overloaded and inelegant airframes into the air and out over the wide expanse of the Pacific to begin the search that would surely provide, before the morning was much older, the first sightings of Nagumo's carriers. Shortly thereafter, against the backdrop of dawn's early light, Lt-Colonel Sweeney's force of 16 Army B-17s was once more sent aloft to visit further destruction on Tanaka's invasion force, still ploughing its slow course towards Midway. With the 'big boys' now departed, the rest of the aircraft spread across the base were armed with bombs and torpedoes and made ready for action. Engines were started and given their preliminary warm-up, their pulsating throb reverberating through the cool of the early morning air.

On both islands of the atoll base, Marines called to their weapons checked their ammunition and practised last-minute gunnery drill, elevating and rotating their pieces while tensely awaiting the first radar sighting of the incoming enemy. Although the two sets on the base were somewhat dated, their maximum detection range of 150 miles gave valuable early warning time. There would be no catching aircraft on the ground this time, as at Pearl Harbor.

Events now began to move quickly. Between 0520 and 0553 a series of sightings from PBYs and on the ground radar galvanised the whole base into frenetic activity. The initial sighting was relayed by a PBY of Flight 58, commanded by Lieutenant Howard P. Ady, at 0520. He reported spotting a Japanese reconnaissance aeroplane. At 0530 came the words that those on Midway, in Fletcher's Task Force and on Oahu had been waiting so tensely to hear: 'Carrier bearing 320, distance 180'. The order now went out to the pilots to man their aircraft. By 0545 all were ready, with engines turning over, awaiting the word to launch. Some minutes later a further flash was received from a second PBY, flying a pattern adjacent to that of Flight 58. It stated that many aeroplanes were heading towards Midway on a bearing of 320 degrees. This provided both Midway and Fletcher with the absolutely vital information that Nagumo had committed his first strike wave, and that it was inbound to the atoll base.

In the meantime, life had become decidely more hazardous for the shadowing PBYs. Far below, keen eyes on the Japanese vessels had spotted one of the Catalinas drifting across the sky, and heavy anti-aircraft fire had opened up on the unwelcome observers, littering the sky around them with ugly smudges of black smoke. 'Zero' fighters had launched from *Kaga* in a bid to shoot down the intruders, but by making good use of the cloud cover the two PBYs successfully avoided them. Finally, at 0552 Lieutenant Ady was able to despatch the clinching sighting fix on Nagumo's force, reporting: 'Two carriers and battleships bearing 320 degrees, distance 180 course 135, speed 25'. Barely a minute thereafter Midway obtained its own radar sighting, when operators poring over their scopes in the shack on Sand Island detected the incoming Japanese strike force at a range of 93 miles and an altitude of 11,000ft. As they moved ever closer to Midway the blips rapidly resolved into one large formation, denoting the approach of a sizable enemy force. Without further ado the order was given to send off the aircraft.

▶ *The pilot of a D3A1 'Val' carrying a single 1,050lb bomb under its centreline opens its throttle as it gains speed for take-off. The 'Vals' in the Midway strike came from* **Kaga** *and* **Akagi**.

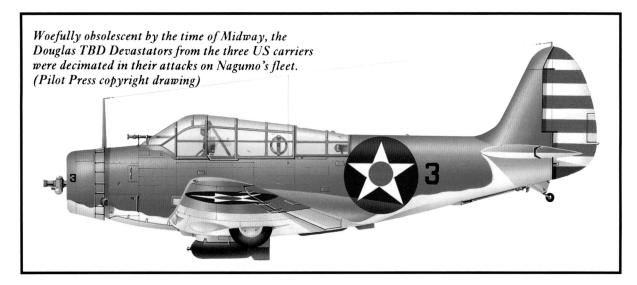

Woefully obsolescent by the time of Midway, the Douglas TBD Devastators from the three US carriers were decimated in their attacks on Nagumo's fleet. (Pilot Press copyright drawing)

As the air raid siren wailed over Midway the Wildcat and Buffalo fighters of VMF-221 took off and, once aloft, headed for the Japanese formation. In their wake the pilots of the bombing aircraft taxied their charges to the runway and prepared in rapid succession to take off before the arrival of the enemy. The first aloft were the dive bombers of VMSB-241 – sixteen Marine SBDs led by Major Lofton Henderson, each armed with a 500lb bomb, followed by the venerable SB2U 'Vibrators' under the command of Major Benjamin Norris. Thereafter came the the six Navy TBFs of VT-6 and the four Army B-26 medium bombers, these two new types making their combat debut. By 0620, with the enemy force just 22 miles from Midway, the airbase on Eastern Island lay deserted, and its former occupants were heading at their best speed towards the northwest and the position of the last sighting of the Japanese carriers, in response to the simple but graphic order '...attack enemy carriers'. Set to join this motley collection of types was Sweeney's force of Flying Fortresses, which was already far out to sea when it received new orders at 0600 to divert and head for the more significant target of Nagumo's carriers. The somewhat limited chances of survival of this uncoordinated, ill-experienced and poorly equipped force had been further reduced by the decision not to employ the Wildcats and Buffaloes as fighter cover for the bombers. Instead, contrary to Nimitz's original orders, they were to be used to protect the airfield.

At 0616 the 25 Buffaloes and Wildcats under the command of Majors Parks and Armistead acquired their first clear picture of Tomonaga's approaching force. Climbing before the advancing Japanese, Parks was able to secure a height advantage, and with his section of twelve fighters began his diving attack on the level bombers, with Armistead's group in tow. The 'Zeros', flying top cover, were stationed slightly behind the formation of level and dive bombers, and although they were not initially well placed to respond to the attackers, they were able to use their superior speed and manoeuvrability to place themselves rapidly on the tails of the slower American fighters.

Within a few minutes a wild and confused swirling melée filled the sky, and it quickly became apparent that the Japanese fighters had the upper hand. The 'Zeros' assailed the Buffaloes and Wildcats with their machine guns and cannon, hacking them from the air. Nevertheless, the gallant impression made by the Marine pilots was enough for one of *Soryu*'s pilots to misidentify the portly and obsolescent Buffaloes and report that they had been attacked by '30 to 40 F4F-3s at a point some 20 miles from Midway'. The Japanese tally for this few minutes of vicious dogfighting was thirteen Buffaloes and two Wildcats shot down, with Major Parks among the pilots lost. Nagumo was later to record that three level bombers and two 'Zeros' were shot down by the Marine pilots while inbound to Midway.

Emerging from the attack virtually unscathed, Tomonaga led the formation on the final run-in to

The debut of the Grumman TBF Avenger was less than auspicious at Midway, but it was subsequently to prove its effectiveness and versatility with a career that extended well into the post-war period. (Pilot Press copyright drawing)

Midway, although it was frustratingly obvious that the airbase was devoid of aeroplanes. The bulk of the level bombers therefore directed their attention on Sand Island, hits on the oil tanks starting fires that lasted for days. In their wake, Chihaya's dive bombers plummeted down, targeting the hangars and other installations with their 500lb bombs while the 'Zeros', now released from their defensive tasks, swooped in at low level, strafing ground targets. The defending fire was of such an order that it was later described by the attackers as 'vicious'. Official Japanese sources admitted the loss of four aircraft over Midway itself. The captain of the Japanese submarine *I-168*, which was lying offshore ten miles to the south of Midway, had an excellent view of the raid, and later spoke of the island being turned into a mass of flames with buildings and fuel tanks exploding.

Nevertheless, when Tomonaga gave the order for the raiding force to withdraw at 0643 it was clear to his experienced eye that, in many respects, the raid had not succeeded. US air power on the island had not been neutralised, and would still be able to use the runways which, most surprisingly, remained undamaged. Neither had the bombing eliminated the bulk of the heavy weapons on the island, and these would certainly be used to oppose the landing of the invasion force. Tomonaga was some minutes into the return flight before he decided what he thought needed to be done. At 0700 he had a message flashed to Nagumo: 'There is need of a second attack wave'. Within moments of receiving his raid

leader's signal, Nagumo himself had just reason for believing Tomonaga's request to be sound.

Task Forces 16 and 17: 0430–0838

Even as Lt Suginami opened the throttle of his 'Zero' and accelerated down the flight deck of the *Soryu* on the dot of 0430, some 220 miles away to the east ten SBDs from the USS *Yorktown* were ordered aloft by Admiral Fletcher to scout the arc of sea 100 miles to the north of Task Forces 16 and 17. Although he was convinced that intelligence was correct in believing Nagumo would strike at Midway from the northwest, in the absence of any firm information he had no intention of allowing the Japanese admiral to catch him with his pants down should he decide to approach the island via a more northerly track. With the last of the scout aeroplanes despatched, the orderly waiting routine of the past few days was re-established, although it was clear that tension was slowly beginning to build as the minutes ticked away.

Aboard *Yorktown* and *Enterprise* Fletcher and Spruance sat patiently waiting for news of the first sighting of the Japanese force. When it came, Lt Ady's initial message contained nothing on which the Task Force commanders could act. However, the message received on *Enterprise* at 0534 not only gave news of the sighting of a carrier, but also contained a vital direction fix on which Spruance could plan his reaction. In principle it had already been determined. Fletcher and Spruance were in agreement that only an all-out strike on the Japanese carriers, launched at the earliest possible moment, would suffice to yield maximum advantage. This explains Spruance's order to his chief of staff that *Enterprise* and *Hornet* be ready to launch everything they had at the earliest possible moment. However, the receipt of later messages sighting Nagumo's inbound Midway strike force, allied to a second fix on two carriers, placed the Japanese force about 200 miles from the American position and prompted the admiral to make a rapid reappraisal of the situation.

Spruance had originally intended to close to half that distance before launching his air strike, but it now became clear that by doing so he would forego the opportunity to realise his principal aim of inflicting maximum damage on the Japanese carriers. He estimated that Tomonaga's strike group would recover aboard their respective carriers at about 0900 and would then be rearmed for a second strike. They would then be at their most vulnerable to an American air attack. To catch them Spruance would have to launch very soon, at least two hours earlier than originally intended, even though to reach Nagumo's carriers at that distance involved a round trip that lay beyond the maximum range of his torpedo bombers. It was presumed that Nagumo would have to maintain his present heading to recover his aircraft, and an intercept course was plotted whereby he could be brought within the maximum strike range of 200 miles by about 0700.

Fletcher also had reason to reflect on the implications of the sightings, governed as he was by his experiences in the Coral Sea. As only two Japanese carriers had been spotted, he decided to hold *Yorktown*'s air group in reserve, pending the receipt of more accurate information locating the other two, or possibly three carriers which intelligence had said Nagumo had in his fleet. Fletcher had no intention of launching all of his aeroplanes, along with those of *Enterprise* and *Hornet*, against two carriers, only to find himself totally vulnerable to a massive air strike from the two or more as yet unlocated enemy flat-tops. He also wished to recover the ten scouting aeroplanes sent out earlier. Realising that this would delay action against the two already located enemy carriers, Fletcher flashed Spruance at 0607 to 'proceed southwesterly and attack enemy carriers when definitely located. I will follow as soon as my planes are recovered.'

Turning to their new course, *Enterprise* and *Hornet* increased speed to 25kts and headed towards Nagumo's presumed position in a bid to close the distance before launching. From the hangar levels the lifts rapidly brought on to their flight decks the SBDs, TBDs and F4Fs with which the two carrier air groups were shortly to launch their strikes. The two carriers then separated, dividing the screening vessels between them to provide air defence if attacked. Spruance now ordered both carriers turned into the wind, and at 0700 *Hornet* started the launching of the 60 aircraft of her strike group. Under her air group leader, Commander Stanhope C. Ring, were the fifteen Devastators of VT-8 led by Lt-Commander John C. Waldron, known as much for his flying and leadership skill as his somewhat idiosyncratic behaviour. Thirty-five Dauntless dive bombers of VB-8 and VS-8, each armed with a 1,000lb bomb in the former unit and a 500lb bomb in the latter, were provided with an escort of just ten Wildcat fighters from VF-8 led by the fighter group commander, Lt-Commander Samuel G. Mitchell.

As *Hornet*'s aircraft assembled they were joined by those from *Enterprise*'s air group, which commenced launching at 0706. The composition of the 61-aircraft group was almost identical to that from *Hornet*. The fourteen torpedo bombers of VT-6 were led by Lt-Commander Eugene E. Lindsey, and the 37 Dauntless dive bombers of VB-8 and VS-8 were commanded by Lts Best and Gallaher. Fighter cover was provided by ten Wildcats from VF-6 under the command of Lt James S. Gray. Spruance's provision of only twenty Wildcats for fighter cover for such a large striking force was governed by caution in protecting his flat-tops. Ever mindful of Nimitz's charge to preserve the carriers, he had retained 36 Wildcats on *Enterprise* and *Hornet* as fighter cover in the event of a Japanese counter-strike.

In the meantime, having recovered his scouting aeroplanes, Fletcher increased his speed to 25kts and headed towards Task Force 16. Upon further reflection he had decided that, although just two carriers had been identified so far, they provided too good an opportunity to miss, so he too would launch. However, he allocated only half of *Yorktown*'s air group to the planned strike, the other half being retained to form a small second strike force.

▶ *Commissioned on 20 October 1941 as the last of the class, USS* Hornet *had a short, albeit dramatic, career. Following Midway she met her end on 26 October 1942 during the Battle of Santa Cruz. (via Roger Chesneau)*

Shortly after 0830 *Yorktown* turned into the wind and began launching seventeen Dauntlesses of VB-3 under the command of Lt-Commander Maxwell F. Leslie. These were then joined by the twelve Devastators of VT-3 led by Lt-Commander Lance E. Massey and a minimal force of six Wildcats from Fighting Squadron 3. Thus by 0910 Fletcher and Spruance had a total of 156 aircraft airborne and heading for the presumed position of Nagumo's fleet.

First Air Fleet: 0700–0920

With the scouting aeroplanes launched, the Japanese carriers were busy once more as the second wave was brought up from the hangar levels and on to the decks. Comprising 108 aircraft, all crewed by battle proven veterans, the force was under the command of Lt-Commander Takashige Egusa of *Soryu*, regarded by many as the *Rengo Kantai*'s leading exponent of dive bombing. Thirty-six D3A1s were spotted on the decks of *Soryu* and *Hiryu*, while eighteen Kates, each loaded with a 24in torpedo, were aboard the *Akagi* and *Kaga* under the command of Lt-Commander Shigeharu Murata. Fighter cover for the whole group was to be provided by 36 Zeros commanded by Lt-Commander Shigeru Itaya, also of *Akagi*. Although they were provisionally tasked with the role of attacking any American carrier fleet spotted by the scout aircraft, the lack of any reported sightings as the hours rolled by served only to confirm the presumptions of

▶ *Although it depicts a Grumman F4F-3 Wildcat (F4F-4s were flown at Midway) this picture is notable because the machine in the foreground is being flown by Lt Commander 'Jimmy' Thach, who commanded* Yorktown's *fighters at Midway. (US Navy)*

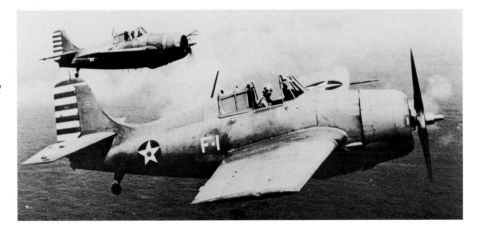

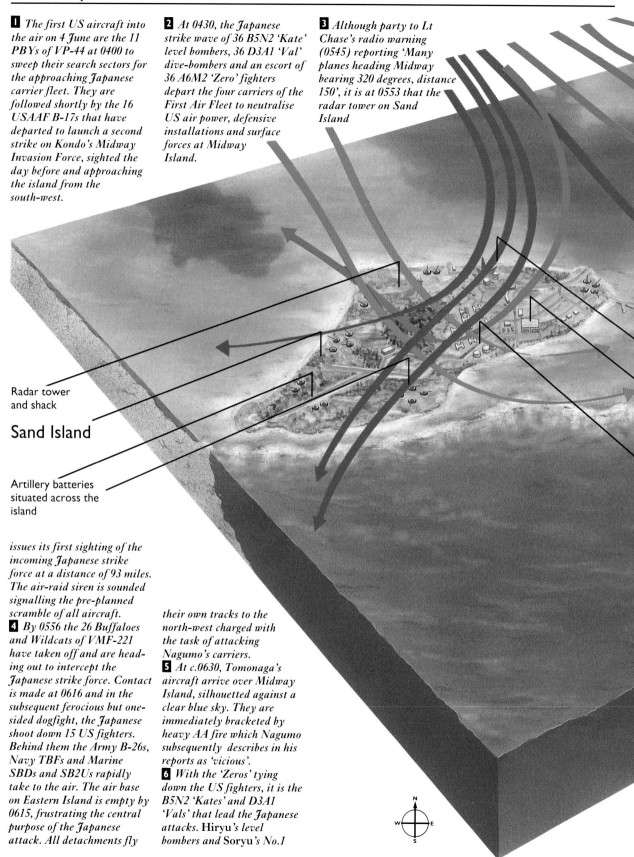

1 *The first US aircraft into the air on 4 June are the 11 PBYs of VP-44 at 0400 to sweep their search sectors for the approaching Japanese carrier fleet. They are followed shortly by the 16 USAAF B-17s that have departed to launch a second strike on Kondo's Midway Invasion Force, sighted the day before and approaching the island from the south-west.*

2 *At 0430, the Japanese strike wave of 36 B5N2 'Kate' level bombers, 36 D3A1 'Val' dive-bombers and an escort of 36 A6M2 'Zero' fighters depart the four carriers of the First Air Fleet to neutralise US air power, defensive installations and surface forces at Midway Island.*

3 *Although party to Lt Chase's radio warning (0545) reporting 'Many planes heading Midway bearing 320 degrees, distance 150', it is at 0553 that the radar tower on Sand Island*

Radar tower and shack

Sand Island

Artillery batteries situated across the island

issues its first sighting of the incoming Japanese strike force at a distance of 93 miles. The air-raid siren is sounded signalling the pre-planned scramble of all aircraft.

4 *By 0556 the 26 Buffaloes and Wildcats of VMF-221 have taken off and are heading out to intercept the Japanese strike force. Contact is made at 0616 and in the subsequent ferocious but one-sided dogfight, the Japanese shoot down 15 US fighters. Behind them the Army B-26s, Navy TBFs and Marine SBDs and SB2Us rapidly take to the air. The air base on Eastern Island is empty by 0615, frustrating the central purpose of the Japanese attack. All detachments fly*

their own tracks to the north-west charged with the task of attacking Nagumo's carriers.

5 *At c.0630, Tomonaga's aircraft arrive over Midway Island, silhouetted against a clear blue sky. They are immediately bracketed by heavy AA fire which Nagumo subsequently describes in his reports as 'vicious'.*

6 *With the 'Zeros' tying down the US fighters, it is the B5N2 'Kates' and D3A1 'Vals' that lead the Japanese attacks.* **Hiryu's** *level bombers and Soryu's No.1*

THE MIDWAY ATTACK

The Japanese air strikes on the island of Midway, 0400 to 0643 hours, 4 June 1942

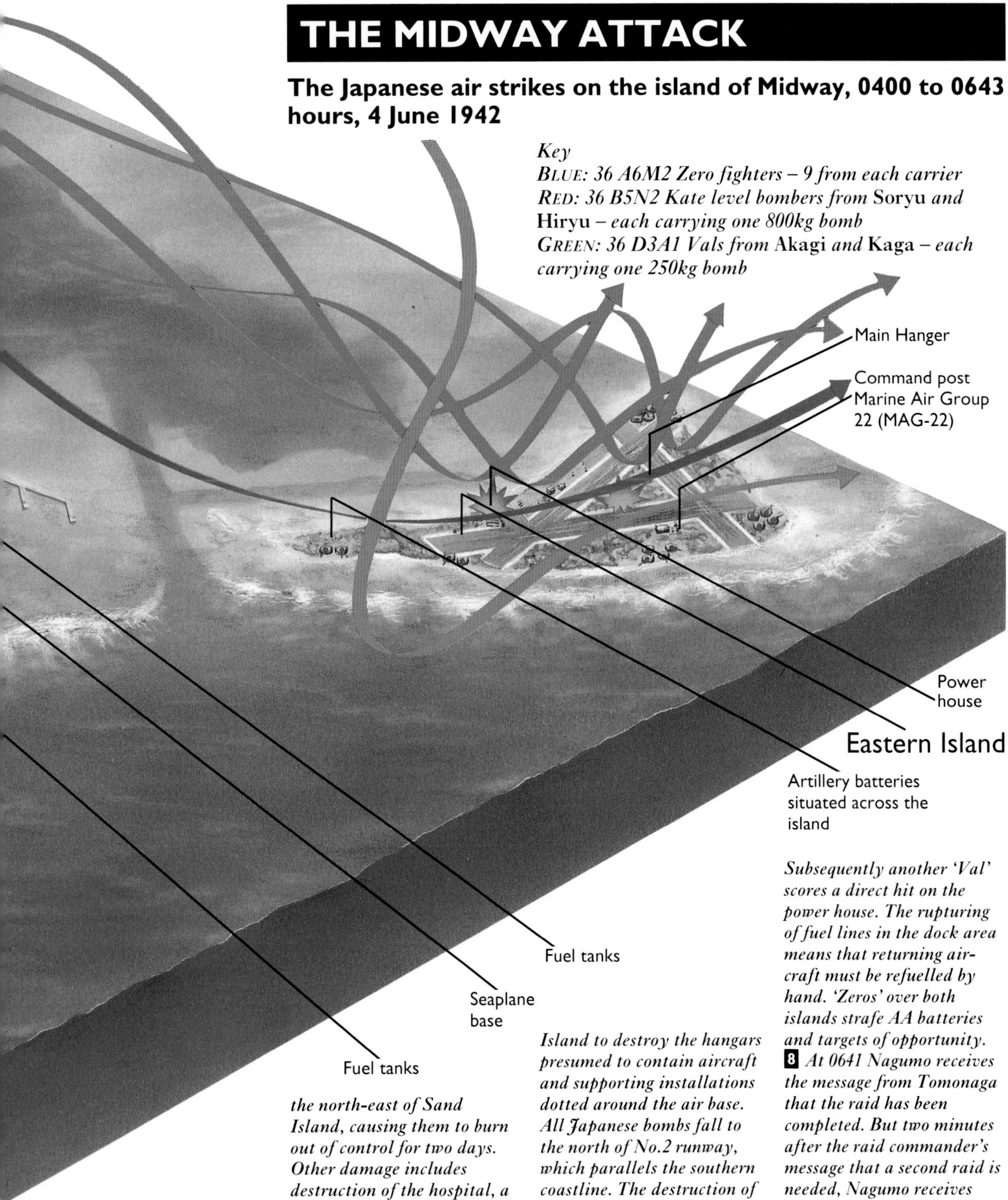

Key
BLUE: 36 A6M2 Zero fighters – 9 from each carrier
RED: 36 B5N2 Kate level bombers from Soryu and Hiryu – each carrying one 800kg bomb
GREEN: 36 D3A1 Vals from Akagi and Kaga – each carrying one 250kg bomb

Main Hanger

Command post
Marine Air Group
22 (MAG-22)

Power
house

Eastern Island

Artillery batteries
situated across the
island

Fuel tanks

Seaplane
base

Fuel tanks

Subsequently another 'Val' scores a direct hit on the power house. The rupturing of fuel lines in the dock area means that returning aircraft must be refuelled by hand. 'Zeros' over both islands strafe AA batteries and targets of opportunity. **8** At 0641 Nagumo receives the message from Tomonaga that the raid has been completed. But two minutes after the raid commander's message that a second raid is needed, Nagumo receives ample confirmation of the obvious failure of the first when US aircraft, launched from Midway over an hour before, begin their first attacks on his fleet.

Squadron concentrate on Sand Island where they are first tasked with the suppression of the AA defences. Level bombers from **Hiryu** also set fire to the three fuel tanks on the north-east of Sand Island, causing them to burn out of control for two days. Other damage includes destruction of the hospital, a seaplane hangar and other sundry buildings.
7 The bulk of **Akagi** and **Kaga**'s dive-bombers and **Soryu**'s No.2 'Kate' Squadron make for Eastern Island to destroy the hangars presumed to contain aircraft and supporting installations dotted around the air base. All Japanese bombs fall to the north of No.2 runway, which parallels the southern coastline. The destruction of the main hangar is caught on celluloid by the film director John Ford, who later incorporates the scene into his Oscar-winning film, 'The Battle of Midway'.

▲ *These SBD Dauntless dive-bombers are shown spotted on the deck of a carrier while refuelling and rearming prior to launch. The Dauntless* *was the standard US Navy dive-bomber and carrier scouting type at the time of Midway. (Philip Jarrett)*

senior officers and aircrew alike that the Americans were not out there at all. It is not surprising, therefore, that, when Nagumo received Tomonaga's 0700 signal requesting a second strike on Midway, he pondered its content with a degree of sympathy that, within minutes, hardened to firm assent as the first US aircraft despatched from the atoll base barely an hour before began their attack on the First Air Fleet.

Approaching the Japanese carriers were the four B-26s under the command of Captain James F. Collins and the six TBFs of VT-8 led by Lt Langdon K. Fieberling. Lookouts on *Akagi* were the first to track the incoming hostiles, and within minutes her speed increased as the ship and her screening vessels turned to face the attackers, thereby offering

them the smallest possible target. Exploding shells and smoke bursts attended the passage of the enemy aeroplanes as the screening destroyers and the heavy cruiser *Tone* added to the barrage of anti-aircraft fire erupting from *Akagi*'s batteries. Behind this curtain of fire, ten of Itaya's 'Zeros' had been sent aloft to join those of the standing air patrol. These rapidly hauled around behind the attackers and soon started wreaking havoc among the incoming aircraft.

The TBFs came in first, their speed much reduced owing to the need to open their bomb bay doors to launch their torpedoes. Maintaining course despite the hail of anti-aircraft fire to their front and the attacking 'Zeros' to their rear, they managed to loose off several torpedoes mainly directed at *Akagi*, which was able to avoid them by deft manoeuvring. Of the TBFs that flew in low to attack the carriers, five were brought down. Only one escaped to limp back to Midway, its hydraulic system shot up, its controls badly damaged and the rear gunner dead in his turret. The B-26s followed, skimming just above the wave tops with the ever present 'Zeros' snapping at their heels. One was destroyed on the run, disintegrating into a thousand pieces as it hit the sea at nearly 200mph. Fuchida clearly recalled seeing another of the bombers, the white star on its fuselage clearly visible, skimming low over the *Akagi* and barely missing its bridge before bursting into flames and crashing into the sea beyond. The two remaining Marauders, including the one flown by Collins, managed to drop their torpedoes and survived the barrage of fire thrown up by the Japanese vessels to return to Midway.

This attack swung the decision for Nagumo. He could hardly retain his second strike force to counter a non-existent threat when a real and very tangible one, in the form of Midway's as yet undestroyed air power, did exist. He snappily ordered that the aeroplanes of the second wave be prepared to attack Midway. That meant a rapid disarming of the 'Kates' on board *Akagi* and *Kaga*, to replace their torpedoes with bombs. Frantically, the deck crews on the two vessels hauled the aeroplanes to the lifts, from whence they were taken down to the hangar levels. Here sweating armourers worked as quickly as possible to change the armament so that the aircraft could be returned topside. Even under normal conditions it took the best part of an hour to carry out this procedure.

As Nagumo and his bridge staff were no doubt convinced of the logic of his decision, it must have come no small shock to them when, 25min later,

they were presented with a splendidly vague message from *Tone*'s Number Four floatplane. It read: 'Sight what appears to be 10 enemy surface ships, in position 10 degrees distance 240 miles from Midway. Course 150 speed over 20 knots.' Minoru Genda observed that the fact and imprecision of the sighting left Nagumo and his staff unable to make an accurate judgement of the situation and how best to respond. The admiral was indeed in a quandary. While his original orders called for the neutralisation of Midway's air power, he clearly could not ignore the potential danger to his own fleet implied by the sighting of these US naval vessels, whatever their type. Furthermore, the aircraft of Tomonaga's strike group were on their way back to the carriers and they would need to land, refuel and rearm, even though aircraft of the second wave were still spotted on the carrier decks. Pondering his options, Nagumo signalled his commanders at 0745 that he had decided to continue preparing for the second strike on Midway, but ordered that those bombers whose armament was as yet unchanged retain their torpedoes, so as to be able to 'carry out attacks on enemy fleet units'.

A few minutes later *Akagi* signalled the pilot of *Tone*'s Number Four aircraft with a curt injunction to 'Ascertain ship types, and maintain contact'. All now turned on the identity of the vessels and the despatch with which any new sighting was sent to the flagship. If no carrier was detected among them,

▶ *By the time of the Battle of Midway, the TBD Devastator torpedo bomber was decidely obsolescent. Its slow speed and poor rate of climb made it a sitting duck for Japanese 'Zero-Sen' fighters. Those shown here are from VT-6, and the pre-war picture dates from 1939 when the planes were resplendent with chrome yellow wings and blue tails. (via Robert F. Dorr)*

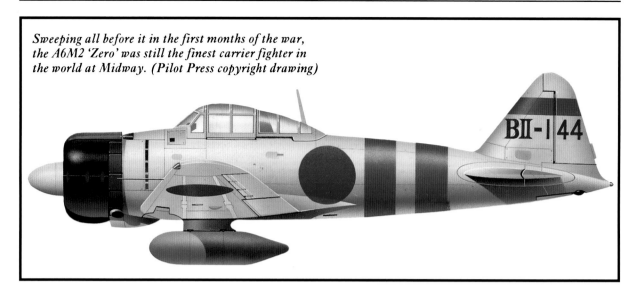

Sweeping all before it in the first months of the war, the A6M2 'Zero' was still the finest carrier fighter in the world at Midway. (Pilot Press copyright drawing)

and they proved only to be surface warships, Nagumo believed he had the time to realise the best of both worlds – launch the second wave against Midway and then recover the returning first strike force. Once they were refuelled and rearmed, Tomonaga's aeroplanes could be launched again, this time to strike at the American vessels. Barely had the Admiral and his staff finished reflecting on their options when, at 0748, a signal from *Soryu* drew their attention to the beginning of yet another air attack on the fleet.

The incoming aircraft on this occasion were the sixteen Dauntlesses of VMSB-241, but their passage towards the carriers was hampered from an early stage by the dogged attention of a swarm of 'Zeros'. Fuchida, watching events from the deck of *Akagi*, expressed surprise that the aeroplanes were employing a low-angle glide attack and not the 'hell-diving' technique that was their forte. He could not know that Major Lofton Henderson, who was commanding the incoming aircraft, had good reason for choosing this tactic, deeming it to be the only one he could realistically employ because most of the young and very green pilots he was leading had almost no experience at the controls of an SBD. The low-angle approach with dive brakes deployed made them easy targets for the 'Zeros', and even before they reached the fleet half of their number had been

◀ *As part of the air search pattern instigated by Nagumo after the launch of the Midway strike force, the battleship Haruna catapulted its old and short-ranged Naka-jima E8N 'Dave' float-plane to survey to the north of the southward-moving carrier fleet. (Philip Jarrett)*

Although inferior to the Zero in many respects, the Grumman F4F Wildcat nevertheless proved a remarkably rugged and effective aircraft. (Pilot Press copyright drawing)

shot down. Seemingly oblivious to the fate of their comrades, the remainder doggedly held their course even as they flew into the curtain of anti-aircraft fire thrown up by the now rapidly manoeuvring warships. At the end of their glide attacks the SBDs released their bombs, most of which were targeted at the *Hiryu*. To observers on the other ships of the fleet it seemed as if the carrier must be hit, as she disappeared behind a wall of water plumes and smoke. Within minutes she emerged, clearly unscathed by the experience.

As the eight surviving SBDs made their escape by flying low across the sea, pursued by the fighters, the pressure on the Japanese was relentlessly main-

tained. High overhead Lt-Colonel Sweeney's Flying Fortresses swung into view. From 20,000ft the B-17s dropped their loads of 500lb bombs on their targets four miles below. As on the previous day, the dramatic view of bombs bursting close to enemy vessels led the Army pilots to claim heavy damage on the Japanese carriers, although none was actually hit.

At 0806 Nagumo received the response he had been awaiting from *Tone*'s Number Four scout. Its content could hardly have carried better tidings for the harassed admiral: 'Enemy is composed of 5 cruisers and 5 destroyers'. Nevertheless Kusaka, the Chief of Staff of the First Air Fleet, was of the opinion that a force so constituted would hardly be at sea

▶ *Delays in launching the Mitsubishi Type 'O' 'Pete' observer floatplanes from the heavy cruiser Tone, and engine problems with that from Chikuna, were to deny the Japanese the intelligence of the approach of the US Task Forces from the east. (Philip Jarrett)*

◄ Six crews of VT-8 had the distinction of taking the new Grumman TBF-1 into combat at Midway. Only one of the aeroplanes survived the attack on the carriers to return, badly shot up, to Midway, where its undercarriage collapsed on landing. The aircraft was thereafter named 'Avenger' in memory of the five crews that did not return. (US Navy)

unless there was a carrier present. Notwithstanding his eminently reasonable deduction, there can be no doubting the very genuine sense of relief fostered by the 0806 message, for as matters now stood the second strike on Midway-could proceed. Even a further attack by Midway based Marine Vindicators after 0820 did nothing to dampen the spirits of Nagumo and his staff. They were not to know that, with the departure of Major Norris's surviving SB2Us, land based air power from Midway had shot its bolt. The results of the combat thus far had been totally in favour of the Japanese. From 0702 until 0830 they had been attacked by 131 aircraft, with numerous US aircraft shot down for no registered hits on any vessels of the First Air Fleet. Fuchida remarked that, in his opinion, the US flyers had not displayed a high level of ability, a view shared on the bridge of *Akagi*. The prevailing sentiment was that, if this was the best that the enemy could throw at them, the Japanese had little to fear.

Into this self-congratulatory atmosphere on the bridge of *Akagi* the latest message from Scout Number Four dropped like a bombshell on Nagumo and his staff officers at 0830: 'The enemy is accompanied by what appears to be a carrier in a position to the rear of the others'. All were momentarily shocked at the news, and it could not have come at a worst moment. For accompanying Nagumo's receipt of this message came the first sighting of Tomonaga's returning aeroplanes. Many of the aircraft were low on fuel or damaged, and on arrival over the fleet they began to circle as they awaited permission to land. Unless the decks of the carriers

were rapidly cleared of the second strike wave the returning aircraft would have no alternative but to ditch in the sea. Speed of decision was therefore of the essence. No discussion was needed for the planned second strike on Midway to be aborted. It was self-evident to all on *Akagi*'s bridge that the American carrier now posed the greater danger and must take first priority.

Herein lay the dilemma for Nagumo. Of the bombers in the second strike wave, the bulk of the 'Kates' were armed with bombs and not with the more efficacious torpedoes. Should they be launched as armed against the carrier? Certainly Admiral Yamaguchi on *Hiryu* believed so, and signalled Nagumo to that effect. But Nagumo knew that to launch the strike aircraft immediately would be to do so without benefit of fighter cover. Itaya's 'Zeros' had been aloft since early morning, helping the small number of fighters of the fleet combat air patrol defeat the repeated US air attacks. They were also waiting in the circuit to land to refuel and rearm. Nagumo was acutely conscious of the questionable value of sending out the bombers without fighter cover, as they would prove highly vulnerable to interception by enemy fighters – a point well made by the Japanese themselves in the previous few hours. He therefore believed he had sound reasons for supposing that a strike despatched immediately would prove to be of dubious value and lead only to the loss of valuable men and machines.

Genda and Kusaka were also fully cognisant of these matters, and were prompted in consequence to advise Nagumo to recover Tomonaga's force first, and only then attack the carrier. That would require the second-strike aircraft at present spotted on the decks to be taken down to the hangar levels to clear the decks. While that was being done, the 'Kates' could then also be rearmed with torpedoes. It could not be said that Nagumo suffered from any agony of indecision on this occasion. Less than two minutes elapsed from his receipt of the scout aeroplane's message to the fateful signal flashed to all carriers, instructing that the Midway attackers be allowed to land and the second-wave strike bombers be rearmed with torpedoes. This was followed at 0835 by a further signal, ordering that once all aircraft had been recovered, the whole fleet would turn north to 'contact and destroy the enemy force'.

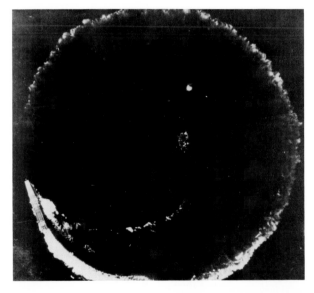

▲ *The Soryu makes nearly a full turn as it seeks to evade the bombs from Lieutenant Colonel Sweeney's B-17s which arrived over the Japanese carriers shortly after 0800. (US National Archives)*

▶ *Of the nine slow and venerable Vought SB2U-3 Vindicators – nicknamed 'Vibrators' by their crews – that left Midway to attack Nagumo's carriers, two were shot down. (Philip Jarrett)*

As the gongs sounded and orders were barked across the flight decks there was an intense flurry of activity on all four carriers as aircraft were manhandled to the lifts and then taken down to the hangar levels. Within minutes they were clear and at 0837 the first of Tomonaga's thirsty charges touched down. On board *Kaga* and *Akagi* sweating armourers once more lowered bombs from shackles and began the laborious and tiring work of reloading the torpedoes. Owing to the pressure of time and the constant demands of officers to speed up the process, safety procedures were ignored as bombs were casually stacked en masse at the sides of the hangars. To acquire a better fix on the American vessels, more scout aeroplanes were launched at about 0845, including one of the new D4Ys from *Soryu*. Scout aeroplane Number Four then came back on the air to inform *Tone*'s captain that he was returning to the ship as, having been airborne since 0500, he was running low on fuel. He was immediately told to postpone and turn on his DF transmitter to allow the carrier fleet to home in on his position.

With the last of the Midway attackers and Itaya's 'Zeros' recovered by 0917, the whole fleet changed course. A shudder was felt throughout *Akagi* as speed was increased to 30kts, and along with the other carriers the fleet turned to its new heading of east-north-east in a bid to close the distance to the American force. Nagumo was confident of being well placed to launch his first strike, comprising 102 aircraft, against the American carrier by 1030. The question on everyone's mind was: would they be

◀ *An unusual view of* **Akagi's** *flight deck, as seen from the gunner's position in a 'Kate' bomber that has just launched. Of note is the island offset to port, a feature found on only one other carrier ever built – the* **Hiryu.** *Note the Imperial symbol of the gold chrysanthemum carried on her bow and on all other warships of the Rengo Kantai.*

◀ *Although another pre-Pearl Harbor photograph, it is nevertheless of interest showing* **Hiryu** *viewed from the rear flight deck of her consort* **Soryu,** *on which 'Val' dive-bombers are warming up for take-off.*

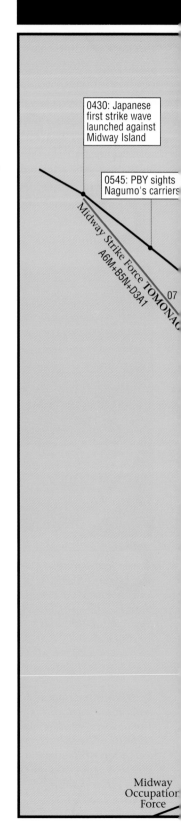

0430: Japanese first strike wave launched against Midway Island

0545: PBY sights Nagumo's carriers

Midway Strike Force **TOMONAG**
A6M+B5N+D3A1

07

Midway
Occupation
Force

Operations on 4 June 1942

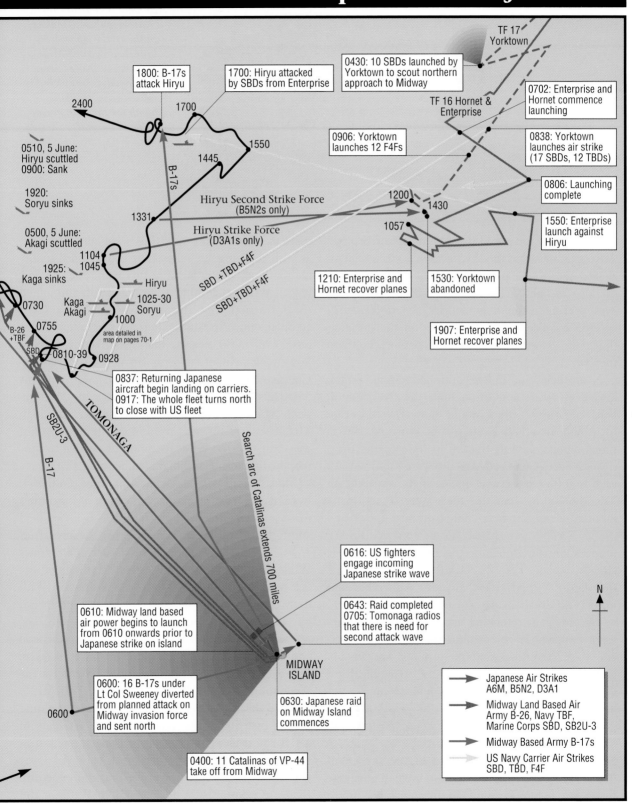

1800: B-17s attack Hiryu

1700: Hiryu attacked by SBDs from Enterprise

0430: 10 SBDs launched by Yorktown to scout northern approach to Midway

TF 17 Yorktown

TF 16 Hornet & Enterprise

0702: Enterprise and Hornet commence launching

2400

1700

1550

1445

B-17s

0906: Yorktown launches 12 F4Fs

0838: Yorktown launches air strike (17 SBDs, 12 TBDs)

0510, 5 June: Hiryu scuttled 0900: Sank

1331

Hiryu Second Strike Force (B5N2s only)

1200

1430

0806: Launching complete

1920: Soryu sinks

Hiryu Strike Force (D3A1 only)

1057

1550: Enterprise launch against Hiryu

0500, 5 June: Akagi scuttled

1104
1045

SBD +TBD+F4F

1210: Enterprise and Hornet recover planes

1530: Yorktown abandoned

1925: Kaga sinks

Hiryu

Kaga Akagi

1025-30 Soryu

SBD +TBD+F4F

0730

1000

area detailed in map on pages 70-1

1907: Enterprise and Hornet recover planes

B-26 +TBF

0755

SBD

0810-39

0928

0837: Returning Japanese aircraft begin landing on carriers. 0917: The whole fleet turns north to close with US fleet

SB2U-3

B-17

TOMONAGA

TOMONAGA

Search arc of Catalinas extends 700 miles

0616: US fighters engage incoming Japanese strike wave

0643: Raid completed 0705: Tomonaga radios that there is need for second attack wave

0610: Midway land based air power begins to launch from 0610 onwards prior to Japanese strike on island

MIDWAY ISLAND

0600: 16 B-17s under Lt Col Sweeney diverted from planned attack on Midway invasion force and sent north

0630: Japanese raid on Midway Island commences

0600

0400: 11 Catalinas of VP-44 take off from Midway

N

	Japanese Air Strikes A6M, B5N2, D3A1
	Midway Land Based Air Army B-26, Navy TBF, Marine Corps SBD, SB2U-3
	Midway Based Army B-17s
	US Navy Carrier Air Strikes SBD, TBD, F4F

◄ *Of the 63 aircraft carried by* **Akagi** *at Midway, 21 were Nakajima B5N2 'Kate' bombers. However, in the strike wave launched against Midway Island, the 'Kates' were employed as level bombers substituting an 800kg bomb for the 24in aerial torpedo normally carried.*

given the time, or would the Americans strike first? Anxious eyes swept the sky for the air strike that all aboard had been expecting ever since the American carrier was sighted. Barely three minutes later, keen eyes peering through binoculars aboard *Chikuma* spotted a collection of black dots on the horizon; they were growing larger by the moment. So, there they were!

Nevertheless, optimism continued to reign on the bridge of *Akagi* and throughout the fleet, for all believed that this attack would be weathered as easily as had the others earlier in the morning. But as the American aircraft tracked in towards the fleet, this confidence proceeded to dissipate rapidly. With each sighting it became increasingly apparent to Nagumo and his staff that there were far too many inbound hostiles to have come from just one enemy carrier. Orders were hastily issued to speed up the preparations for launching the air strike, but it was already too late. The US Navy flyers had caught the four Japanese carriers at their most vulnerable, and in just the situation that Spruance had hoped for – in the midst of refuelling and rearming their aircraft. Unbeknown to Nagumo, the fate of the carriers, their aeroplanes and their pilots was already sealed. The life of the seemingly invincible First Carrier Strike Force had but one hour to run.

The Courageous Sacrifice

Spruance had intended to have all the aircraft of Task Force 16's Striking Force assemble in one large formation before heading off to attack Nagumo's carriers. To that end the SBDs were launched first, as with their greater range they could afford to circle the Task Force, burning fuel while the shorter-legged Wildcats and Devastators took off and joined the formation. But the discovery of *Tone*'s scout aeroplane hovering on the horizon prompted him to change his mind. Fearing that the strike force would lose its element of surprise, Spruance ordered Lt-Commander Wade McClusky, already aloft with his 33 SBDs, to depart immediately, leaving the torpedo bombers and fighters to follow. Although McClusky was thus deprived of any fighter cover, it was clear that the Wildcats would be needed to protect the lumbering and highly vulnerable TBDs.

Shortly before 0800 McClusky turned southeast, heading towards the assumed position of Nagumo's force. He was followed by *Hornet*'s dive bombers and fighters and Waldron's VT-8. As the aircraft of *Hornet*'s strike group took their leave, *Enterprise*'s Wildcats were circling the carrier, waiting for the last of the TBDs of VT-6 to take to the air. With their departure the strike force had become spread out into four distinct bodies: McClusky's SBDs, *Hornet*'s SBDs and F4Fs, and the two torpedo bombing squadrons. In addition, the onset of layers of broken cloud made it increasingly difficult for the dive bombers and fighters flying at 19,000ft to observe the torpedo bombers, which were holding course just above the wavetops. The Wildcats of VF-6 had been tasked with protecting VT-6, but in the confusion caused by the cloud cover Lt Gray had unknowingly lost track of VT-6, and ended up flying top cover to Waldron's VT-8. Waldron did

▶ *Seen here early on 4 June is the USS* Hornet *and her attendant screening vessels comprising the light cruiser* Atlanta *on the left, a* New Orleans-*class heavy cruiser mid-field, and the destroyer* Phelps. *(via Robert C. Stern)*

not know of the prearranged signal whereby Gray's fighters would descend to aid VT-6, and in consequence both squadrons of torpedo bombers ended up attacking the Japanese carriers devoid of fighter support.

At the time of the launch neither Spruance nor Fletcher had received any update on the position of Nagumo's force since their receipt of Ady's original sighting report. They were therefore totally unaware of Nagumo's change of course away from Midway and his subsequent run to the north to close with the American carrier group. Thus Task Force 16's attack force had struck out on a direct route towards the estimated position of Nagumo's carriers, on the erroneous assumption he was still holding his southeasterly course towards Midway. Anticipating that contact would be made with the enemy between 0915 and 0939, *Hornet*'s dive bombers and fighters arrived in position only to find themselves over a wide and empty expanse of the Pacific. Choosing to hold this same course, Ring then decided — wrongly, as it transpired — that Nagumo must have moved even further south towards Midway. Consequently, the SBDs and F4Fs of *Hornet*'s Air Group were drawn even further away from Nagumo's actual position. Unable to locate the Japanese fleet, and with fuel running low,

Ring led some of the SBDs back to the carrier while others landed on Midway. The Wildcats, however, were forced to ditch as, one after another, their fuel tanks ran dry.

Following his own hunch, Waldron led his squadron for only part of the way along the identified route before changing course and heading northwest. In his final briefing to his men he had confided in them that he believed that, once Nagumo became aware of the presence of the American carriers, he would change his course and heading. He said that he would do the same, and told his men to follow him as he knew where he was going. Waldron was under no illusions about the prospects of survival for his squadron, but told them that if

▶ *Lieutenant Commander John C. Waldron was squadron commander of VT-8 aboard* Hornet, *and led the first of the attacks* *by the carrier-based air-craft on the Japanese Fleet. All 15 of Waldron's aircraft were shot down. (US National Archives)*

The Carrier Air Strikes on Nagumo's Carriers, 0920-1200

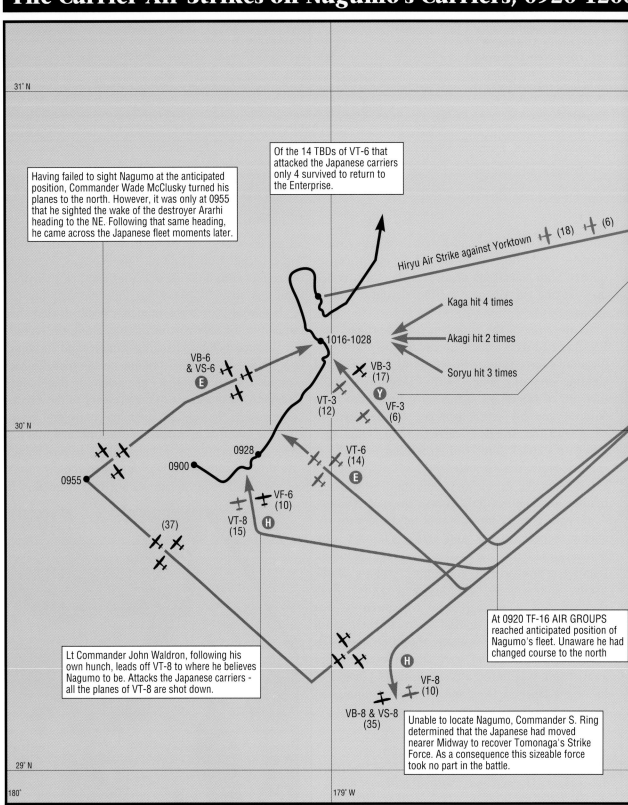

Having failed to sight Nagumo at the anticipated position, Commander Wade McClusky turned his planes to the north. However, it was only at 0955 that he sighted the wake of the destroyer Ararhi heading to the NE. Following that same heading, he came across the Japanese fleet moments later.

Of the 14 TBDs of VT-6 that attacked the Japanese carriers only 4 survived to return to the Enterprise.

Hiryu Air Strike against Yorktown ╪ (18) ╪ (6)

Kaga hit 4 times

Akagi hit 2 times

Soryu hit 3 times

1016-1028

VB-6 & VS-6 **E**

VB-3 (17)

VT-3 (12)

Y

VF-3 (6)

31° N

30° N

0928

0900

0955

(37)

VT-6 (14) **E**

VF-6 (10)

VT-8 (15) **H**

Lt Commander John Waldron, following his own hunch, leads off VT-8 to where he believes Nagumo to be. Attacks the Japanese carriers - all the planes of VT-8 are shot down.

At 0920 TF-16 AIR GROUPS reached anticipated position of Nagumo's fleet. Unaware he had changed course to the north

H

VF-8 (10)

VB-8 & VS-8 (35)

Unable to locate Nagumo, Commander S. Ring determined that the Japanese had moved nearer Midway to recover Tomonaga's Strike Force. As a consequence this sizeable force took no part in the battle.

29° N

180°

179° W

only one of them survived the run-in, he wanted him to go in and get a hit. Flying his squadron as straight as a die, Waldron found the Japanese Fleet exactly where he believed it would be. At 0920 the fifteen Devastators of VT-8 began their lone and suicidal assault on the enemy fleet.

As Nagumo's command accelerated on to its new heading its vessels deployed to provide maximum defensive coverage for the carriers in the event of air attack. In the van of the advancing fleet the light cruiser *Nagara* shepherded the destroyers which screened the advancing fleet to its fore and flanks. To the rear of *Nagara*, sailing in line ahead, were the fast battleships *Kirishima* and *Haruna*, flanked to port and starboard by the carriers *Akagi* and *Hiryu* and *Kaga* and *Soryu* respectively. The battleships were so placed to bring to bear the firepower of their heavy anti-aircraft batteries in defence of the carriers. The heavy cruisers *Tone* and *Chikuma* provided flank cover for the inner group of warships and the outermost anti-aircraft screen. No fewer than 50 'Zeros' were aloft to provide a comprehensive standing air patrol. As soon as Waldron's squadron was spotted at 0920 the fighters veered off and accelerated towards the incoming torpedo bombers.

Waggling his wings, Waldron signalled his squadron to begin their attack. As he was unable to call down Gray's Wildcats circling uselessly above him at 20,000ft, his attack went in without fighter cover. It seems that he intended to target *Akagi*, but eight miles out from the fleet the first of the 'Zeros' swept down on the low-flying squadron and began hacking the TBDs from the air in a hail of machine-gun and cannon fire. Within seconds they had

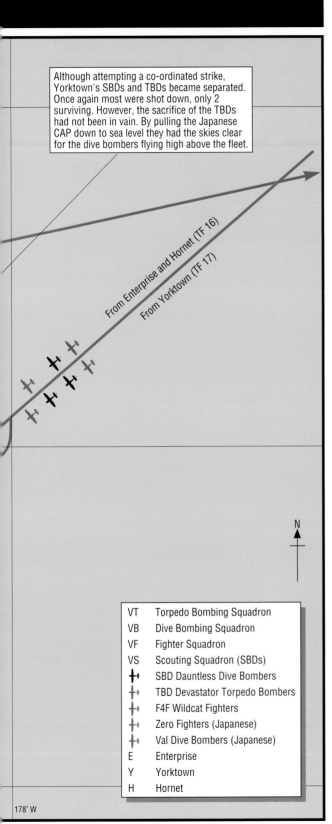

Although attempting a co-ordinated strike, Yorktown's SBDs and TBDs became separated. Once again most were shot down, only 2 surviving. However, the sacrifice of the TBDs had not been in vain. By pulling the Japanese CAP down to sea level they had the skies clear for the dive bombers flying high above the fleet.

From Enterprise and Hornet (TF 16)

From Yorktown (TF 17)

N

VT	Torpedo Bombing Squadron
VB	Dive Bombing Squadron
VF	Fighter Squadron
VS	Scouting Squadron (SBDs)
✈	SBD Dauntless Dive Bombers
✈	TBD Devastator Torpedo Bombers
✈	F4F Wildcat Fighters
✈	Zero Fighters (Japanese)
✈	Val Dive Bombers (Japanese)
E	Enterprise
Y	Yorktown
H	Hornet

178° W

◀ *Just five minutes was sufficient for the balance of naval power in the Pacific to be changed for ever. Between 1020 and 1025 on the morning of 4 June 1942, the dive-bombers of Task Forces 16 and 17 destroyed three of Admiral Nagumo's carriers.* Hiryu *followed later that day. In one fell swoop the US Navy Dauntlesses had eliminated an overwhelming Japanese superiority in naval air power, the vital key to the successful prosecution of war in the vast expanse of the Pacific theatre. Those five minutes transformed an empire at the zenith of its power into one facing the prospect of defeat and inevitable ruin. The battle of Midway is for that reason one of the most decisive battles ever fought.*

The pilots of VT-8 pose for the camera aboard **Hornet** *shortly before their fatal attack on the Japanese carriers at Midway. Only Ensign George Gay, fourth from the left in the front row, survived the attack. Clutching a piece of wreckage, he witnessed the rest of the battle from the water. (US Navy)*

accounted for four of them. As the survivors flew ever nearer they encountered a wall of anti-aircraft fire that tore apart the airframes and killed the crews. Fuchida, who was watching from the flagship, recounted how 'occasionally one of the specks burst into a spark of flame and trailed black smoke as it fell into the water'. Although all of TBDs were lost, there was one survivor. Ensign George Gay, who was flying in the last of the Devastators, later recounted how, as he flew through the flak and towards *Akagi*, he heard his gunner cry out as he was killed by fire from the 'Zeros' on his tail. Even though he had been wounded by a 20mm cannon shell in his left foot and his aeroplane had been riddled and holed, he managed to release his torpedo. Pulling up over the carrier, he nearly hit its bridge before the fire from the 'Zeros' that were chasing him sent his aircraft crashing into the sea beyond. Gay managed to abandon his sinking Devastator and, by catching hold of an inflatable life raft, floated free of the wreckage to became an unwitting spectator of the dramatic events of the next few hours.

Even as it was announced that all fifteen of the torpedo bombers had been shot down, the work of preparing the strike force went on. Amid the violent defensive manoeuvres aircraft were still being brought up and spotted on deck and having their engines run up. Nagumo now needed a period of relative calm to enable the aeroplanes to be launched, but the gallant sacrifice of VT-8 meant that the carrier fleet had been forced to waste vital minutes in defensive action. This delay was further

compounded when it was announced that yet another enemy force had been spotted. Inbound to the fleet were Lindsay's fourteen Devastators from VT-6. From *Akagi* it appeared that they were attempting a concerted attack from either bow in single columns.

Although their designated fighter cover was still circling high overhead, Lindsay did not give the signal that would have brought Gray's Wildcats plummeting down on the 'Zeros' that were even now tearing into his two columns. As the Devastators bore in towards the fleet, skimming the wave tops, the Japanese fighters began to scythe down the American torpedo bombers. Ripped apart by shellfire, they exploded, disintegrated and fell into the sea. By the time they reached the torpedo release point for *Akagi*, only seven of the bombers were still airborne. For some reason these then peeled away from from the flagship and headed instead for the *Hiryu*. Flying through the hail of flak being thrown up by the warships, and pursued by the 'Zeros', the seven surviving aircraft launched their torpedoes at Yamaguchi's carrier. By turning hard to port the *Hiryu* succeeded in avoiding them all. As the TBDs pulled away from the fleet a further three were hacked down, only four managing to return to the *Enterprise*.

Hardly had the 'Zeros' landed to refuel and rearm when, at 1015, lookouts on the *Akagi* sighted yet another incoming attack of torpedo bombers. Unlike the previous two attacks, *Yorktown*'s contingent of Massey's twelve Devastators had arrived as part of a coherent strike group. In addition to a small fighter force of six Wildcats under Jimmy Thach, high overhead cruised Leslie's seventeen dive bombers. The intention was to launch a combined assault on the Japanese warships in the hope of swamping the defences, thus increasing the chance of at least some of the aircraft getting through. All was going well as the Americans approached the Japanese force. Visibility was good, for when first spotted, some 40 miles distant, Nagumo's vessels were seen to be manoeuvring violently, indicating that they were clearly under attack. But as the *Yorktown*'s group deployed for action, the dive bombers flew into heavy cloud and radio contact was lost with the TBDs and the F4Fs far below.

For Massey and his eleven charges, what now unfolded was nothing more than a replay of the slaughter of the earlier Devastator attacks. The presence of Thach's Wildcats became somewhat academic. So many 'Zeros' were airborne that, once the American fighters were embroiled in a dogfight with some of the Japanese aircraft, more than sufficient were left over to attack Massey's torpedo bombers with impunity. Of the twelve Devastators that began the run-in, only seven were still in the air some minutes later as they reached their final run-in positions to their targets. Two more, including Massey's, blew up as they ran into the hail of fire thrown up by the ships. The remaining five lunged ahead, splitting their attacks on the Hiryu and Kaga, but in the face of the devastating wall of flak and the omnipresent 'Zeros' their torpedoes, once launched, veered wide of their targets. Freed of the weight of their weapons, the surviving TBDs struggled desperately to escape, but two more fell flaming into the sea and another disintegrated as it crossed the outer screen of warships. Only two of VT-3's Devastators returned to land forlornly on *Enterprise*'s deck at 1020.

Nemesis

There was a grim sense of satisfaction on the bridge of *Akagi* as the last of the TBDs staggered away from the carriers. Once again, wave after wave of American torpedo bombers had been thrown at the First Air Fleet and destroyed with no damage incurred. Now was the moment for the riposte. Without further delay Nagumo ordered all carriers turned into the wind to make ready for launching. Who could doubt that, with the cream of the *Rengo Kantai*'s pilots about to take off from the decks of the four carriers, Japan was on the verge of realising the decisive victory she so desired? Yet the sacrifice of the 37 American torpedo bombers and their crews had not been in vain. By their repeated attacks the TBD squadrons had thoroughly disrupted the integrity of the defensive screen around Nagumo's carriers. More significantly, their low-level attacks had pulled down the 'Zero' fighter screen from medium to high altitude, where they normally patrolled, to sea level. This left the skies above the fleet unprotected and the carriers totally vulnerable to attack from the US dive bombers hidden in the clouds above. The engines of the strike group on all four carriers rose to a crescendo as pilots eagerly awaited the signal for take-off. At almost the same moment as Nagumo gave the order to launch the strike force, a lookout on *Kaga* made the first sighting of the plummeting US dive bombers. The time was 1020.

Overhead were McClusky's and Leslie's SBD squadrons. The former had almost not made it. He had initially proceeded to Nagumo's estimated position but, finding nothing there, chose, unlike Ring, to fly north rather than south. As he had already used up half of his fuel, his decision to proceed was brave, for if the Japanese had not been spotted soon the whole squadron would have had to ditch. Just after 1000 McClusky saw the faint wake of a Japanese destroyer racing to the north. Following the same heading, he was soon rewarded by the sight of three of the carriers under attack. Although Leslie's passage to the fleet had been more direct, it was not without incident. In the process of arming their weapons, faulty electrical circuits caused a number of the SBDs, including Leslie's, to drop their bombs. When both SBD groups finally located the Japanese fleet, Leslie's SBDs approached from the southeast and McClusky's came up from the southwest. Their respective approaches gave the pilots differing perspectives of the positions of the enemy carriers, resulting in a dispute that continues to this day regarding whose aeroplanes subsequently hit which carriers. This account has no space to investigate the respective claims of either group, but these can be explored by examining a number of the texts in the bibliography. Needless to say, such matters were somewhat academic to those in the Japanese carriers that now became the targets and victims of the US 'helldivers'.

Only a few desultory bursts of anti-aircraft fire greeted the first of the Dauntlesses as they came hurtling out of the sun. *Kaga* was the first to be struck, the pilots no doubt attracted by her huge size. Four bombs were sufficient to reduce her to a blazing wreck in a matter of minutes. The first three missed her, but the fourth dropped squarely amidst the mass of fully armed and fuelled aircraft waiting to take off on the rear of her flight deck. In the eruption of fuel and bombs, aircrew were cremated in their cockpits as the flight deck became a massive funeral pyre. Burning fuel seeped from the deck to the lower levels, filling the passageways and cutting off crew members. Two other bombs hit near the forward elevator, one penetrating to the hangar level where aircraft of the second wave were being fuelled and armed. The explosion detonated their fuel tanks and the many 800kg bombs that had been so casually stashed during the first rearming earlier in the

morning. The eruption of the high-octane fuel transformed the hangar level into a conflagration, killing the mechanics and armourers at work there. The deck became an inferno when the explosion of the fourth bomb generated a shock wave which ruptured a fuel bowser. This then exploded, killing Captain Okada and his command staff on the bridge.

Kaga's air officer assumed command, but it was clear that the fire fighting teams were conducting a losing battle, for the ship was now blazing from stem to stern. Anti-aircraft guns began firing of their own accord as the ferocious heat set off their magazines. All lights went out as the power failed, and the carrier began to list. For three hours fire fighting teams tried to control the flames that were ravaging what was now little more than a blazing hulk. The ship had become so hot that even the paint had begun to burn on what remained of the superstructure. Although many of the crew had already jumped overboard, Captain Amagai did not give the final order to abandon ship until 1640. By this time *Kaga* was alone and forlorn, with just the

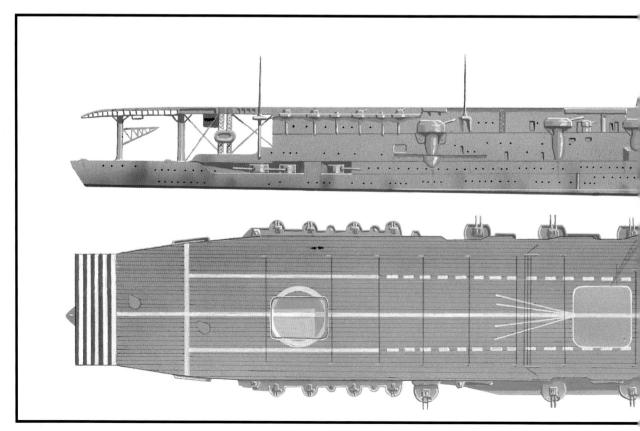

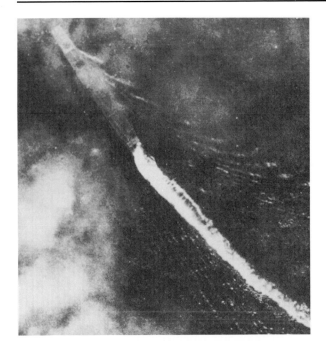

▲ Akagi *prior to being hit by three bombs from SBDs of VF-8 commanded by Lieutenant Richard H.* Best. Akagi *was hit at 1026. (US Navy)*

destroyers *Maikaze* and *Hagikaze* picking up survivors. An attack by the US submarine *Nautilus* on the *Kaga* (which was mistaken for the *Soryu*) does not seem to have contributed to her sinking. The end did not come until 1925, when observers saw her hull rent by two massive explosions as the fires reached the magazines. Shortly thereafter the flaming hulk turned over and sank into the deep, taking with her over 800 of her crew and virtually all of her aircraft and aircrew.

A similar fate befell *Akagi*. The first 'Zero' was already beginning its take-off run when three SBDs were seen plummeting towards the flagship. The first released its bomb at 2,500ft, but this missed the ship and fell into the sea on the starboard side. The second hit the target, exploding close to the rear lift and twisting it so badly that it fell into the hangar below. The third fell among the packed aircraft waiting to take off on the rear of the deck. These erupted and flared in a sheet of burning fuel and exploding bombs, incinerating the élite of the Air Fleet where they sat. The rear of the carrier was transformed into an inferno likened by one of the

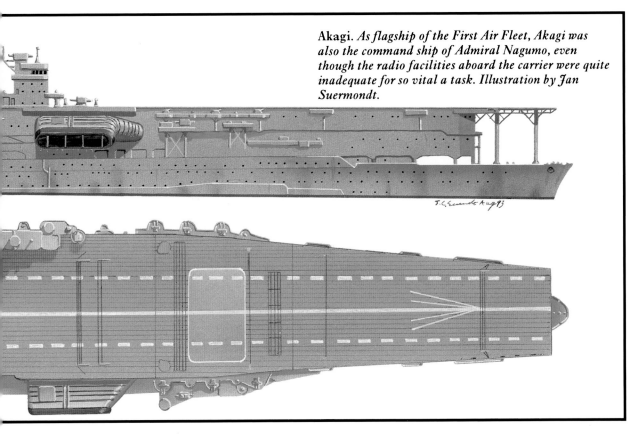

Akagi. *As flagship of the First Air Fleet, Akagi was also the command ship of Admiral Nagumo, even though the radio facilities aboard the carrier were quite inadequate for so vital a task. Illustration by Jan Suermondt.*

▲ *With air brakes deployed, the Dauntlesses begin their power-dives from 15,000ft on the Japanese carriers below.* Akagi, Kaga *and* Soryu *were hit within minutes of each other and were reduced to blazing wrecks by the Navy dive-bombers. (via Robert F. Dorr)*

survivors to a burning hell. As the flames reached the hangar level the stacked bombs blew up, along with the aeroplanes of the second wave that were still being armed. Within minutes the whole of the the lower levels of the carrier were afire and cut off. Just ten minutes after the attack the steering gear failed. Periodically, explosions were felt in the interior of the vessel.

When the news reached the bridge that even the escape passages below were afire, Nagumo was advised to transfer his flag to another vessel. The hapless admiral, however, gazed around as if in a trance, unable to comprehend how the fortunes of his proud and mighty fleet had changed so quickly and so brutally in the space of but five minutes. When finally led from the bridge, Nagumo and his staff could only vacate it by sliding down a rope hanging out of one of the windows. Relocating to the *Nagara*, the admiral and his staff contemplated their flame-engulfed flagship as the light cruiser moved away from her at speed. Not until early the following morning did Yamamoto himself give the order for her still burning hulk to be given the *coup de grace*. Dawn was just breaking as four destroyers launched their torpedoes into the mighty ship. She slipped beneath the waves, one last mighty explosion marking her passing as she headed down into the deep, taking with her nearly 300 of her crew.

Observers on *Soryu* hardly had time to register the explosions aboard *Kaga* before they, too, became victims of the 'helldivers'. Three SBDs plummeted out of the sky just after 1025 to deposit their bombs along her flight deck. Accounts differ as to where the bombs actually hit, but it seems that the first exploded between the second and third lifts. The second hit just in front of the forward lift, penetrated the flight deck, crashed into the hangar level below and exploded amidst the aircraft parked there. The subsequent detonation caused the fuel tanks and weapons stores to explode, vaporizing everything within the hangar level and generating a

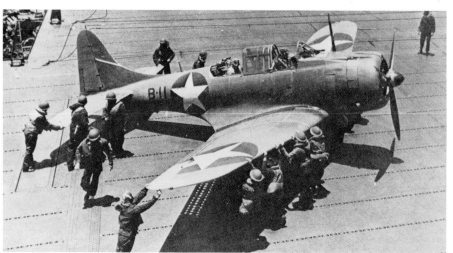

◀ *An SBD of VB-3 recovers aboard the* Hornet *having missed the entire battle. A shortage of fuel meant that the whole fighter escort protecting the Dauntlesses had to ditch in the sea. Only the TBDs of* Hornet's *Air Group attacked the Japanese carrier fleet. (US Navy)*

heat so fierce that within a short time even the metal began to melt. Such was the force of this explosion that the forward lift was flung from its mounting and smashed into the island. Simultaneously, the third bomb fell on the rear deck amid the waiting aircraft, transforming it, as on *Kaga* and *Akagi*, into yet another funeral pyre for the élite flyers of the Air Fleet.

Twenty minutes later a huge explosion tore through the innards of the ship, throwing large numbers of men into the water. Such was the destruction and ferocity of the fires aboard *Soryu* that, half an hour after the strike, her engines had stopped, all steering was gone and the whole carrier was ablaze from stem to stern. Seeing that all was lost, her captain gave the order to abandon ship. The destroyers *Hamakaze* and *Isokaze* closed with the blazing hulk and picked up survivors. Attempts to talk Captain Yanagimoto down from the bridge were to no avail, and he was still aboard with sword drawn when, at 1913, a series of massive explosions swept the carrier. It sank shortly afterwards, taking 718 men down with her.

The End of *Yorktown*

Nagumo now devolved command to Rear Admiral Abe Hiraoki in *Tone*, who in turn ordered Yamaguchi and the as yet undamaged *Hiryu* to strike back at the American carriers. At 1058 the first of two strike waves was launched from *Hiryu*, comprising eighteen dive bombers escorted by six 'Zeros' and led by the redoubtable Lt Kobayashi. They were guided by radio reports from *Chikuma*'s Number Five floatplane, which had Task Force 17 under discreet surveillance.

Shortly before midday, as *Yorktown* was preparing to recover her dive bombers and refuel her fighters, her radar detected Kobayashi's incoming strike group. A combat air patrol of twelve fighters was already aloft, and a further fifteen were on deck being refuelled when the order was given to launch. The dive bombers were warned off, and the carrier prepared for attack. All her petrol pumps were closed down and the carbonic acid gas fire suppression system was readied. *Yorktown*'s escorts were pulled in closer to add their own firepower to that of the carrier. Fighters were despatched from Task Force 16, so that 28 Wildcats were now available to tackle the incoming Japanese aircraft.

Running in at 10,000ft, the 'Val' dive bombers were assailed by the Wildcats and ten, including Kobayashi's, were shot down. The heavy flak curtain sent aloft by the Task Force then accounted for a further three, but five survived. They were sufficient to do the damage. They plummeted down on the *Yorktown*, and three bombs found their mark. The first exploded on the carrier's deck, making a large hole and causing fires which quickly spread below deck. The second crashed down the smokestack and exploded in the engine room, leaving only one boiler working and wrecking the bridge's radar, communications systems and plotting room. The third penetrated the deck and exploded deep in the bowels of the ship, but deft use of the carbonic acid gas system and selective flooding prevented the nearby petrol tanks and a magazine from exploding.

As he was now unable to maintain effective command over the Task Force, Fletcher shifted his flag to the cruiser *Astoria*. However, although *Yorktown* was badly damaged, she was rapidly brought back into action. By 1340 four of her engines were working, the fires were out and she was able to work up 20kts. Rapid deck repairs had been improvised, and she began to recover and refuel her fighters in preparation for *Hiryu*'s second wave.

Meanwhile, the 'Judy' reconnaissance aircraft despatched some hours earlier from the *Soryu* to watch the American force had been recovered aboard *Hiryu*, and Yamaguchi had received the dramatic news that there were three American carriers, not the two suspected. He therefore decided to launch his second strike wave with despatch. The chosen strike leader was the same Lt Tomonaga who had led the Midway attack earlier in the day. He accepted without hesitation, even though he knew that his trip would be one way – there had not been enough time to repair the damage to the fuel tank in his port wing. The rapid depletion of Japanese aircraft was apparent in the fact that only sixteen aircraft were available, and even some of these were strays from *Kaga* and *Akagi*. Ten torpedo bombers and six escorting 'Zeros' were launched at 1331. Although guided once more by *Chikuma*'s floatplane, Tomonaga's group had been informed that

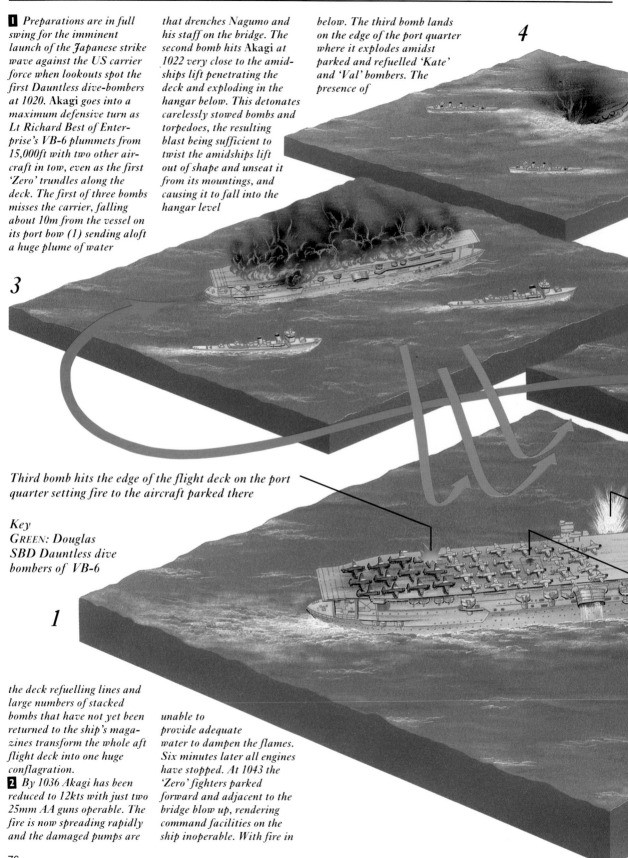

1 *Preparations are in full swing for the imminent launch of the Japanese strike wave against the US carrier force when lookouts spot the first Dauntless dive-bombers at 1020.* Akagi *goes into a maximum defensive turn as Lt Richard Best of Enterprise's VB-6 plummets from 15,000ft with two other aircraft in tow, even as the first 'Zero' trundles along the deck. The first of three bombs misses the carrier, falling about 10m from the vessel on its port bow (1) sending aloft a huge plume of water*

that drenches Nagumo and his staff on the bridge. The second bomb hits Akagi *at 1022 very close to the amidships lift penetrating the deck and exploding in the hangar below. This detonates carelessly stowed bombs and torpedoes, the resulting blast being sufficient to twist the amidships lift out of shape and unseat it from its mountings, and causing it to fall into the hangar level*

below. The third bomb lands on the edge of the port quarter where it explodes amidst parked and refuelled 'Kate' and 'Val' bombers. The presence of

4

3

Third bomb hits the edge of the flight deck on the port quarter setting fire to the aircraft parked there

Key
GREEN: Douglas
SBD Dauntless dive
bombers of VB-6

1

the deck refuelling lines and large numbers of stacked bombs that have not yet been returned to the ship's magazines transform the whole aft flight deck into one huge conflagration.
2 *By 1036* Akagi *has been reduced to 12kts with just two 25mm AA guns operable. The fire is now spreading rapidly and the damaged pumps are*

unable to provide adequate water to dampen the flames. Six minutes later all engines have stopped. At 1043 the 'Zero' fighters parked forward and adjacent to the bridge blow up, rendering command facilities on the ship inoperable. With fire in all the passages below and unable to exercise control over his ravaged carrier fleet, Nagumo reluctantly agrees to evacuate the ship, boarding the screening destroyer *Nowaki* before transferring his command flag to the light cruiser *Nagara*.

3 With engine room dead and fires engulfing the ship, Captain Aoki calls up the destroyers *Arashi* and *Nowaki* to evacuate all crew not fighting fires. Such is the ferocity of the fires that Aoki and his staff are driven down to the anchor deck where he tries to exercise command over the fire-fighting teams, but to no avail. The Emperor's portrait is transferred at 1338 and shortly thereafter all power from the engines ceases and the blazing hulk begins to drift. Crew evacuation is completed by *Arashi* and *Nowaki* by 1600, but it is not until nearly 3½hrs later that Aoki bows to the inevitable when he signals Nagumo that *Akagi* cannot be saved and requests permission to scuttle the vessel. By 2000 the two attending destroyers have evacuated the last of the survivors.

4 Meanwhile Yamamoto, having intercepted Aoki's request to scuttle, orders a delay, no doubt influenced by his own sentimental attachment to the carrier of which once he had been captain. At the same time

Amidships elevator has fallen into the hangar deck below

2

Aoki returns to *Akagi* and lashes himself to the ship's anchor, determined to go down with his ship, but he is eventually persuaded to come down and is in due course evacuated by *Arashi*.

In spite of the terrible damage wrought by the fires and explosions, *Akagi* stays afloat throughout the night of 4/5 June, but at 0450 Yamamoto reluctantly gives the final order to despatch the blackened hulk. Shortly after 0450, four destroyers close in on the carrier and launch torpedoes. Just before sunrise, the flagship of the Pearl Harbor Strike Fleet sinks, taking down to the depths some 270 of her crew.

First bomb hits the sea off the port bow approximately 30ft from the carrier

Second bomb hits the amidships elevator at 1022 penetrating and exploding in the hangar below

THE LOSS OF *AKAGI*

The destruction of the Japanese flagship *Akagi*, 1026 hours to 0500 hours, 4 June 1942

◄ *As the only surviving carrier capable of retaliation, Hiryu launched a strike against Yorktown at 1200. This remarkable photograph was taken literally at the moment of impact when one of three bombs hit the vessel. (via Robert C. Stern)*

◄ *The following sequence of photographs should be 'read' with the diagram on pages 82–3 to give a comprehensive account of the fate of Yorktown. Here she is seen manoeuvring to avoid the Japanese bombs while in the next shot she is seen burning after being hit by three bombs from 'Val' dive-bombers. (via Robert C. Stern)*

▼ *Smoke belches forth from the bomb hit that penetrated the stack, extinguishing a large number of her boilers. This damage also led to Fletcher transferring his command flag to the cruiser Astoria. Already, teams can be seen dealing with the damage. (via Robert C. Stern)*

▼ *Work has already started on repairs to Yorktown's flight deck. Clearly seen is the hole in the splintered flight deck* *caused by one of the Japanese bombs. Fast work of this sort enabled the carrier able to operate her aircraft just in time to* *receive the second Japanese strike. (via Robert C. Stern)*

Yorktown had been left ablaze and belching huge columns of smoke, and was presumed to be sinking. So when they arrived in the vicinity of *Yorktown* to discover no evidence of the damage caused by the earlier raid, they assumed that they were about to attack either *Hornet* or *Enterprise*.

Radar had picked up the Japanese group at 1430, and once more the decks of the carrier were rapidly cleared. The twelve Wildcats of the combat air patrol intercepted the incoming force, and as before succeeded in accounting for a number of the attackers, as did anti-aircraft fire. Although five bombers and three fighters were lost, the attackers continued to bore in on *Yorktown*. Led by Tomonaga, the five survivors deployed to launch their torpedoes. Having released his own, and knowing he could not return, the Midway attack leader deliberately crashed his aeroplane on to *Yorktown*'s flight deck. Two torpedoes then hit the carrier's port side less than 60ft apart, causing a series of explosions and fires. The carrier shuddered under the twin impact and came to a stop, all power was lost and the vessel began to list to port. Fearing that the carrier might capsize, Captain Buckmaster gave the order to abandon ship at 1500 and some 2,270 of her crew were recovered. Although abandoned, she remained afloat and was attended throughout the night by the destroyer *Hughes*, and was still there the following morning. However, the life of this remarkable vessel had not yet run its course. *Yorktown* refused to sink and was still afloat early the next morning, and her captain believed it was still possible to salvage her.

▶ **Yorktown** *is seen here shortly after 1220 by which time she was dead in the water. Most of the fires however have been contained, although a small amount of smoke is still emerging from the stack. (via Robert C. Stern)*

▶ *By 1437,* **Yorktown,** *able to make speed once again, prepares to launch eight of the ten fighters left on board against the incoming second Japanese strike. (via Robert C. Stern)*

▶*Although a grainy photograph, this picture captures the second strike on the* **Yorktown** *which was carried out only by 'Kate' torpedo bombers. Nevertheless, such had been the success of the US repair teams that Japanese flyers believed they had hit a second* **Yorktown**-*class carrier. (via Robert Stern)*

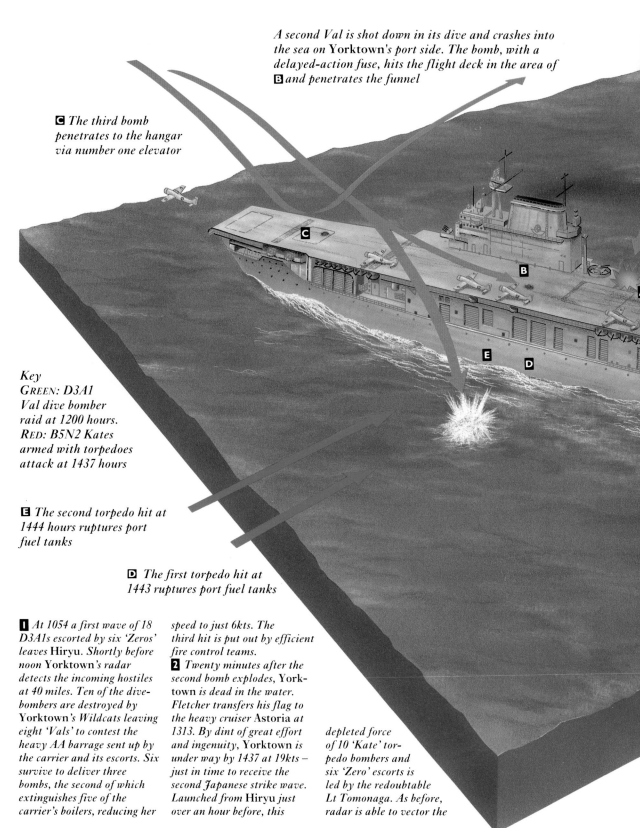

A second Val is shot down in its dive and crashes into the sea on **Yorktown**'s port side. The bomb, with a delayed-action fuse, hits the flight deck in the area of **B** and penetrates the funnel

C The third bomb penetrates to the hangar via number one elevator

Key
GREEN: *D3A1 Val dive bomber raid at 1200 hours.* RED: *B5N2 Kates armed with torpedoes attack at 1437 hours*

E The second torpedo hit at 1444 hours ruptures port fuel tanks

D The first torpedo hit at 1443 ruptures port fuel tanks

1 *At 1054 a first wave of 18 D3A1s escorted by six 'Zeros' leaves* **Hiryu**. *Shortly before noon* **Yorktown**'s *radar detects the incoming hostiles at 40 miles. Ten of the dive-bombers are destroyed by* **Yorktown**'s *Wildcats leaving eight 'Vals' to contest the heavy AA barrage sent up by the carrier and its escorts. Six survive to deliver three bombs, the second of which extinguishes five of the carrier's boilers, reducing her* speed to just 6kts. The third hit is put out by efficient fire control teams.
2 *Twenty minutes after the second bomb explodes,* **Yorktown** *is dead in the water. Fletcher transfers his flag to the heavy cruiser* **Astoria** *at 1313. By dint of great effort and ingenuity,* **Yorktown** *is under way by 1437 at 19kts – just in time to receive the second Japanese strike wave. Launched from* **Hiryu** *just over an hour before, this* depleted force of 10 'Kate' tor-pedo bombers and six 'Zero' escorts is led by the redoubtable Lt Tomonaga. As before, radar is able to vector the

80

THE LOSS OF *YORKTOWN*

The saga of *Yorktown*, 1050 hours on 4 June to 0500 hours on 7 June 1942

Approaching on a curving path, the first Val dives but disintegrates under Yorktown's AA fire and falls into the sea in three pieces, but the bomb hits the flight deck and explodes **A**

Wildcats of the CAP to the incoming force. With the F4Fs tied up by the 'Zeros', the surviving 'Kates' speed in on Task Force 17 at low level. Although five are hacked down by the 'splash barrage', four break through to launch their torpedoes. Having successfully avoided two of these by deft manoeuvring Yorktown succumbs to two strikes. The consequences are dramatic: her

port fuel tanks are destroyed and her rudder jammed; almost immediately she begins to take on a 26° list to port. **3** Unable to maintain watertight integrity, the carrier is in danger of capsizing, so at about 1500 Captain Buckmaster orders the vessel abandoned. Four destroyers, Balch, Benham, Russell *and* Anderson *close with* Yorktown saving some 2,270 of her crew. She is now abandoned, Fletcher and Buckmaster presuming her list is such that it is only a matter of time before she sinks.

When **Yorktown** *detects the incoming second strike, at approximately 1320, only 10 Wildcats are on board. Only 8 possess enough fuel for combat and are launched immediately to intercept the torpedo bombers, along with 6 F4Fs of VF-3 that are already on patrol*

minesweeper **Vireo** *and fleet tug* **Navajo** *to assist and also strengthens the anti-submarine screen around the ship. At 1436* Vireo *begins to tow* Yorktown *towards Pearl Harbor at 2kts, while aboard the carrier the salvage team lightens the vessel by ejecting over the side extraneous materials until nightfall when the vessel is without*

power and illumination. **5** *At 0410 in the early light of 6 June the Japanese submarine* I-168 *sights* Yorktown *screened by six destroyers: not until 1331 can torpedoes be fired. The first hits the destroyer* Hamman *which sinks almost immediately; two torpedoes run under the destroyer's keel and slam into the* Yorktown's

vitals, but still the carrier refuses to die. **6** *Ironically, the water pouring into* Yorktown's *starboard side now levels up the list, and Buckmaster is optimistic. The carrier hangs on through the night but it becomes ever clearer that she is doomed. USS* Yorktown *sinks as the sun rises, at 0458 on 7 June.*

4 *But the following morning* Yorktown *is still afloat. The decision is taken to re-board her, and a determined effort is made to salvage the stricken carrier. Nimitz despatches the*

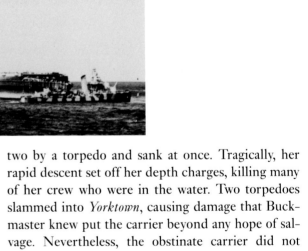

◀ *Attempts to salvage* **Yorktown** *and tow her to Pearl Harbor were finally abandoned on 6 June when she was torpedoed by the Japanese submarine* **I-168**. *Hit by two 'fish', it rapidly became clear that she was beyond saving. In the two centre photographs she is seen having taken on a heavy list to port while still surrounded by her destroyer screen. Bottom: With the ever-increasing list, salvage teams are ordered to abandon ship and they can be seen moving down the starboard hull to be picked up by an attendant destroyer. The cross on the hull marks the likely position of a torpedo hit from* **I-168**. *(via Robert C. Stern)*

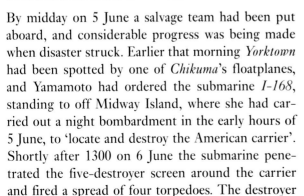

By midday on 5 June a salvage team had been put aboard, and considerable progress was being made when disaster struck. Earlier that morning *Yorktown* had been spotted by one of *Chikuma*'s floatplanes, and Yamamoto had ordered the submarine *I-168*, standing to off Midway Island, where she had carried out a night bombardment in the early hours of 5 June, to 'locate and destroy the American carrier'. Shortly after 1300 on 6 June the submarine penetrated the five-destroyer screen around the carrier and fired a spread of four torpedoes. The destroyer *Hamman*, which was lashed to the carrier, was cut in

two by a torpedo and sank at once. Tragically, her rapid descent set off her depth charges, killing many of her crew who were in the water. Two torpedoes slammed into *Yorktown*, causing damage that Buckmaster knew put the carrier beyond any hope of salvage. Nevertheless, the obstinate carrier did not finally succumb until 0600 the following morning.

Just as the survivors of *Hiryu*'s strike force returned to the carrier, she was finally spotted by one of the ten scout aircraft Fletcher had despatched earlier to seek her out. Lieutenant Wallace Short found her and her screening vessels approximately 100 miles to the northwest of *Yorktown*. When the news was received by Spruance aboard *Enterprise*, the decision was taken to launch an all-out strike against *Hiryu*. At 1530 *Enterprise* despatched a force of 24 Dauntlesses, and *Hornet* launched another sixteen. The few Wildcats that had survived the day's combat were retained to defend the carriers, so the dive bombers made way towards their prey without fighter cover.

By 1630 the remnant of the second strike group had been recovered by the *Hiryu*. Only three 'Zeros' and five 'Kates' had returned, but the pilots of the torpedo bombers were convinced that, rather than attacking *Yorktown* again, they had successfully destroyed a second US carrier. Yamaguchi now believed that, with the odds reduced to one-to-one, it might still be possible to resurrect a possible victory out of the ashes of the morning's disaster. To that end he ordered a third air strike made ready. However, the aircraft available were but a pale shadow of *Hiryu*'s air group and of the First Air Fleet's aeroplane strength launched against Midway barely twelve hours before. Only four 'Kates', five 'Vals' and six 'Zeros' of the combat air patrol, along with their exhausted crews, could be mustered. Nevertheless, the order went out to refuel and rearm them for a twilight strike. The deck of *Hiryu* rapidly became a hive of activity as fuel lines, bombs, torpedoes and ammunition were deployed to arm and equip the skeleton strike force. In the meantime, the aircrew were treated to a meal of sweet rice balls before their anticipated launch at 1800. While the Japanese flyers were in the middle of their meal the first Dauntlesses began their dive on the last of Nagumo's carriers.

The Death of *Hiryu*

Although there was a small combat air patrol aloft, the 'Zeros' did not detect the incoming dive bombers, so when the first thirteen of the SBDs began their power dives they achieved complete surprise. They came out of the sun, as they had done against the other carriers earlier in the day, allowing the *Hiryu* and its screening vessels to put up only a desultory defensive barrage before the first bombs struck. Sharp commands from the bridge to the engine room saw the speed of the *Hiryu* race up to

30kts as the rudder was put hard to starboard. From the diving SBDs it could be seen that she was attempting to turn full circle, but it was to no avail. Although three bombs were avoided, Nemesis struck with number four and three others followed in rapid succession. Two hit amidships and the other two forward of the island. The first blew the forward lift against the island bridge, and the whole deck forward of that position became a vast flaming void. As before, bombs penetrated to the hangar levels, causing casually stashed bombs to explode and fuel tanks to erupt. Many dead lay on the flight deck, and large numbers of the crew who survived the initial explosions below succumbed to the thick smoke from oil fires. The small strike group spotted on the rear of the carrier also blew up, spewing flaming fuel across the deck and adding further misery to the suffering crew.

Judging that *Hiryu* was already fatally damaged, the other SBDs turned their attention to the vessels of the screening force. *Haruna*, *Tone* and *Chikuma* were all subjected to heavy attack, but none were hit. With the departure of the American aeroplanes attempts were made to control the fires raging on the carrier. However, such was the damage that all the fire-fighting equipment had been destroyed, and the surviving crewmen were reduced to using buckets on lines and seawater in a pathetic attempt to control the flames. Four destroyers pulled alongside and poured seawater from their hoses on to the flaming hull. It was to no avail. Having maintained speed for some while after the attack, the engines finally died when flames reached the lower levels, killing many of the engineering crew. Heat caused rupturing of the lower hull plates, which led to flooding, and as she took on water *Hiryu* developed a fifteen-degree list.

A large explosion at 0158, which caused the fires to increase in intensity, finally decided Admiral Yamaguchi to abandon ship. When ordered to muster at 0250, approximately half of the crew of 1,500 had survived to present themselves. While the officers and crew were transferred to the destroyers alongside, Admiral Yamaguchi and Captain Kaku stayed aboard the stricken vessel, having stated their intention of going down with her. Lashing themselves to the helm, they awaited the end. On the order of Captain Abe, the destroyer *Makigumo*

launched a spread of torpedoes at the flaming hulk, and it was assumed that in the wake of the subsequent explosions the carrier would inevitably sink. But, like the *Yorktown*, the *Hiryu* did not want to die. She did not finally founder until about 0820, carrying with her to the bottom 416 of her crew, her captain and Admiral Yamaguchi. The last carrier of Nagumo's victorious and proud First Air Fleet had been consigned to the depths.

Operation MI Cancelled

Although Yamamoto and his staff had been party to the messages despatched by the *Tone*'s floatplane throughout the morning, the only signal they received from Nagumo came shortly after 0835. It announced the sighting of a carrier and other vessels, its position, and the decision to head for it. Although the operational plan had made no allowance for this contingency, Yamamoto and his staff displayed no anxiety, remaining secure in the conviction that Nagumo could handle the situation and resolve it to their advantage. The shock at the

▲ *Caught by the SBDs, the* **Hiryu** *tried desperately to avoid the plummeting dive-bombers but to no avail. At 1705 she was bracketed by four bombs and her fate became very quickly that of her sister carriers. (US National Archives)*

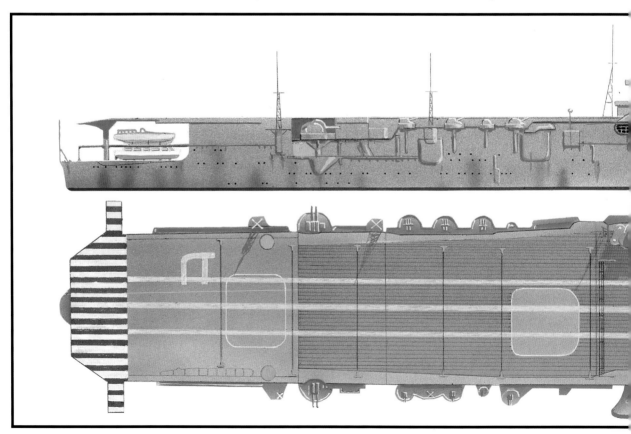

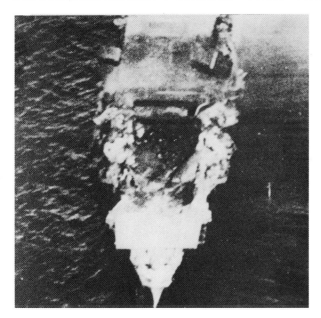

▲ Hiryu *is seen here dead in the water. A tremendous explosion has flipped her forward lift through the air to rest against the vessel's island structure. The whole of the flight deck just forward of the island is a gaping void and the hangar level below can be clearly seen. (US National Archives)*

receipt of Admiral Abe's 1050 signal announcing: 'Fires raging aboard *Kaga*, *Soryu* and *Akagi* resulting from attacks by enemy carrier and land based planes' was therefore profound and traumatic. Reputedly, Yamamoto's response was to emit a deep groan, and the mood of his staff moved rapidly from bright optimism to deep despair. The only saving grace was that Abe reported *Hiryu* untouched and fighting back.

Pondering his options in the wake of these dire tidings, Yamamoto decided on a course of action that he believed still offered the Japanese the chance to retrieve the situation. At 1220 he issued a signal ordering a concentration of Kondo's Second Fleet with his own Main Body to the northwest of Midway at 1200 the following day. AL was suspended, and Kakuta was ordered to send his two carriers southwards post haste to effect a junction with Yamamoto, but it soon became apparent that *Ryujo* and *Junyo* could not arrive before the afternoon of 6 June. At this stage Yamamoto still believed he could overwhelm the enemy by sheer weight of numbers in a night battle.

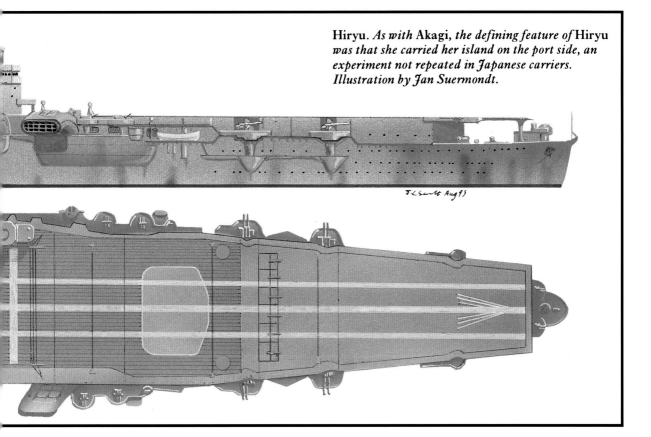

Hiryu. *As with* **Akagi,** *the defining feature of* **Hiryu** *was that she carried her island on the port side, an experiment not repeated in Japanese carriers. Illustration by Jan Suermondt.*

Subsequently, Kondo was further ordered to detach Kurita's four heavy cruisers from his Main Body and send them towards Midway to continue a night bombardment to be initiated by submarine *I-168* shortly after midnight on 5 June. As the day wore on, however, the news feeding back to Yamamoto became increasingly serious. Shortly after 1700 he knew that he had also lost *Hiryu*, the linchpin of his updated plan. Although intelligence on the size of the American force was confusing, it was now known to contain at least three carriers. By 1915, as he received word of Spruance's withdrawal of Task Force 16 to the east, he knew his chances of catching them in a night battle were rapidly receding. At 2130 Nagumo signalled that he was in essence unable to co-operate with the Main Body in any night attack. Adjudging him to be too 'conservative' Yamamoto replaced Nagumo with Kondo at 0055.

As the hours wore on it became increasingly clear that the American force was moving away from the Japanese at too fast a rate to allow them to be caught in a night engagement. Furthermore, Kurita's cruisers could not begin their bombardment of Midway before 0300. They and Kondo's battleships would then be exposed to air attack, not just from Midway, but also from the US carriers that were expected to make another appearance with the onset of daylight at 0400. So it was that, with great reluctance, Yamamoto had the signal flashed to all vessels cancelling Operation MI and ordering a general withdrawal at 0255 on 5 June. Kondo's main force linked up with the Main Body at about 0700 when they were some 320 miles northwest of Midway, to be joined at mid-day by the remnants of Nagumo's once proud and mighty First Air Fleet. But as the still-powerful Japanese fleet turned west and headed for home, the agony of the Combined Fleet had not yet run its course.

5 June: The Demise of *Mikuma* and *Mogami*

Far to the southwest of Yamamoto's Main Body, Kurita's Cruiser Division 7 was but 80 miles from Midway when calamity struck early on 5 June. The four cruisers were in single column when, at about 0118, the sighting of a US submarine led Kurita to order an emergency 45-degree turn. As a conse-

quence of confusion *Mogami* rammed *Mikuma* on her port quarter. Damage to both vessels was severe, with *Mogami*'s bow bent back right to her No.1 turret and *Mikuma*'s port side oil tanks holed. Leaving the destroyers *Asashio* and *Arashio* to escort the two cruisers, Kurita headed off to rendezvous with Yamamoto. Although *Mogami* was still able to make 12kts, *Mikuma* was leaving a wide oil slick in her wake, and this tell-tale trail allowed a PBY to locate the four vessels shortly after 0630. Between 0805 and 0828 the cruisers were attacked by Dauntlesses, Vindicators and B-17s from Midway. There were no bomb hits, but one Vindicator hit by anti-aircraft fire crashed on to the aft turret of the *Mikuma*, and the ensuing fire spread down into the engine compartment. *Mikuma*'s speed was now reduced to that of *Mogami*.

The following day *Hornet* and *Enterprise* both launched strikes against the two cruisers. In three attacks through to 1445 *Mogami* was extensively damaged by at least six bomb hits from SBDs, but was able to limp back to Truk by 14 June. However, her sister ship was so extensively damaged in the attacks that her captain ordered her abandoned even before the third strike. She was afire from stem to stern, and *Arashio* had great difficulty closing to rescue survivors because of the intensity of the heat. A further bomb hit by the last SBD strike set off her torpedoes, and she was abandoned and sank after sunset on 6 June. Nearly 300 crewmen were killed, and her demise marked the end of the Battle of Midway.

THE AFTERMATH

There can be little doubt that, with the news of the destruction of the *Hiryu*, Admiral Yamamoto knew that more than just the battle had been lost. Midway marked the moment when Japan lost the war, and was for that reason the decisive battle of the Pacific conflict. The four carriers of Nagumo's First Air Fleet had been Japan's primary offensive instrument in her bid for hegemony in the Pacific. With their destruction, Japan's superiority in naval air power – the key to the successful execution of offensive warfare in the vast Pacific theatre – was eliminated. In one fell swoop Nimitz had wrested the offensive initiative from Japan, and thereafter the United States was never to surrender it. Whereas before Midway Japanese naval strategy had been predicated upon *shinko sakusen*, or offensive operations, thereafter all was perceived in terms of *yogeki sakusen* – defensive operations.

The reality of the catastrophic defeat at Midway was the elimination of irreplaceable assets from the Japanese order of battle. Above all, there were the experienced pilots now lost for ever as a consequence of the totally inadequate pilot replacement programme with which Japan had entered the war.

Nor could Japanese shipyards hope to replace the four lost fleet carriers. At the time of the outbreak of the Pacific conflict, Japanese shipyards had yet to adopt the mass-production shipbuilding techniques practised so successfully in the United States. An indication of the production differential between American and Japanese yards in the construction of aircraft carriers can be gauged by a comparison of the production figures for this class of warship in the two-and-a-half years from Pearl Harbor through to June 1944.

The United States completed 18 of the formidable Essex-class fleet carriers and 99 escort carriers, whereas Japan produced just twelve carriers of all types. Furthermore, this superiority was not just numerical but also qualitative, the US vessels being better built and fitted out with superior technical equipment. This was already discernible at the time of Midway. Nearly all US vessels in the battle were provided with radar, whereas in the Combined Fleet this vital equipment had been fitted in an experimental capacity only to the battleships *Ise* and *Hyuga*, which were engaged in the Aleutians sideshow and were therefore put to no good use. In the months and years following Midway, the relentless destruction of the once proud and mighty Combined Fleet by the most powerful navy the world has yet seen completely shattered the falla-

◀ *For the Rengo Kantai, the agony of Midway did not end with the loss of the carriers. Due to a collision, the heavy cruiser* **Mikuma** *of Admiral Kurita's unfortunately named Midway Bombardment Force was heavily damaged in a collision* *with her sister ship* **Mogami** *in the early hours of 5 June. Throughout the day both vessels were subjected to heavy air attacks. This is* **Mikuma** *having been hit by SBDs from USS* **Enterprise***. (US National Archives)*

cious notion of the primacy of *Nihon Seishin* over the material and technological superiority of the United States.

The American victory at Midway was a remarkable testimony to the bravery, self-sacrifice, foresight and technical expertise of the US Navy. Indeed, Professor Samuel Morison emphasised the latter point when he spoke of Midway as 'a victory of intelligence'. The breaking of the Japanese code JN-25 provided Nimitz with a remarkable oversight of his enemy's intentions, but a very great deal could have gone awry between planning and victory. Nor was the American performance in the battle flawless. In the final analysis, however, those errors were far fewer and less profound by degrees of magnitude than those of the Japanese.

What if Midway had indeed proved to be Yamamoto's *kantai kessen*? It is almost certain that he would have been profoundly disappointed in his expectations of the benefits that he hoped Japan would gain from victory. In this sense it would have transpired that victory was anything but 'decisive'. Any material damage the Japanese might have inflicted on the Pacific Fleet could never have been enough to bring the United States to the peace table. Indeed, this could have been the only tangible consequence that would have shown Midway to have been the 'decisive' battle for Japan. In this, his hopes for the results of a Midway 'victory' would have been totally forlorn. Indeed, it could be argued that the very fact that Yamamoto entertained such hopes was evidence of a profound misunderstanding of the psychology of the nation he professed to know so well.

Yamamoto's failure to perceive that no lasting political benefit could accrue to Japan from what would have been a purely military victory at Midway is symptomatic of the intellectual failure that lay at the heart of the Combined Fleet's war-making strategy. In seeing 'victory' purely in terms of territory and resources captured and battles won, the Japanese had truly misunderstood the nature of the war they had unleashed. Yamamoto had cast the die for the nature of the Pacific conflict with his attack on Pearl Harbor. The images of the devastated warships and the dead personnel created by his flyers on 7 December 1941 had succeeded in unifying the politically disparate American people in a way no domestic politician had ever done, filling them with a bitter resolve to see the perpetrators of that attack utterly and totally defeated, no matter what the cost. That, indeed, was the point. Japan had unwittingly initiated a 'total war' with a power that not only possessed the resources and expertise to prosecute such a war, but was above all else animated by the moral conviction and certitude to harness and direct its national resources to serve such a conflict and see it through to its bitter end. Had the Japanese triumphed at Midway, it certainly would have taken the United States longer to achieve the same end they realised in August 1945. The cost in blood and treasure would have been far higher, but the result would have been the same – the inevitable and total ruin of the Japanese Empire.

◀ Mikuma *some hours before her demise: on top of her 8in turret No.4 can be seen the remains of a Marine Vindicator dive-bomber. Hanging out over the side of the vessel are her torpedo tubes.* Mikuma *finally sank after sunset on 6 June. (US National Archives)*

CHRONOLOGY

Note: Japanese dates are given in Japanese time until 3 June, after which the time used is local; i.e. Japanese time for N-Day = 7 June, by local time becomes 6 June. All dates and times in parentheses are approximate.

1941

7 Dec Japanese attack Pearl Harbor.

31 Dec Admiral Chester Nimitz assumes command of the Pacific Fleet.

1942

1-14 Jan Admiral Ugaki, on instructions from Yamamoto, prepares plans identifying possible future operations.

20-25 Feb Army turns down Navy project to invade Ceylon.

Mid March Combined Fleet turns to Midway proposal.

28 March Combined Fleet staff under Kuroshima begin work on Midway operation.

2-5 April Kuroshima and Watanabe discuss Midway plan with Naval General Staff. They reluctantly agree to accept Midway plan after Yamamoto threatens to resign.

18 April Doolittle raid.

22 April First Air Fleet returns to Japan. Nagumo learns of Midway operation for first time.

28 & 29 April Conference aboard *Yamato* to explore Midway operation.

1-4 May Preliminary war games for MI held on *Yamato*.

2 May Nimitz flies to Midway to inspect defences of base.

5 May Admiral Nagano issues Naval Order 18, ordering MI and AL.

7-8 May Battle of Coral Sea. US loses *Lexington*. *Yorktown* badly damaged. Japan loses *Shoho*. *Shokaku* and *Zuikaku* unavailable to take part in MI because of battle damage/aeroplane losses.

10 May Midway despatches false message under Hypo's direction that Midway is short of water.

12 May Hypo intercepts Japanese signal that 'AF' is short of water.

15 May Halsey ordered to Pearl Harbor.

20 May Yamamoto issues estimate of US strength.

20 May Midway Transport Group & Seaplane Tender Group leave Japan for Saipan.

21 May Midway begins Alert Phase.

22 May Midway begins search and reconnaissance phase.

24 May Final wargames on *Yamato*.

25 May Commander Rochefort gives Nimitz breakdown of Japanese order of battle.

25 May Nimitz informs Midway that D-Day is postponed to June 3.

22-26 May Air and Marine reinforcements arrive at Midway.

26 May Halsey too ill to command TF 16. Recommends Spruance.

27 May First Carrier Strike Force sorties from Japan. Midway Invasion Force and Seaplane Tender Group sorties from Saipan. Close Support Group sorties from Guam.

27 May Nimitz briefs Spruance. *Yorktown* enters harbour. Emergency repair work begins.

28 May Northern Force sorties from Japan.

28 May Fletcher named commander of Task Forces 16 & 17. Nimitz briefs Fletcher and Spruance. Task Force 16 sorties from Pearl Harbor.

29 May Yamamoto's Main Body sorties from Hasharijima.

30 May Submarine finds US vessels at French Frigate Shoals. Operation K postponed.

30 May Task Force 17 sorties from Pearl.

30 May Midway begins air search. Time uncertain: Japanese submarine cordon arrives on station 2 days late. Does not detect passage of either US Task Force.

31 May Operation K cancelled.

1 June Japanese detect US vessels sending many 'urgent' messages.

2 June Nagumo breaks radio silence by transmitting course change.

2 June TF 16 & TF 17 meet at 'Point Luck'.

3 June :

0300 Second Carrier Strike Force launches air strike.

0800-0808 Attacks Dutch Harbor.

0904 PBY 6-V-55 sights Japanese vessels.

0925 Ensign Reid sends message 'Sighted Main Body'. Time uncertain: Tanaka informs Yamamoto Invasion Force sighted.

1125 Read sends report listing 11 vessels sighted.

1200 2nd Carrier Strike Force withdraws towards Adak.

1225 Sweeney leads 9 B-17s to hit Invasion Force.

1640 Invasion force bombed by B-17s. No hits.

1950 Fletcher orders TF 16 & 17 south.

2115 4 PBYs leave Midway to attack Invasion Force.

4 June :

0130 3 PBYs attack invasion force. *Akebono Maru* hit.

0245 Aircrew awoken on Japanese carriers.

0300 Reveille on Midway.

0400 Midway launches PBYs followed by B-17s.

0430 108 aeroplanes of First Strike Wave launched. *Akagi*, *Kaga* and *Haruna* launch scout aircraft.

0430 *Yorktown* launches ten scout SBDs.

0438 *Chikuma* launches No.5 floatplane.

0437 Dawn.

0438 *Chikuma* launches No.6 floatplane.

0442 *Tone* launches No.3 floatplane.

0500 *Tone* launches No.4 floatplane.

0530 Ensign Ady reports a carrier.

0534 *Enterprise* receives same report.

0553 Midway radar picks up Strike Wave.

0556 Fighters take off from Midway. Air Raid alert sounded.

0600 Sweeney's B-17s diverted to attack carriers.

0603 Spruance receives news of two enemy carriers.

0607 Fletcher orders Spruance to move towards carriers and launch attack.

0610 VMSB aeroplanes take off from Midway.

0615 VT-8 TBFs take off from Midway.

0616 Midway fighters attack Japanese strike group.

0630–0643 Japanese strike on Midway.

0700 *Hornet* launches aeroplanes.

0705 Tomonaga radios 'need for second strike on Midway'.

0706 *Enterprise* launches her strike group.

0702–0830 Successive waves of Midway based aircraft attack First Air Fleet. Heavy US losses, no Japanese carriers hit.

0715 Nagumo orders second wave 'Kates' re-equipped with bombs.

0728 *Tone*'s No.4 aeroplane signals what appears to be ten enemy surface ships.

0745 Nagumo orders torpedoes still on 'Kates' to be left on.

0800 *Tone* No.4 aeroplane ordered to 'ascertain ship types'.

0806 Reports back 'enemy fleet consists of five cruisers and five destroyers'.

0830 No.4 aeroplane now reports enemy ships include 'what appears to be a carrier'.

0837 Tomonaga's aircraft begin recovery aboard carriers.

0838 *Yorktown* begins launch of aeroplanes.

0845 More scout aircraft launched to ascertain more details of US vessels.

0855 Nagumo orders carrier force northward once Midway aeroplanes recovered.

0917 Fleet turns on to new heading ENE to close with US carrier.

0918 All aircraft recovered by Japanese carriers.

0918 *Chikuma* sights VT-8.

0920 VT-8 attacks.

0955 McClusky sights wake of Japanese destroyer.

0958 VT-6 attacks Carrier Fleet.

1005 McClusky sights Japanese fleet. Leslie does same.

1015–1020 VT-3 begins attack on First Air Fleet.

1020 SBDs sighted over Fleet. *Akagi* goes into maximum turn.

1022 *Kaga* dive bombed.

1024 Extensive fires break out on *Kaga*.

1025 *Soryu* bombed three times.

1026 *Akagi* hit by two bombs.

1046 Nagumo and staff abandon *Akagi* for *Nagara*.

1050 Nagumo informs Yamamoto of fate of three carriers.

1055 Crew aboard *Soryu* ordered to abandon ship.

1058 *Hiryu* launches first strike wave.

1127 *Akagi* stopped.

1200 *Hiryu* attacks *Yorktown*.

1220 Yamamoto orders concentration of Main Body, Invasion Force and 2nd Mobile Carrier Force.

1310 Yamamoto temporarily suspends MI and AL.

1320 *Hiryu* launches second strike.

1437 *Yorktown* still making 19kts.

1445 *Hiryu* located. Spruance orders immediate attack.

1454 *Hiryu* reports two definite hits on *Yorktown*, although Japanese believe it to be a second carrier.

1455 Abandon ship ordered on *Yorktown*.

1550 All aircraft launched from *Hornet* and *Enterprise*.

1640 Captain Amagai orders abandon ship on *Kaga*.

1705 *Hiryu* attacked, hit by four bombs.

1913 *Soryu* sinks.

1925 *Kaga* sinks.

2000 All hands abandon *Akagi*.

5 June:

0130 Submarine *I-168* bombards Midway.

0200 Spruance turns west.

0255 Yamamoto cancels MI.

0300 *Mikuma* crashes into *Mogami*.

0500 *Akagi* scuttled.

0820 *Hiryu* sinks.

0840 First air attack on Japanese cruisers.

6 June:

0945–1445 Air attacks on *Mikuma* and *Mogami*.

1331 *I-168* torpedoes *Yorktown*.

After sunset *Mikuma* sinks. *Mogami* limps back to Truk.

7 June *Yorktown* sinks at 0458.

A GUIDE TO FURTHER READING

AGAWA, H. *The Reluctant Admiral*, Kodansha International Ltd., 1979.

CALVOCORESSI, P., WINT, G. and PRITCHARD, J. *Total War: The Causes and Courses of the Second World War*, Vol II, Penguin Books, 1989.

DULL, P. S. *A Battle History of the Imperial Japanese Navy*, US Naval Institute Press, 1978.

FUCHIDA, M. and OKUMIYA, M. *Midway*, US Naval Institute Press, 1955, reprinted 1992.

HOWARTH, S. *Morning Glory*, Hamish Hamilton, 1983.

IENAGA, S. *The Pacific War, 1931–1945*, Pantheon Books, 1968.

OKUMIYA, M., HORIKOSHI, J. *Zero*, Cassell, 1957.

PRANGE, G. *At Dawn We Slept*, McGraw Hill, 1981.

— *Miracle At Midway*, McGraw Hill, 1982.

UGAKI, M. (ed. D. M. Goldstein and K. V. Dillon) *Fading Victory: The Diary of Admiral Ugaki*, University of Pittsburgh Press, 1991.

VAN DER VAT, D. *The Pacific Campaign*, Hodder & Stoughton, 1991.

WILMOT, H. P. *Empires in the Balance*, US Naval Institute Press, 1982.

General Reference:

KEEGAN, J. (ed.) *The Times Atlas of the Second World War*, Times Books, 1989.

PITT, B. *Purnell's History of the Second World War*, Macdonald Phoebus/BPC Publishing Ltd., 1966.

The Strategic Situation, July-August 1942

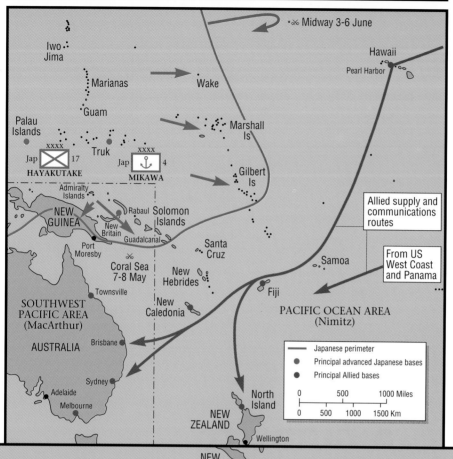

The Japanese takeover of Guadalcanal represented the farthest limit of their Pacific advance in the Second World War. With bases established throughout New Guinea, the Bismarck Archipelago and the Solomon Islands, they began to pose a serious threat to the communications lifeline that ran between Hawaii and Australia.

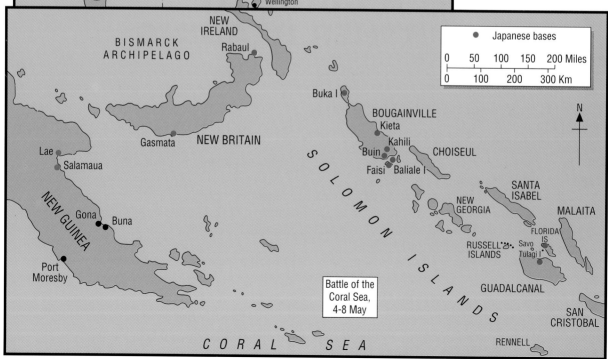

PART 2
GUADALCANAL

Guadalcanal was the first American amphibious counteroffensive of the Second World War. It was on this virtually unheard of island that the Americans shattered the myth of Japanese invincibility in the Pacific. Although the Battles of Midway and the Coral Sea are described as turning-point battles, it was at Guadalcanal that the Japanese war machine was ground to a halt. After Guadalcanal there were no other advances made by the Japanese in the Pacific.

The Battle for Guadalcanal was a unique battle for many reasons. Both the American and Japanese forces fought at the farthest end of their supply lines. The battle itself would be among the longest in duration of the Pacific campaign. It would take six months of fierce and savage fighting, testing the endurance of both sides, before the Japanese were driven off the island; the climate and terrain, which were equally harsh, proved an enemy to both sides. Ship losses off Guadalcanal, comparable to those suffered later off the Philippines and Okinawa, were so great that the waters along the north coast of Guadalcanal would become known as 'Iron Bottom Sound' – a name that continues to this day.

The burden of the conflict was endured by the United States Navy and the Marine Corps. However the army forces soon joined in and saw their fair share of combat as well. The troops first to experience the cruel realities of jungle warfare were the Marines of the newly formed 1st Marine Division. This division was deployed from the east coast of the United States to Wellington, New Zealand, where it was to complete its training; the Division was not expected to see combat until after January 1943.

The movement of the Marines overseas was accomplished without incident. The advance echelon, consisting primarily of Major General Vandegrift's divisional headquarters and the 5th Marine Regiment under Colonel Leroy P. Hunt, with the 2nd Battalion, 11th Marine Regiment and twelve other unit detachments, arrived in Wellington on 14 June 1942. Training and camp sites had been selected before their arrival by a small group of officers working in conjunction with the New Zealand military. The camp sites were ideally chosen and were in close proximity to good training areas on the south-western tip of North Island.

The Japanese on the other hand were operating to a different time table. Their advance took them to the North Coast of New Guinea and into the Admiralty Islands. They continued their unopposed advance into the Solomon Islands and pushed south, seizing Tulagi and Guadalcanal, there to begin construction of an airfield.

As these events were occurring on the local level, strategic planning commenced on the American Joint Chiefs of Staff level. The Joint Chiefs were aware that the Japanese advance in the Pacific threatened the communications lifeline to Australia. Furthermore, American bases that lay in the path of the Japanese advance would be endangered. The Joint Chiefs concluded that an American offensive in the Pacific was now a matter of necessity.

Once it was determined that the Japanese were constructing an airfield on Guadalcanal, the 1st Marine Division was given the mission of seizing that island. The date set for the amphibious assault was 1 August 1942, nearly eight months to the day after the Japanese attacked Pearl Harbor.

THE OPPOSING PLANS

The Japanese Plan

From 7 December 1941 to 7 May 1942, the Japanese advanced with seeming precision, sweeping through east Asia, the Indies and a large portion of Melanesia. They overran the Philippines, Wake Island, Guam and Singapore. As their seemingly unstoppable advance continued, they seized Rabaul on the island of New Britain on 23 January 1943. They thereby acquired a key objective. Rabaul was just 1,200 nautical miles from their bases in the Palau Islands and 640 nautical miles from their base at Truk. It could easily be defended and converted to a bastion from which future offensive operations could be launched. It also had the best harbour in the region and excellent terrain for the construction of airfields.

From Rabaul the Japanese could dominate New Guinea and the Solomon Islands. Once these two areas could be controlled, the Japanese could sever the communications lifeline between Hawaii and Australia.

In March 1942, the Japanese seized Bougainville in the Northern Solomons. From there they proceeded down the Solomons to the centre of British Government, Tulagi. After seizing operational bases on the northern coast of New Guinea

▼ *Officers and petty officer of the 3rd Kure Special Landing Force who seized Tulagi and Gavutu on 3 May. This picture was taken prior to the invasion, at their base in Japan. The majority of the men in this picture were killed between 7 and 9 August in action against the Marines. (USMC)*

and in the Solomon Islands, they attacked Tulagi on 1 May 1942. Unable to defend Tulagi adequately, the British withdrew from the area. Then, on 3 May 1942, the 2nd and 3rd Companies of the Kure Special Landing Force, supported by a small naval force, made an unopposed landing on Tulagi and Gavutu.

The operation did not go unhindered. The next day, dive-bombers and torpedo planes from the American aircraft carriers *Enterprise* and *Yorktown* raided Tulagi sinking the destroyer *Kikutsuki* and damaging other ships. This attack was the opening phase of the Battle of the Coral Sea. In that battle, the Americans turned back a large Japanese task force that was advancing on Port Moresby, New Guinea. After the Battle of the Coral Sea, the Japanese commander at Rabaul advised his subordinates that the battle had depleted Japanese naval forces in the area. He further advised that supply lines to Lae and Tulagi were in great danger. His greatest concern was for the New Guinea area.

Tulagi did not receive much attention. After landing, the small 380 man Japanese force began improving existing facilities by building seaplane bases on Tulagi and Gavutu. Once this was accomplished, they began generally exploring their new conquests. For about a month, no immediate steps were taken to develop bases in the area. Then, in late June 1942, survey parties went ashore at Lunga Point on the north coast of the

▲ The Japanese destroyer Kikutsuki *participated in the Japanese invasion of Tulagi on 3 May 1942. She gave fire support to the Kure Special Landing Force that made an unopposed landing. On the following day she was sunk in an air raid by pilots from the American aircraft carrier* Yorktown. *In October 1943 she was raised and used as a floating repair ship by the 34th Construction Battalion. (National Archives 80-G-89212)*

big island of Guadalcanal. There they explored the possibility of building an airfield. By mid-July construction had started, with completion estimated by mid-August.

According to Japanese documents captured later, the objective of capturing Tulagi and building an airfield on Guadalcanal was to protect their flank while carrying out their main attack on Port Moresby, New Guinea. The secondary objective was to secure a favourable base of operations to move south through New Caledonia to attack Australia. This attack was to take place after the capture of New Guinea.

The American Plan

The American plan for the invasion of Guadalcanal began with inter-service rivalries. After the Battle of the Coral Sea, in early May 1942, General Douglas MacArthur, Commander of the Southwest Pacific Forces (CINCSWPA), realized that the Japanese would eventually attempt to sever the lines of communication between Hawaii and

Australia. He felt that a Japanese attack on New Guinea was inevitable. To prevent such an attack he wanted to take the offensive against the Japanese in the New Britain–New Ireland areas. An attack of this nature would force the Japanese out of the region and back to Truk. MacArthur's plan found favour with General George C. Marshall, US Army Chief of Staff. However, MacArthur did not have the resources available to launch such an offensive. Further, he had no troops under his command that had any experience of amphibious warfare.

Simultaneously, Admiral Chester W. Nimitz, Commander in Chief Pacific Fleet (CINCPAC)

and Pacific Ocean Area (CINCPOA), was contemplating a strike on Tulagi, a plan that found favour with Admiral Ernest J. King, Chief of Naval Operations, Joint Chiefs of Staff. Originally, Nimitz had advocated the taking of Tulagi with a Marine Raider Battalion, but the concept was rejected by King, who felt the force was not suitable. However, King felt that the immediate objectives should be in the Solomon and Santa Cruz Islands, with the ultimate objective in the New Guinea and New Britain area.

The Operations Division of the War Department (OPD), did not favour the Navy plan to attack and occupy Tulagi and move progressively against Rabaul: they felt that the quick strike at Rabaul had the most merit. Once Rabaul was taken the Japanese would be driven from the area and other positions could be isolated.

To complicate the issue further, neither side in the debate could agree on an operational commander. The Navy felt that MacArthur might

▼ *Joint Chiefs of Staff during the Guadalcanal campaign. From left to right: Lieutenant General Henry H. Arnold, Admiral William D. Leahy, Admiral Ernest J. King and the Chairman,* *General George C. Marshall. It was interservice rivalries between King and Marshall that caused some friction during the planning stages of the campaign. (National Archives)*

unnecessarily expose its carriers to land based aircraft while they would be operating in restricted waters with limited aircraft carrier capability. They also felt Tulagi should be taken first to lessen the Japanese danger, at the same time establishing a base in the Solomons for future operations. This would allow a build-up of naval power for future operations. The Navy concluded that command should be through Nimitz, to his subordinate, Vice Admiral Robert L. Ghormley, Commander South Pacific Area and South Pacific Force (COMSO-PAC). MacArthur objected strenuously. He felt he was the logical choice for command since the amphibious objectives were in his area. However he lacked the ground troops to initiate an amphibious mission.

Between 29 June and 2 July 1942, the Joint Chiefs of Staff met and came up with a compromise plan. It called for Admiral Ghormley to command the Tulagi portion of the upcoming offensive; thereafter General MacArthur would command the advance to Rabaul. The American Navy with the Marine Corps would attack, seize and defend Tulagi, Guadalcanal and the surrounding area, while MacArthur made a parallel advance on New Guinea. Both drives would aim at Rabaul. The boundary between Southwest Pacific Area and the South Pacific Area was moved to reflect this, and South Pacific Forces were given the go-ahead to initiate planning. Admiral King had not waited for the final approval: on 25 June 1942 he notified Nimitz to alert Ghormley to start planning. Ghormley in turn contacted Major General Alexander A. Vandegrift, the Commanding General, 1st Marine Division (reinforced), that his division would spearhead the amphibious assault, scheduled to take place on 1 August 1942.

For General Vandegrift the problems were just beginning. He had not expected to go into combat until after January 1943. Only a third of his division was at Wellington; a third was still at sea; and the other third had been detached to garrison Samoa. In little less than a month Vandegrift would have to prepare operational and logistical plans, unload part of his ships, reload for combat, sail from Wellington to the Fiji Islands for an amphibious rehearsal, and then sail to the Solomon Islands to drive out the Japanese.

To make the amphibious assault, the cargo that had been loaded in America would have to be reconfigured into a combat load. This in itself would pose a difficult set of problems and take place in New Zealand at Aotea Quay, a confined area that could only berth five ships at a time. To make bad matters worse, two other events compounded the misery. First, the dock workers went on strike so that the Marines had do all the stevedore work themselves. Next came the rains, which were steady for almost the entire period and were driven by a cold, persistent wind. The Marines worked around the clock in three eight-hour shifts, and the docks offered no protection from the weather. Space was adequate for stacking cargo, but it was left unprotected. The net result was the loss of food and clothing, which had been packaged in cardboard cartons that virtually dissolved. Morale of the Marines also suffered while working in such conditions – and, to make matters even worse, an influenza epidemic broke out. Once the combat loading task was completed, it was discovered that there was not enough room for all the motor transport to go back aboard: nearly all one-ton vehicles and below were put aboard, but 75 per cent of the heavier prime movers had to be left behind.

In addition to all this, Vandegrift would have to gather intelligence on an amphibious objective that most people had never heard of nor been to. Information on Guadalcanal in the summer of 1942 ranged from sketchy to completely unreliable. There were two main sources of information available to the Division's intelligence officer, Lieutenant Colonel Frank B. Goettge. The first source was obtainable from former residents of the area, who were now scattered throughout New Zealand and Australia. Goettge set up an extensive interview programme to gain as much information as possible. The second source of intelligence was from maps and hydrographic charts of the region. Unfortunately, these proved to be virtually non-existent.

The most useful source of information came from aerial photos taken by Lieutenant Colonel Merril B. Twining and Major William B. Kean on

17 July 1942. The flight was made in an Army B-17 bomber based at Port Moresby, New Guinea, but it was cut short when three Japanese float planes were observed taking off from the Tulagi area to attack the B-17. The aerial photographs did not clearly identify the Japanese airfield, but they did give an excellent view of the north coast of Guadalcanal and the Tulagi area. It would be maps made from these photographs of the northern coast that the Marines would use for the majority of the campaign.

Realizing the enormity of the task ahead. Vandegrift asked for an extension of the invasion date. He was given one week: the amphibious assault would take place on 7 August 1942. There would be no further postponements, for the Japanese had most of the airfield completed.

With logistical preparations completed so far as time permitted, General Vandegrift issued the tactical orders. The grouping of the Marines for the operation was based on intelligence estimates of Japanese forces in the area. It was estimated that of the 8,400 Japanese believed in the area, 1,400 were on Tulagi and its neighbouring islands. The remaining 7,000 were thought to be on Guadalcanal, but this later turned out to be an erroneous estimate; only about half that number were there.

It was anticipated that Tulagi would be the more difficult of the two amphibious objectives. The Marines going ashore there would have to make a direct assault against a small, defended island. To protect the flanks of the Marines landing on Tulagi, it was decided first to seize key points overlooking Tulagi on nearby Florida Island. Later in the day, Gavutu, Tanambogo and the other smaller islands would be taken. With their seizure, the Tulagi portion of the operation would be completed.

▶ *Lieutenant General Harukichi Hyakutake, Commanding General of the Japanese Seventeenth Army, was assigned the mission of recapturing Guadalcanal. Preoccupied with the capture of New Guinea, he did not grasp the seriousness of the Guadalcanal battle until it was too late, and his piecemeal attacks were defeated by the Americans in detail. (National Archives)*

THE OPPOSING COMMANDERS

The Japanese Commanders

Japanese troops in the Solomon Islands in the summer of 1942 constituted a force to be concerned with, but were not numerically superior, while the Japanese command structure was disjointed and plagued with a lack of cooperation between the Army and Navy.

Army forces in the area centred around the Japanese Seventeenth Army under the command of Lieutenant General Harukichi Hayakutake, who was preoccupied with the conquest of New Guinea.

The naval commander tasked with defence of the area was Vice Admiral Gunichi Mikawa, a seasoned officer who had commanded the escort for Admiral Nagumo's carrier force from Pearl Harbor to the Indian Ocean. Mikawa was in command of the 4th Fleet (Inner South Seas Force), not a large force and composed of either middle-aged or older ships.

Although Mikawa was tasked with defence of the area, he did not have control over the air units at Rabaul. They were controlled by Vice Admiral Nishizo Tuskahara, Commander of the 11th Air Fleet. Mikawa was justifiably concerned with the command and control measures utilized by the Japanese forces in the area. He was also disturbed by the lack of preparedness on the part of forces in the Solomons. The members of his staff thought he was an alarmist.

▲ *Vice Admiral Gunichi Mikawa, Imperial Japanese Navy, was the architect of the Battle of Savo Island. This battle was the worst defeat suffered by the American Navy since Pearl Harbor.*

Mikawa was appalled by the lack of a cohesive command in the Solomon Islands area. By his staff he was considered an alarmist. (Naval Historical Center)

The American Commanders

For the Guadalcanal campaign the American command was set up under Admiral Nimitz, with Admiral Ghormley as Commander of the South Pacific Area (COMSOPAC) and the South Pacific Force. Ghormley would be in overall command of the operation, code named 'Watchtower'. Ghorm-ley, in turn, would appoint Vice Admiral Frank J. Fletcher as commander of the entire task force. This naval task force, designated an Expeditionary Force, was made up of two groups: the aircraft carriers constituted the Air Support Force, under Rear Admiral Leigh Noyes; other warships and the

◀ *General Vandegrift, Commanding General, 1st Marine Division, Guadalcanal. This portrait depicts him some time after Guadalcanal when he became Commandant of the Marine Corps. The senior, or topmost, ribbon on his uniform, is the Congressional Medal of Honor, America's highest award for valour; it was presented to him for his skills as commanding general on Guadalcanal. (USMC A413197)*

▶ *Vice Admiral Robert L. Ghormley, Commander of the South Pacific area and South Pacific Force (COMSOPAC) was in command of the Guadalcanal phase of the Joint Chiefs of Staff plan. Ghormley was a competent leader and planner; however, he never left his command centre at Noumea, New Caledonia, to get a first-hand account of the fighting. (Naval Historical Center)*

transports were organized as the Amphibious Force, under Rear Admiral Richmond K. Turner. Major General Alexander A. Vandegrift would command the Marines as part of the Landing Force.

This command set up, which placed Vandegrift's Marines under the Amphibious Force commander, stemmed back to an earlier era. The Navy felt the Marines were an extension of the forces afloat and still connected to the Navy. The Navy would therefore not only designate the Landing Force Objective, but the manner in which the land campaign would be prosecuted. The Marines, knowing the intricacies of an amphibious assault, were not overjoyed with this relationship. They believed that, once they were ashore and firmly established, command should be transferred

from the Navy: the Marine commander ashore could then best control the battlefield.

Rear Admiral V. A. C. Crutchley, Royal Australian Navy, would provide the anti-aircraft protection and the naval gunfire support for the operation. His forces were detached from MacArthur to assist in the operation.

To assist Admiral Ghormley in any dealings with the US Army, Major General Millard F. Harmon, Commanding General US Army Forces South Pacific Area (COMGENSOPAC), was assigned to his command. Further, General Harmon would also be responsible for the administration and supply of Army units in the South Pacific Area. This, then, was the command that propelled the American forces towards the amphibious objective area.

▲Vice Admiral Frank J. Fletcher was the commander of the naval task force at the invasion of Guadalcanal. His decision to withdraw the aircraft carriers on 9 August caused disastrous consequences in the early stages of the campaign, for it left the Marines ashore virtually unsupported and without adequate supplies. (National Archives)

◄En route to Guadalcanal, Rear Admiral Richmond K. Turner goes over the movement to objective area with Major General Vandegrift. Turner was a brilliant amphibious planner; however, his relationship with Vandegrift was sometimes strained by philosophical differences. Turner was the commander of the amphibious task force and was senior to Vandegrift, who was commander of the landing force. (Naval Historical Center)

◀In the aftermath of the Tenaru battle, many Japanese weapons were captured. This particular weapon, a Japanese Nambu light machine-gun, is examined by 1st Lieutenant Soule. The Nambu was a gun based on the British Bren-gun system, and had an accurate, high rate of fire. This picture was taken on the east or Japanese side of the river. The Nambu's gunner lies dead in the background. (USMC 50491)

◀A Marine tests a captured Japanese flame-thrower on Guadalcanal. Neither side used this type of weapon in the campaign, but it was to be used quite effectively by the Marines against the Japanese in the later Pacific campaigns. (USMC 50046)

◀Captured Japanese weapons. The Marine in this picture is holding a Japanese Arisaka Model 38 bolt-action rifle. The rifle fired a 6.5mm (.25-cal) bullet which was inferior to the .30/06 Springfield rifle used by the Marines. The machine-gun mounted on the tripod is a Model 92 heavy machine-gun, which fired a 7.7mm bullet. It was serviced by a crew who could carry it into battle assembled with the pole carrying handles seen attached to the tripod legs. The weapons in the foreground are Model 99 Nambu light machine-guns; they fired a 7.7mm bullet and were extremely effective weapons. (USMC 108575)

THE OPPOSING FORCES

Guadalcanal would set the tone for the future campaigns of the war in the Pacific – not just one battle of quick duration, but a series of land, air and sea battles 'slugged out' along a narrow coastal belt, in restricted waterways and in the air space over Guadalcanal.

The reason why the campaign was to be so prolonged was that neither side would be able to mass its forces at a critical juncture to obtain a decisive victory. The Japanese and the Americans were operating at the farthest points of their supply lines. The Americans were hampered further by the fact that the bulk of their Pacific Fleet (with the exception of their aircraft carriers) had been sunk at Pearl Harbor, and that they were fighting a two-ocean war. The eventual outcome would be decided by the dogged determination of the American forces committed to the campaign and the release of critically needed supplies and equipment – coupled with luck.

The Japanese Forces

Initially, the Japanese were successful in the early naval battles. With the Battle of Savo Island (8-9 August) they achieved a great naval victory that severely crippled the American Navy's ability to support the operations ashore and in the waters surrounding Guadalcanal. And initially, with their land based fighters they also were able to control the air space overhead. Their ground forces were seasoned fighters and had achieved notable military successes up to Guadalcanal.

Japanese soldiers were masters of camouflage and reputably masters of jungle warfare. Their artillery was accurate, but not mobile enough for the type of jungle warfare engaged in. The tanks they used were also inadequate. The tactics the Japanese used, or were forced to use, were not conducive to success. For the most part, they attempted to conceal the movement of their forces in the jungle of Guadalcanal. This of course restricted their movements considerably. Much of the terrain they traversed was rain forest with few footpaths to travel on. Communications in the jungle were poor, and supplies were limited to what could be manpacked. Couple all of these disadvantages with a tropical disease factor second to none and you have a formula for disaster. Of the 21,500 casualties suffered by the Japanese in the campaign, 9,000 were to die of tropical diseases. By the end of the campaign the Japanese would be reduced to scavenging their food from the jungle.

As for the Japanese soldier, he was hardy and more than likely had some prior combat experience. He was tenacious, and subscribed to the code of 'bushido', or warrior, preferring death to capture. As he was subject to privations and stern discipline, those who became his prisoners were shown little mercy.

The Japanese Army was fairly well organized at the regimental level and below, but rarely did it operate at a divisional level. It consistently underestimated the capabilities of its enemies, a course of action that would prove disastrous on Guadalcanal. It also lacked security consciousness, and many of its soldiers carried detailed diaries into combat. Small unit leadership was not stressed: the running of the command and its employment was centred around the officers and senior sergeants.

The Japanese Navy on the other hand was an efficient organization. Tactically it could operate by day as well as by night. It was a disciplined aggressive force that carried out its assigned tasks without hesitation, using its weapons systems with deadly efficiency. Most notable was the infamous 'Long Lance' 24-inch diameter torpedo, which was used in conjunction with naval gunfire to

This Second lieutenant of the Imperial Japanese Army is armed with a Taisho 14 (1925) 8mm pistol. (Shirley Mallinson)

inflict maximum damage upon American warships.

The most serious failing of the Japanese Navy was its inability to exploit its successes. Time and time again throughout the naval campaign the Japanese achieved a tactical victory and then departed. By exploiting their successes they could have achieved a strategic victory.

In the air, the Japanese had clearly achieved a technological masterpiece with the zero fighter. This aircraft, with its lightweight construction and high rate of climb, could outmanoeuvre any American plane on Guadalcanal, but its diving capability was poor and it was not well suited to absorb punishment inflicted on it in aerial combat. Another disadvantage the Japanese had in the air was the amount of time they could spend over Guadalcanal: their time of flight and fuel consumption meant that their air missions were extremely restricted.

The American Forces

The American troops who invaded Guadalcanal were for the most part untried volunteers. The bulk of the initial combat forces were from the newly formed 1st Marine Division, of which only the advance elements were in Wellington at the time the decision was made for the amphibious assault on Guadalcanal. The remainder were to arrive just prior to embarkation.

The majority of the equipment that the Marines had was First World War vintage. Although it was time tested, in many cases it was either antiquated or worn out; either way, it was generally not suited for conditions on Guadalcanal.

Medical technology, although better than the Japanese, was inadequate in coping with the jungle diseases, primarily malaria. Communications were a problem, but since the Marines had mostly internal lines, these were not as severe as the problems experienced by the Japanese.

The tactics used by the Marines to encounter the Japanese were basic. Preparing to seize and then defend the airfield, they held the key terrain features that were encompassed by the Lunga Perimeter. On these they created strongpoints, forcing the Japanese to attack at a disadvantage. The Marines also discovered that in the jungle

▲This 37mm Model 97 anti-tank gun was one of the few Japanese weapons that had an equivalent American counterpart. Although not a heavy weapon, it was not easily transportable in the jungle. (USMC 53480)

▶ A captured Japanese Model 92 mountain gun. This 70mm light field piece was used throughout the campaign by Japanese troops. It was one of the few pieces of artillery that could be broken down and manpacked. However, even when broken down it proved too much for the Japanese to carry over the terrain of Guadalcanal. The square box with leather handle contains the sight optics for the gun. The oblong metal box contains the tools and cleaning kit, and the upright metal box is the fixed ammunition container. (USMC 51015)

◀On Guadalcanal, Marines used a variety of weapons. In this picture, two types of the Reising .45-calibre submachine-gun are visible. The Marine in the left of the picture is holding the folding stock variant, while the Marine in the centre has the fixed stock. The Reising was not a preferred weapon and was prone to malfunctioning. The third Marine is cleaning a .30-calibre Browning Automatic Rifle (BAR), which was used as the squad automatic rifle and was a reliable, proven weapon. (USMC 51366)

flanking attacks on dug-in positions worked much better than frontal assaults.

American artillery was accurate and could deliver a high volume of high-angle fire either in the attack or on the defensive. The Japanese on the other hand launched most of their attacks unsupported, taking appalling losses. The M3A1 light tanks (Stuarts) brought ashore by the Marines were utilized effectively. They were light enough to be employed in the jungle clearings and superior to their Japanese counterparts.

Later, when the Army was brought in to reinforce and eventually to relieve the Marines, they also learned valuable lessons in jungle warfare. The fighting endured by the soldiers did not differ greatly from that of the Marines, but in most cases the equipment they carried and used was

◀ *Once ashore on Tulagi the Marines took over abandoned Japanese positions. Here a Marine 75mm Pak howitzer crew occupies a camouflaged Japanese gun position.*

The 75mm Pak was a light-weight infantry support weapon capable of being emplaced in confined spaces. (USMC 50515)

◀ *Sergeant Charles C. 'Monk' Arndt, dressed in the garb of a Japanese sniper, demonstrates how a sniper would ascend a palm tree on Guadalcanal. To assist his climb, Arndt uses Japanese climbing spikes which tie on to his field shoes and ease the climb. He is also wearing a woven fabric vest designed to blend the wearer into the tree top. Arndt was one of the three survivors of the ill-fated Goettge Patrol of 12-13 August. (USMC-50988)*

▼ *M3A1 Stuart tanks of the 1st Tank Battalion on patrol, at Kukum Beach. These tanks operated primarily along the coastal plain and performed reconnaissance, screening and defensive roles. The Kukum area was the initial western boundary of the Marine perimeter. In the background are supply ships offloading at Lunga Point. (USMC 53256)*

Both the two piece fatigue suit of herringbone twill and the Marine inside it are starting to show the strain of the battle. Although of World War I vintage the M1918A2 Browning Automatic Rifle was still a reliable and popular weapon. (Shirley Mallinson)

newer and better. And when the Army arrived it came in force. Supply and communications problems were being solved, and the campaign was passing from a defensive into an offensive phase. By this time, the Americans had taken control of both sea and air lanes to the island.

(For purposes of clarifying Marine and Army unit regimental designators for the remainder of the text, Marine regiments are referred to as 'Marines' and Army regiments are referred to by branch. Thus the 1st Battalion, 5th Marine Regiment, is listed as the 1st Battalion, 5th Marines. The 1st Battalion, 164th Infantry Regiment, is listed as the 1st Battalion, 164th Infantry.)

The American Navy's entry to the campaign did not start off on a good note. The Battle of Savo Island was the worst naval disaster since Pearl Harbor. Most of the equipment on board the ships was First World War vintage. Radar was virtually new technology and was not effectively exploited.

The Navy learned its lessons in battle, and once an error was made it was seldom repeated. The naval battles fought for control of the waters surrounding Guadalcanal were violent in nature and occurred mostly during the hours of darkness. They were fought by ships ranging in size from PT boats up to battleships. The aircraft carrier, a mainstay for both sides, also played a decisive role in the campaign.

Damage control was another key aspect of the naval war. If a Japanese ship was damaged in a naval engagement it would have to be out of range of American aircraft from Guadalcanal by daylight – if not, it would be sunk by those planes. On the other hand, damaged American ships could be repaired at a series of 'local advanced naval bases' and be returned to fight again.

In the air the Americans had an advantage. Aircraft taking off from Guadalcanal could quickly engage the enemy and not use up tremendous quantities of fuel. Damaged aircraft could make emergency landings, and pilots could easily be rescued. The Grumman Wildcat fighter (F4F-4), was the mainstay Navy-Marine fighter for the campaign; although not as agile as the Zero it could out-dive it and absorb more punishment. And what the American pilots lacked in technology they made up for in skill and daring.

THE LANDINGS

Prior to the amhibious assault, very few people in the outside world had ever heard of Guadalcanal. Up to that point in time probably the only person who had mentioned it was Jack London in a turn of the century novel. The only information available was from planters and missionaries who had lived there in the past. Due to time constraints and fear that operational security would be compromised, there was no opportunity for intelligence patrols to conduct a reconnaissance. So, with somewhat sketchy information, the American forces departed for the objective area.

The Solomon Islands are a chain that extend from 163° E 12° S and run in a north-westerly direction to 153° E 5° S. They lie just below New Britain and New Ireland and are directly north and east of the tail of New Guinea. The larger islands of the group form two parallel chains separated by a long enclosed stretch of water that was later nicknamed the 'Slot'. Each of the longer islands, of which Guadalcanal is one, has a long axis that lies parallel to the chain as a whole. Several smaller islands and islets abound in the region: Florida, Tulagi, Gavutu and Tanambogo fall into these categories.

Because of their remoteness, there was not a great deal known about the Solomon Islands prior to the amphibious assault. What was known was not encouraging. Guadalcanal seemed a beautiful island from the air, but from the ground it would be difficult to conduct military operations. It is covered by a dense tropical rain forest that carpets the bulk of the island. Not far from the coastal area there are mountains, deep rivers, swamps, heat, humidity, rains and mud – all of which, when combined with the jungle, makes movement difficult. Here too was a breeding ground for various tropical diseases and fungi that would plague the soldiers of both sides.

The island itself is shaped like a rather large kidney bean, roughly sixty miles long by thirty miles wide. It has a large northern coastal plain, on which the Japanese had started their airfield. The coastal plain is covered by stretches of high, tough, razor-sharp kunai grass and is cut by many rivers that had no names or bridges across them. They generally ran from south to north stopping at the coast where their mouths were usually blocked by sand, forming stagnant pools. It was in this tropical wilderness, with its strange smells and animal sounds, that one of the major battles of the Pacific would take place.

▶ *A posed picture taken on 7 August showing. General Vandegrift discussing invasion plans with his staff. Clockwise from the left are General Vandegrift, Commanding General; Lieutenant Colonel Thomas, Operations Officer; Lieutenant Colonel Pate, Logistics Officer; Lieutenant Colonel Goettge, Intelligence Officer; and Colonel James, Chief of Staff. (National Archives)*

It was still dark (0400) on 7 August 1942 when the amphibious task force silently separated into two groups as it approached Savo Island. The Transport Division (TRANSDIV) was divided into two groups, X-RAY Guadalcanal and Y-OKE (Tulagi). The regiments of the 1st Marine Division consisted of two groups:

● The 5th Marines (Reinforced) less its 2nd Battalion, under the command of Colonel Leroy P. Hunt, was designated Combat Group A.

● Combat Group B was made up of the 1st Marines (Reinforced) under Colonel Clifton B. Cates.

These two combat groups, under Major General Alexander A. Vandegrift, the Division Commander, were to land on Guadalcanal, while smaller, more specialized groups of Y-OKE were organized to assault Florida, Tulagi, Gavutu and Tanambogo:

● The 1st Battalion, Second Marines, under Major Robert E. Hill, made up the Florida group.

● The Tulagi group was under Colonel Merritt A. Edson of the 1st Raider Battalion and included the 2nd Battalion, Fifth Marines, under Lieutenant Colonel Harold E. Rosecrans, and the 3rd Defense Battalion under Colonel Robert Pepper.

● The Gavutu and Tanambogo group were under Major Robert H. Williams of the 1st Parachute Battalion.

These smaller groups were under the command of Brigadier General William H. Rupertus, the Assistant Division Commander.

Both groups were task organized for the invasion: that is to say the 1st Marine Division had been reduced to a two-regiment division. The third regiment (7th Marines) had been detached for duty in British Samoa. (In reality, this was not the case and the division was actually far stronger than implied.) The 2nd Marines, who were normally part of the 2nd Marine Division, were added as were specialized units such as the 3rd Defense Battalion, the 1st Raider Battalion and the 1st Parachute Battalion. The division support group under Colonel Pedro A. Del Valle of the 11th Marines completed the force. A total of 1,959 officers and 18,146 enlisted Marines and Navy Corpsmen comprised the amphibious landing force on 7 August 1942.

Prior to their arrival in the area, the task force had conducted an amphibious rehearsal at Koro, in a remote portion of the Fiji Islands. The rehearsal, conducted in high surf conditions on beaches obstructed by coral reefs, was a disaster and was aborted to avoid injury to the personnel and damage to the precious landing craft. The planners who observed the rehearsal hoped that it would not be indicative of the upcoming landing!

The American amphibious forces were embarked on nineteen transports and four destroyer/transports. There were five cargo ships, eight cruisers, fourteen destroyers and five minesweepers. The accompanying carrier support group consisted of three carrier battle groups, *Saratoga*, *Enterprise* and *Wasp*. One battleship, *North Carolina*, and a force of cruisers and destroyers screened the battle groups. This force stayed to the south of Guadalcanal while the amphibious force sailed north, dividing in two when they approached Savo Island.

The movement to the amphibious objective area was shielded from the Japanese on Guadalcanal by one of the many tropical rain storms that frequent the region. Once the two groups separated they proceeded to their assigned beaches. After arriving on station, naval gunfire and carrier aircraft began to bombard their respective targets in accordance with the landing plan. The pattern of future campaigns in the Pacific was about to be demonstrated on the beaches of Tulagi and Guadalcanal.

Tulagi

The plan for the conquest of Tulagi was somewhat complicated. The Marine planners felt that in before Tulagi could be taken, certain key terrain features on nearby Florida Island would have to be captured.

At 0740 on 7 August 1942, 20 minutes before H-Hour, the first amphibious landing operation in the Solomon Islands was undertaken. It was made near the village of Haleta on Florida Island to secure a promontory that overlooked Beach Blue, the Tulagi invasion beach. The unit selected for the landing was reinforced Company B of the 1st Battalion, 2nd Marines, 2nd Marine Division, commanded by Captain Edgar J. Crane. The landing was unopposed and the western flank was secured quickly. An unopposed landing was also made by the remainder of the 1st Battalion, 2nd Marines, which landed at 0845 at Halavo on Florida Island to secure the eastern flank of the Gavutu landing.

Tulagi was attacked at 0800, according to schedule. The first to see action were the Marines of the 1st Raider Battalion, commanded by Colonel Merrit A. Edson, and they were followed by the 2nd Battalion, 5th Marines. As the landing craft approached Beach Blue, they ground to a halt on coral formations ranging from 30 to 100 yards out from the beach. The assault waves then began to make their way into the beach through water ranging from waist to armpit level. Upon reaching the shore, the Raiders and the 2nd Battalion, 5th Marines, began to make their way inland, the

▼*The landing on Tulagi was made on the beach just south of the golf course by Marines of the 1st Raider Battalion, followed by the 2nd Battalion, 5th Marines. The Raiders then moved west and the 5th Marines moved east to capture the island. The date of the photograph (17.5.42) indicates it is an early intelligence photo and was undoubtedly one used to plan the assault. (USMC)*

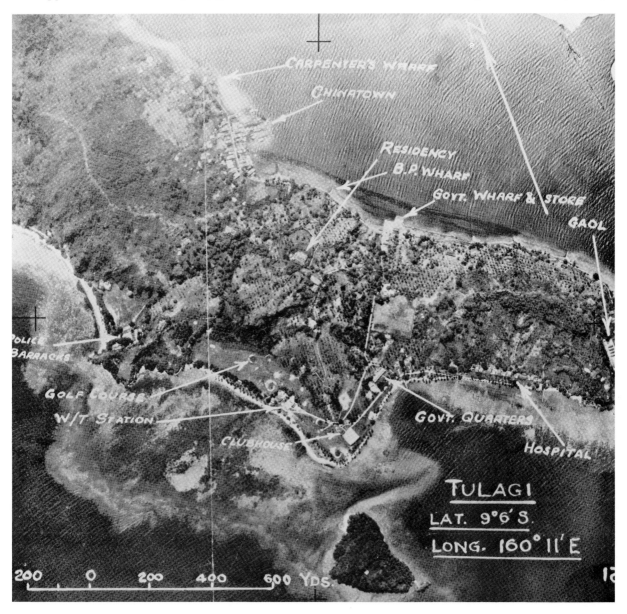

Raiders moving east and the 2nd Battalion, 5th Marines, moving north-west. Japanese resistance was encountered almost immediately by the Raiders but was systematically overcome. The advance continued slowly until dusk, when they consolidated and dug in for the night. This first night on Tulagi was to be indicative of many future nights in the Pacific: four separate attacks were launched by the Japanese to dislodge the Raiders

▶ *The advance west along Tulagi was made during the morning of 7 August by the Raiders. By 1120 they had advanced as far as Phase Line A. It took them the next day and a half to drive the remaining* *Japanese from the island. The fighting around Hill 280 with its cave complex was the most intense in the entire battle. (USMC)*

American Landing on Guadalcanal

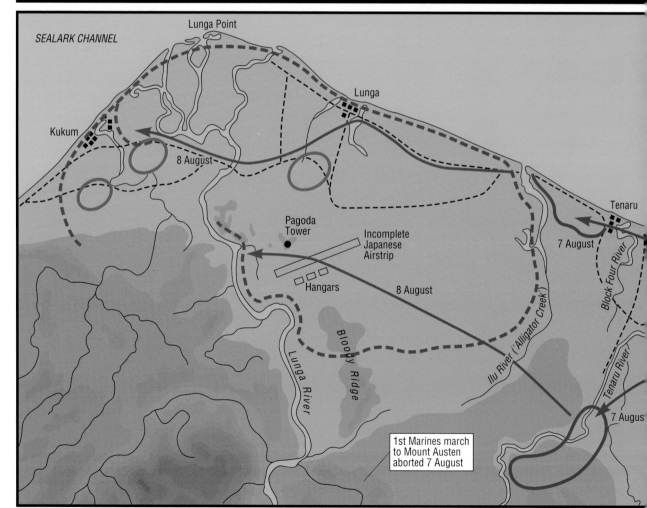

American Landings on Florida, Tulagi, Tanambogo and Gavutu Islands

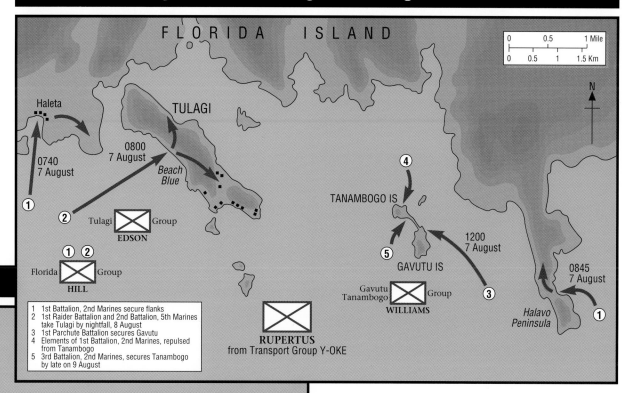

F L O R I D A   I S L A N D

Haleta

TULAGI

0740
7 August

0800
7 August

Beach
Blue

①

② Tulagi ⊠ Group
EDSON

① ②

Florida ⊠ Group
HILL

TANAMBOGO IS

④

⑤

GAVUTU IS

1200
7 August

Gavutu
Tanambogo ⊠ Group
WILLIAMS

③

0845
7 August

①

Halavo
Peninsula

⊠
RUPERTUS
from Transport Group Y-OKE

1 1st Battalion, 2nd Marines secure flanks
2 1st Raider Battalion and 2nd Battalion, 5th Marines
  take Tulagi by nightfall, 8 August
3 1st Parchute Battalion secures Gavutu
4 Elements of 1st Battalion, 2nd Marines, repulsed
  from Tanambogo
5 3rd Battalion, 2nd Marines, secures Tanambogo
  by late on 9 August

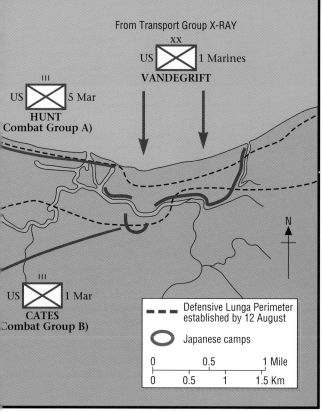

From Transport Group X-RAY
XX
US ⊠ 1 Marines
VANDEGRIFT

III
US ⊠ 5 Mar
HUNT
Combat Group A)

III
US ⊠ 1 Mar
CATES
Combat Group B)

- - - Defensive Lunga Perimeter
       established by 12 August

⬯ Japanese camps

0   0.5   1 Mile
0   0.5   1   1.5 Km

from their positions; each attack was beaten back.

The next day, the Marines resumed the offensive and encountered a stiff pocket of resistance in a deep man-made cut that ran north-south in the north-eastern portion of the island. The Japanese, taking advantage of the cut, dug positions into its base, from where they could bring fire to bear on the Raiders. Bringing up reinforcements, the Raiders isolated the enemy position on three sides; then, using improvised TNT-gasoline explosives, they systematically cleared this troublesome terrain feature and by the evening of the second day had eliminated effective Japanese resistance. For several days afterwards, isolated individuals and groups of Japanese continued to resist, but by nightfall on 8 August 1942, Tulagi was in Marine hands.

Gavutu and Tanambogo

These two small islets, each with prominent hills and connected by a causeway, were to be seized by two companies of the 1st Parachute Battalion led

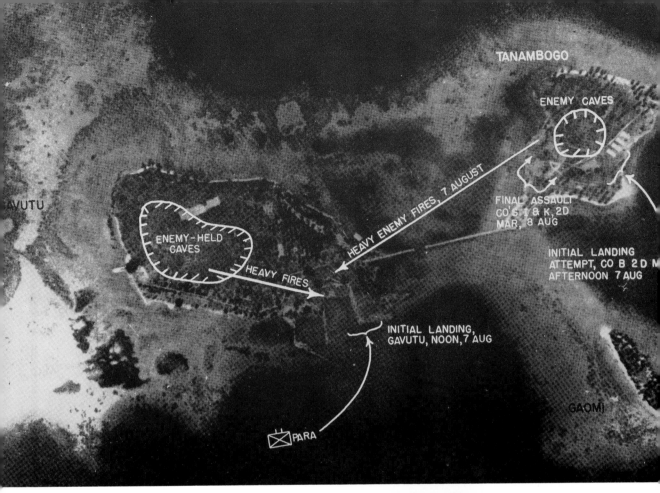

TANAMBOGO

ENEMY CAVES

GAVUTU

ENEMY-HELD CAVES

HEAVY ENEMY FIRES, 7 AUGUST

FINAL ASSAULT
CO'S I & K, 2D
MAR, 8 AUG

HEAVY FIRES

INITIAL LANDING
ATTEMPT, CO B 2D M
AFTERNOON 7 AUG

INITIAL LANDING,
GAVUTU, NOON, 7 AUG

GAOMI

PARA

▲ The fighting on Gavutu and Tanambogo was fierce. This photograph shows the landing site of the Parachute Battalion and the locations from which they received heavy Japanese fire. Also shown are the landing sites of the companies from the 2nd Marine Division who attacked Tanambogo. (USMC)

◄ Smoke rises from the gasoline supply dump on Tanambogo. It was struck by a shell from a naval gunfire ship supporting the landing on the night of 7 August. The photograph was taken the next day and shows the initial landing beach just to the right of the base of the column of smoke, and the final assault position located to the left and rear of the column. (USMC)

by Major Robert H. Williams. A third company would be held in reserve support for the assault companies. Gavutu, the higher in elevation of the two islands, was to be taken first.

The amphibious assault was to take place at H-Hour + 4 (1200) on 7 August. The plan called for a landing on the north-east coast. The naval gunfire support for the Gavutu amphibious assault was so effective, however, that it actually began to work against the Marines: so complete was the destruction that the original landing site, a concrete seaplane ramp, was reduced to rubble. The landing craft were forced to divert farther north to land the Parachutists and in so doing were exposed to flanking fire from Tanambogo. Despite heavy casualties, the Parachutists took the north-eastern portion of the island and its dominating hill, but to secure Gavutu, Tanambogo would have to be taken to stop its flanking fire, which was delaying the operation. Reinforcements were requested to undertake this phase of the operation.

Not being informed as to the number of reinforcements needed for Tanambogo, and with the bulk of his forces tied up on Tulagi, General Rupertus attached Company B, 1st Battalion, 2nd Marines, to the Parachutists. The Company reported to the Parachutists at 1800 and was informed that only a small Japanese force was on Tanambogo. It was felt that a night landing could be made and the Japanese quickly routed. The night amphibious assault was undertaken by Company B, minus one platoon, which did not take part as its landing craft had become stuck on the coral coming to Gavutu. The first boat came ashore without incident. As the second boat ground to a halt on the landing beach, a shell from a naval gunfire ship struck a nearby Japanese gasoline storage area, the explosion and resulting glare exposing the assaulting Marines. The ensuing battle was a nightmare. Unable to be reinforced, the attacking Marines were forced to withdraw under the most haphazardous conditions, the last making it back to Gavutu by 2200. Throughout the night, groups of Japanese counterattacked on Gavutu but were quickly repulsed.

On 8 August, the 3rd Battalion, 2nd Marines, was ordered to reinforce the parachutists on Gavutu and then attack Tanambogo. Supported by tanks from the 2nd Tank Battalion and with air and naval gunfire support, the 3rd Battalion, 2nd Marines made an amphibious landing at 1620 on 8 August 1942 on Tanambogo. Once a beachhead was established, reinforcements crossed the causeway, and by 2300, two-thirds of the island was secured. After a lot of fighting during the night, the island was completely secured by late on 9th.

Once Tanambogo fell, organized resistance in the Tulagi, Gavutu, Tanambogo and Florida Islands ceased. In all, the operation had taken three days. American losses overall were light, and the Japanese lost 1,500 troops. Only a handful of prisoners were taken.

Guadalcanal

On Guadalcanal an unopposed landing was made at Beach Red, about 6,000 yards east of Lunga Point. It was spearheaded by the 5th Marines, followed by the 1st Marines, and by 0930 the assault forces were ashore and moving inland. Their plan was simple: the 5th Marines would proceed along the coast, securing that flank, while the 1st Marines would move inland through the jungle and secure Mount Austen, described as a grassy knoll and reportedly only a short distance away. Now came the realization that intelligence concerning the terrain on Guadalcanal was faulty – Mount Austen was by no means a short way off, nor was it the grassy knoll as described. It was in fact the most prominent terrain feature in the area, more than four miles away and well outside the planned perimeter. It was not be captured until months later.

The remainder of the first day was spent consolidating positions and attempting to disperse the supplies that were stockpiling on the beach. Meanwhile the strongest Japanese countermeasure came at 1400 in the form of an air raid by eighteen twin-engined Type 97 bombers, two of which were shot down. A second wave of Type 99 Aichi bombers that came later was also repulsed with the loss of two aircraft; the cost to the Americans was a bomb hit on the destroyer *Mugford*.

At 2200, General Vandegrift issued the attack order for the next day. With Mount Austen out of

◀ Beach Red, which was about 6,000 yards east of Lunga Point, was the selected landing beach for Guadalcanal. Expecting to land under heavy fire, the Marines were relieved that the landing was unopposed. These Marines coming ashore are part of the initial waves. After crossing the beach, they moved inland to establish a beachhead. (National Achieves)

◀ The Japanese airfield on the morning of 7 August shows clearly how close the airfield was to completion. Hangers are seen in the left foreground, and the taxi way is clearly depicted. Smoke is billowing from a gasoline blaze set by off by fire from an American destroyer, seen to left of the column of smoke.

◀ Taxi-way to main runway is clearly defined, as are circular plane revetments. The structure to left is the pagoda type control tower that was set up by the Japanese to control airfield operations. The preparations made on the ground are clearly indicative of how far the Japanese had progressed to complete the airfield. (USMC)

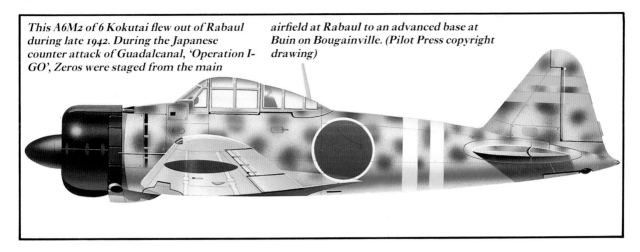

This A6M2 of 6 Kokutai flew out of Rabaul during late 1942. During the Japanese counter attack of Guadalcanal, 'Operation I-GO', Zeros were staged from the main *airfield at Rabaul to an advanced base at Buin on Bougainville. (Pilot Press copyright drawing)*

reach and only 10,000 Marines ashore, he ordered the airfield to be taken and a defensive perimeter set up. The beachhead would be held temporarily to protect the off-loaded supplies until they could be moved into the perimeter. The next day, 8 August, therefore began with a westward advance by all Marine forces on Guadalcanal. The original objectives out of necessity had been changed, but the airfield remained the primary objective.

Contact with small groups of Japanese began to occur as the Marines closed on the airfield. In the Lunga region, just south of the airfield, defensive positions consisting of trenches and anti-aircraft emplacements, well built and equipped, were discovered deserted. The airfield, nearly 3,600 feet long and in its last stages of construction, was defended by a small group of Japanese who were attacked and killed. The hangers,

revetments and machine shops were all captured intact. Two large camps each with radio stations and other technical equipment were also captured.

By the end of the day, the airfield had been taken and a defensive perimeter established. As the Marines took over the Japanese camps in the area they came across large quantities of food, ammunition, weapons, trucks and other equipment

▼*After the assault troops had moved inland, Beach Red became somewhat chaotic. Not enough manpower was allocated to move the masses of supplies from the landing craft to the beach, and there was not enough motor transport to move supplies from the beach to* *the dumps. By the end of the first day the unloading of supplies had to be suspended, as there was no place on the beach to put them. The congestion depicted here is indicative of the problems experienced. (USMC 52193B)*

(some of which, unfortunately, was destroyed by improperly indoctrinated Marines). Except for some token resistance by Japanese stragglers, air action constituted the only major threat.

Originally it was thought that the Japanese were taken by surprise. Intelligence sources later revealed that the Japanese had been aware of the impending American assault but had thought it was only to be a raid. The Japanese higher command therefore had instructed the Japanese troops in the area to withdraw into the hills until the Americans departed.

A report from a Coastwatcher, Cecil J. Mason, on Bougainville, warned of a large group of Japanese aircraft heading toward Guadalcanal. This early warning message and many others that would follow from other Coastwatcher stations throughout the Solomon Islands would save many American lives throughout the campaign. (The Coastwatcher organization was started by Commander Eric Feldt of the Royal Australian Navy, the purpose being to report on Japanese activities in the Solomon Islands. The group was carefully recruited from local inhabitants of the area. The intelligence gathered by these individuals was passed back to the Coastwatcher HQ in Townesville, Australia, for processing and dissemination.) About an hour after Mason's message was received, forty twin-engined Japanese torpedo planes appeared, to find the amphibious task force alerted and manoeuvring at high speed.

So far the Japanese resistance had been less

▲ *The Coastwatchers were an organization set up by Lieutenant Commander Eric Feldt (middle row, second from left). Their mission was to* *gather intelligence in the Solomon Islands and forward it on via radio communications to the Townesville, Australia, headquarters.*

than effective. In the air, attacks were repulsed with minimum damage to the Americans. However, the Japanese had no intention of giving up the Solomon Islands without a fight.

◄ *As the Marines moved through the Lunga area south of the airfield they captured vast stocks of Japanese equipment and foodstuffs. This particular building, which housed a vast quantity of rice, was captured in the first few days. Note the palm frond camouflage hastily applied to the roof by the Japanese. (USMC 53436)*

▼ Some captured buildings were immediately converted for effective use. This particular one houses the 1st Marine Division switchboard and has been named the Guadalcanal Telephone and Telegraph. The smaller sign over the door says USO Club and was typical of Marine humour throughout the campaign. (USMC 61556)

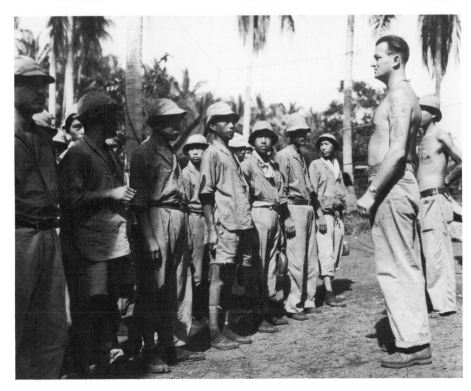

▲The Japanese ice plant, which was initially vandalized by Marines and later repaired. The plant was the only steady source of ice for the Marines throughout the campaign. Luxuries such as this were few and far between on Guadalcanal and demonstrated the primitive conditions encountered. (USMC 50493)

▶ Japanese captured on Guadalcanal were a valuable source of information for the Marines. Once captured, prisoners were usually cooperative. In this picture, a daily roll call is taken. The Japanese soldier to the right of the Marine in the picture is the translator. (USMC-51430)

AUGUST

Early on 8 August, part of the Japanese 8th Fleet under Admiral Mikawa made preparations to strike at the American amphibious task force. Mikawa's battle group consisted of five heavy cruisers and two light cruisers plus a destroyer. With this formidable force he began to move south. En route, he was spotted by an Allied patrol plane and there began a tragic chain of events that would lead to one of the greatest naval disasters ever suffered by the American Navy.

The Battle of Savo Island

Perceiving that he had been spotted, Mikawa reversed course until the plane had left the area; then he came back to his original course. The spotter pilot did not report the sighting until after returning to his base – and then only after having tea. The message was then sent to Australia in code and then decoded; it was then encoded and sent to the American Navy at Guadalcanal. When it arrived at its destination at 1800, there was some confusion about which direction the Japanese were heading.

After receiving the warning about the approaching Japanese, Admiral Turner positioned two destroyers, *Blue* and *Ralph Talbot*, north-west of Savo Island, to maintain a radar watch on the channel. He then positioned three cruisers, the *Australia*, *Canberra* and *Chicago*, along with two destroyers, the *Bagley* and *Patterson* to patrol between Savo Island and Cape Esperance. Three additional cruisers, *Vincennes*, *Astoria* and *Quincy*, along with two destroyers, *Helm* and *Jarvis*, were to patrol between Savo Island and Florida Island. Two other cruisers and two destroyers guarded the transports.

As these events were occurring, Admiral Fletcher, in command of the carrier support group, felt that operational losses to his aircraft and dwindling fuel oil for his ships limited his effectiveness. Predicated on this, he asked Admiral Ghormley for permission to retire from the area. Permission was granted and Fletcher announced that the aircraft carriers would be withdrawn from the area on 9 August. Once Admiral Turner was aware of Fletcher's plans he called General Vandegrift and Admiral Crutchley to his flagship, the latter arriving on one of his cruisers, thus removing a major warship from the protective screen at a critical time. Turner informed his officers that once Fletcher retired from the area he would not be able to remain. Vandegrift argued that over half his supplies were still on the transports. Turner informed him that with the absence of air cover,

◀ *This early view of Henderson Field shows that the Japanese had nearly completed its construction. Only the north-west corner of the runway remains to be levelled and surfaced. Note that the trees in the coconut plantation to the right have been cut down to make room for the airfield. (National Archives)*

▶ *One of General Vandegrift's primary concerns was the threat of a Japanese seaborne invasion, so the bulk of the Division's assets were set up to repel a counter-landing. This M3A1 light tank is dug in and camouflaged as part of a beach defensive position. (USMC 50934)*

he would withdraw the transports the next morning.

General Vandegrift complained bitterly. The withdrawal of the amphibious task force at a time as critical as this could have disastrous effects. The landing plan was predicated on amphibious shipping to remain in the area until 11 August 1942. This was set up in order to off-load the supplies essential for successful prosecution of the campaign ashore. Turner understood – but his decision would remain unchanged. And, at 1810 on 8 August, Fletcher began to withdraw his carriers.

Meanwhile, the Japanese cruisers were approaching Savo Island undetected. Shortly before arriving there, they launched float planes, which flew over the American and Australian ships. The ships did not fire as they assumed the float planes were American since they were flying with their recognition lights on. About 0145 on 9 August, the planes began to drop flares illuminating the American ships. At the same time, the Japanese naval force miraculously slipped past the radar picket destroyers.

In the ensuing night naval engagement, which developed into a wild mêlée, the Japanese scored a major victory. In what is now referred to as the Battle of Savo Island, the Allies lost four cruisers, with one cruiser and one destroyer damaged. The Japanese sustained damage to only one of their destroyers.

The Battle of Savo Island was one of the worst defeats ever suffered by the American Navy. The Japanese had achieved the element of surprise and defeated the American force in detail. *Vincennes* and *Quincy* were sunk within the first hour of the attack. *Canberra* was hit badly; she burned all night and was sunk the next day by American destroyers to prevent possible capture, while *Astoria* sank at about 1130 on the 9th. *Chicago* and the destroyer *Ralph Talbot* were badly damaged.

Fortunately, Admiral Mikawa did not attack the transport area. Had he done so he could have effectively curtailed American operations in the area. Instead he broke contact and headed back to Rabaul to be out of range of American carrier aircraft. Meanwhile, the damage inflicted by the Japanese on the amphibious task force delayed its departure until 1200 on 9 August. By 1500, the first group of ships had departed; the last group left at 1830.

The First Week

With the withdrawal of the amphibious task force the Marines were left without air support. They began to take stock of their perimeter and inventoried their captured supplies. The withdrawal of the transports had left the Marines with only part of their supplies: ammunition was adequate, but food was a much more serious issue. Even with the acquisition of a considerable quantity of Japanese foodstuffs, supplies were so short that on 12 August the division went on a two meal a day programme.

The captured airfield, which had nearly been completed by its former occupants, was renamed Henderson Field in honour of Major Lofton E. Henderson, a Marine pilot killed at the Battle of Midway.

It was realized early on that for the Guadalcanal operation to have a successful outcome,

◀ *On the morning of 9 August, General Vandegrift called his principal staff officers to his command post, which was located near a small ridge east of the Lunga River. Vandegrift informed them of the losses sustained by the American Navy at the Battle of Savo Island and of the subsequent withdrawal of the amphibious shipping. Shortly after the meeting adjourned the officers were asked to pose for this photograph. Vandegrift, fourth from left, is seated among the officers who would not only lead the division to victory on Guadalcanal but through the entire Pacific war. (USMC 50509)*

◀ *Patrols such as this one were sent out to gather intelligence on the Japanese. In the early days of the campaign, these patrols proved invaluable. Patrols travelled light but were usually heavily armed. This particular patrol carries a variety of weapons: M1903 Springfield rifles, M-1 Garands and BARs. They have captured a Japanese soldier who will hopefully provide intelligence on Japanese forces in the area. (USMC 58860)*

Henderson Field would have to be developed. Until it was completed, the Marines would be at the mercy of any air or naval attacks the Japanese cared to launch. A survey of the field conducted on the day of its capture indicated that 2,600 feet of runway could be finished in two days and that the remaining stretch of 1,178 feet could be completed in a week. The task could have been completed much faster, but the engineers had virtually no earth moving equipment. Fortunately there was some Japanese equipment available, and it was quickly pressed into service.

It would not be until 20 August that the Marines would have aircraft based on the island. On that day, nineteen planes of VMF-223 (F4F–4s under Major John L. Smith) and twelve dive-bombers of VMSB 232 (SBD–3s under Lieutenant Colonel Richard C. Mangrum) would land, their first mission being to assist at the Battle of the Tenaru. The Marine planes would be followed on 22 and 27 August by elements of the Army Air Corps 667 Fighter Squadron with 14 P-400s. The P-400 was an export version of the P-39, and was a Lend-Lease aircraft that did not have adapters for the American oxygen system, which necessitated their use in a ground support role. (The standard joke at the time was that a P-400 was a P-40 with a Zero on its tail.)

In the first week the tone of the campaign was set. Daily – and this was to continue for months – except when weather and American fighter aircraft were present, Japanese planes made incessant air raids. The targets were either Henderson Field or resupply shipping at Lunga Point. At night the perimeter was bombarded by Japanese warships offshore or by submarines (nicknamed 'Oscar'), which were more a nuisance than anything else. Two other characters that fell into this latter category were: 'Louie the Louse', a Japanese plane that periodically flew over dropping flares, which usually preceded a naval bombardment; and, 'Washing Machine Charlie', a Japanese plane with its engines set deliberately out of synchronization, the mission of which was more harassment than bombing.

All in all, the situation looked pretty bleak for the Marines, virtually abandoned by the Navy and left to fend for themselves on a remote tropical island. With the lack of adequate supplies and equipment, necessity became the mother of invention. They adapted to their new jungle home and began to carve out some creature comforts.

Having quickly established themselves ashore, they began to improve the perimeter. Considering a Japanese invasion more than likely, General Vandegrift concentrated the bulk of his combat units along the beach. A defensive line was dug along the beach running east from 'Alligator Creek', where the eastern flank was denied to the south, giving the defending Marines holding the river line a tactical advantage. To the west the line ran to Kukum, and then the flank was refused south towards a low range of jungle hills. The southern sector was initially dismissed as an avenue of approach for the Japanese, as it was almost impenetrable. This line was held by support troops manning a series of outposts on the grassy hills that dotted the region.

Once the Lunga Perimeter was established, patrols were sent out to gain information on the Japanese forces on the island. So far as could be determined, the bulk of the Japanese forces were concentrated west of the perimeter, in the Matanikau River and Point Cruz area. To verify this information it was decided to send out two patrols on 12 August 1942: one would head east to Tetere, and one would reconnoitre west past the Matanikau.

The Goettge Patrol

The western patrol, commanded by the Division Intelligence Officer, Colonel Frank B. Goettge, departed with 23 Marines, one Navy surgeon and a Japanese prisoner. Originally intended as a reconnaissance mission, the patrol was to depart during the day. It was scheduled to land west of Point Cruz and to conduct a reconnaissance of the western Matanikau region, move into the hills to the south and bivouac overnight. Next day it would move eastwards and return to the Marine perimeter. Once Goettge assumed command of the patrol, however, certain outside influences began to cause changes in its composition. A Japanese prisoner, a naval warrant officer, had disclosed under repeated questioning that some of his

▲*Colonel Frank B. Goettge, the Division intelligence officer who led the ill-fated patrol that landed near the Matanikau River on 12-13 August. The patrol encountered strong Japanese resistance and was overwhelmed. Only three Marines escaped to give an account of the fight. (Author's Collection)*

comrades in the Matanikau region might be induced to surrender. The fact that he was notably reticent and did not volunteer the information contributed to his credibility. Also, some Marines who had turned a Japanese triple barrelled pom-pom gun in the direction of the Matanikau and fired off some rounds reported a white surrender flag. The flag probably was an ordinary Japanese flag with the red centre not visible to the observers. Based on this sketchy information, Goettge persuaded General Vandegrift to allow him to lead a patrol down to the Matanikau region possibly to accept the surrender of the Japanese.

Believing in the possibility of a Japanese surrender Goettge changed the primary patrol mission from reconnaissance to 'humanitarian'. These additional details caused a considerable delay, and the patrol did not depart until dusk. It left from Kukum beach on 12 August and either by intention or by accident, landed east instead of west of Point Cruz, near the Matanikau River.

Shortly after landing, Goettge and a few selected Marines made a quick reconnaissance. As they approached Matanikau village, they ran into a small Japanese force. Goettge was killed, and one Marine was wounded. The Marines pulled back to the beach to join the main body of the patrol. Had they all moved south or west at that moment, they would have undoubtedly survived. However, it was decided to form a defensive position at the water's edge and signal for assistance.

In a battle that raged through the night, the small patrol fought an even increasing number of Japanese. Two Marines, Sergeant Charles C. 'Monk' Arndt and Corporal Joseph Spaulding, were sent out at different intervals to bring help. Despite heroic efforts on their part, the terrain and Japanese forces in the area slowed their travel time to the Marine Perimeter, and by the time they got back and made their reports it was too late to save the beleaguered Marines. The patrol, which fought on through the night, was finally over-whelmed at dawn. The lone survivor, Sergeant Frank L. Few, stated he had observed the Japanese mutilating the dead as he swam away from the battle area.

A relief force was sent out the next morning and landed west of Point Cruz, the patrol's original destination, but could find no trace of it or a battle.

This, of course, started a rumour that the clever Japanese had killed the patrol and obliterated any trace of the battle. In reality, the rescuing Marines who were not familiar with the area, had landed at the wrong location and had bypassed the battle area as they returned to the perimeter.

The loss of the patrol overshadowed the good news that Henderson Field was declared operational. The first plane to land was a Navy PBY-5A Catalina, which evacuated two Marines, a method that was to be used throughout the campaign.

The Brush Patrol

The progress of the patrol sent east was less eventful. As it moved through a native village it came across a Catholic priest, who advised them that the Japanese had landed a force to the east near Koli Point; two days later, on 14 August, this information was verified by a Coastwatcher, W. F.

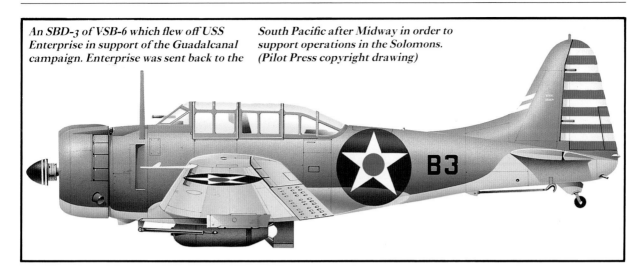

An SBD-3 of VSB-6 which flew off USS Enterprise in support of the Guadalcanal campaign. Enterprise was sent back to the South Pacific after Midway in order to support operations in the Solomons. (Pilot Press copyright drawing)

Martin Clemens, a District Officer assigned to Guadalcanal and a Captain in the British Protectorate Defence Force Solomon Islands Civil Government who had been hiding up in the hills from the Japanese. He had been instrumental in keeping information on Japanese activity flowing back to Australia prior to the Americans coming ashore. As soon as he was convinced that the Americans were going to stay, he came down from his hiding place and rendered valuable assistance. Making full use of his knowledge of Guadalcanal and its natives, he established an intelligence network of native scouts that proved invaluable during the campaign.

To verify the strength of the Japanese in the region, another patrol was sent out on 19 August. This patrol was led by Captain Charles C. Brush, and although its primary mission was reconnaissance, it had sufficient combat power to take care of itself. As it made its way toward Koli Point it stumbled into a large party of Japanese. In the ensuing fire-fight, 31 Japanese were killed.

▶ *Captain Martin Clemens and some of his Solomon Islander scouts. Clemens had been a district officer with the British Government before the war. After entering the American lines, Clemens helped organize a scouting force made up of local natives that provided a valuable source of accurate information throughout the campaign. (USMC 50505)*

◀ The Grumman F4F-4 (Wildcat) was the first type of aircraft to be based at Henderson Field. It was a sturdy, dependable aircraft capable of sustained operations in punishing conditions. This particular plane is an early variant and has the heavy propeller. Note the propeller itself is bullet scarred, indicating that the aircraft has seen combat. This aircraft was saved to fight again by the quick-thinking Marines who extinguished the flames when it was set afire during one of the daily bombing raids. (USMC 50516)

◀ The SBD Douglas (Dauntless) dive-bomber was another mainstay aircraft used by the Marines on Guadalcanal. Normally it carried a crew of two, pilot and rear gunner, and could drop a 500-pound bomb from a mount under the fuselage. It was also capable of carrying two 250-pound bombs mounted on bomb racks located under each wing. (USMC 55786)

◀ These P-400s were used by the Army 67th Fighter Squadron. It was an export version of the P-39 and could not be fitted with oxygen bottles, so it had a 12,000 feet ceiling. It was used in a ground support role. Its 120mm nose cannon, two .50-calibre and four .30-calibre machine-guns, coupled with the ability to carry a 500-pound bomb, made this plane an extremely effective close support weapon. (USMC 50467)

The uniforms and insignia of the dead Japanese indicated that this was a group of high ranking officers and senior enlisted men. Apparently they were on a reconnaissance mission to verify the Marine lines in preparation for a concentrated attack from the east.

The First Battle of the Matanikau

That same day, the 19th, on the western side of the perimeter a battalion sized operation was being launched against the Japanese in the Matanikau area, its mission being to drive the Japanese out of

▶ *The steep banks and jungle terrain are evident in this ground level view of the Matanikau River. This peaceful looking river was made almost impossible to cross by the Japanese troops who tenaciously defended its western banks. (USMC 59649)*

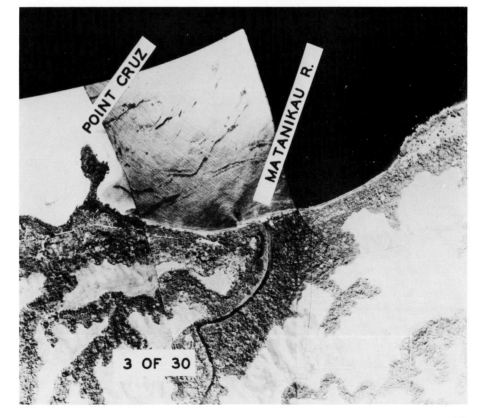

▶ *The Matanikau region was the most hotly contested area of the entire Guadalcanal campaign. The river, which had steep banks, cut through a deep valley and gave the Japanese, who were usually concentrated between it and Point Cruz, an excellent defensive line. This aerial photograph provides an excellent overall perspective of the region. (USMC)*

POINT CRUZ

MATANIKAU R.

3 OF 30

August-September 1942 Operations on Guadalcanal

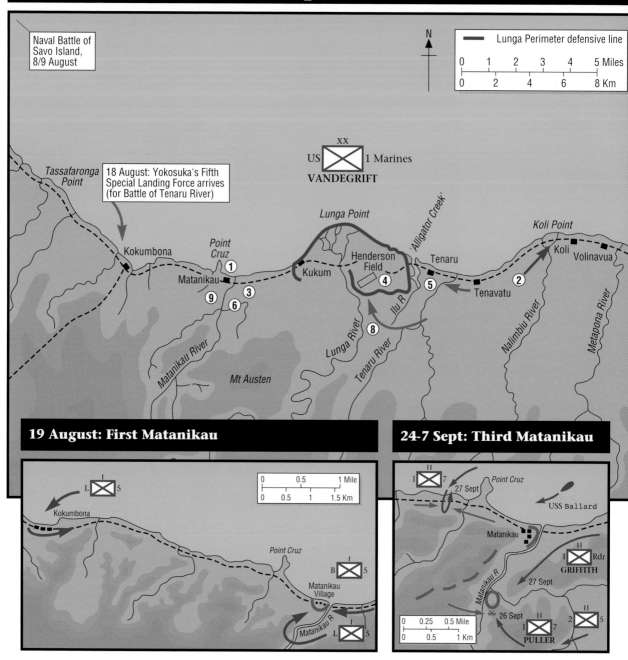

Naval Battle of Savo Island, 8/9 August

Lunga Perimeter defensive line

0 1 2 3 4 5 Miles
0 2 4 6 8 Km

N

US XX 1 Marines
VANDEGRIFT

18 August: Yokosuka's Fifth Special Landing Force arrives (for Battle of Tenaru River)

Tassafaronga Point

Kokumbona

Point Cruz

Matanikau

Lunga Point

Kukum

Henderson Field

Alligator Creek

Tenaru

Koli Point

Koli

Volinavua

Tenavatu

Ilu R.

Lunga River

Tenaru River

Nalimbiu River

Metapona River

Matanikau River

Mt Austen

19 August: First Matanikau

L 5

Kokumbona

Point Cruz

B 5

Matanikau Village

Matanikau R.

L 5

0 0.5 1 Mile
0 0.5 1 1.5 Km

24-7 Sept: Third Matanikau

7

27 Sept

Point Cruz

USS Ballard

Matanikau

I Rdr
GRIFFITH

27 Sept

Matanikau R.

26 Sept

1 7
PULLER

2 5

0 0.25 0.5 Mile
0 0.5 1 Km

the region. One Company (Company B, 1st Battalion, 5th Marines) was to approach using the coastal road and fight a spoiling action at the river mouth, while a second company (Company L, 3rd Battalion, 5th Marines) was to move overland through the jungle and deliver the main attack from the south. The third company (Company I, 3rd Battalion, 5th Marines) would make a seaborne landing to the west near Kokumbona village and cut off any retreating Japanese.

In what would be called the First Battle of the Matanikau, the Marines conducted an attack that succeeded in destroying the small Japanese garrison in the area. During the consolidation phase

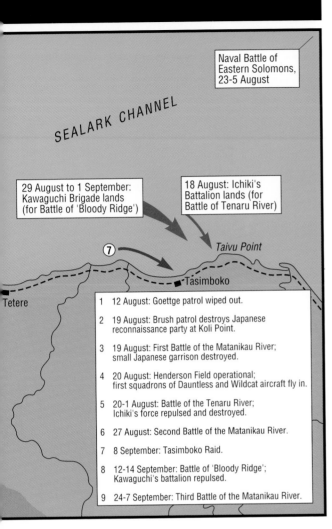

Naval Battle of Eastern Solomons, 23-5 August

SEALARK CHANNEL

29 August to 1 September: Kawaguchi Brigade lands (for Battle of 'Bloody Ridge')

18 August: Ichiki's Battalion lands (for Battle of Tenaru River)

⑦

Taivu Point

Tetere

Tasimboko

1	12 August: Goettge patrol wiped out.
2	19 August: Brush patrol destroys Japanese reconnaissance party at Koli Point.
3	19 August: First Battle of the Matanikau River; small Japanese garrison destroyed.
4	20 August: Henderson Field operational; first squadrons of Dauntless and Wildcat aircraft fly in.
5	20-1 August: Battle of the Tenaru River; Ichiki's force repulsed and destroyed.
6	27 August: Second Battle of the Matanikau River.
7	8 September: Tasimboko Raid.
8	12-14 September: Battle of 'Bloody Ridge'; Kawaguchi's battalion repulsed.
9	24-7 September: Third Battle of the Matanikau River.

of the action, the mutilated remains of the Marines of Colonel Goettge's patrol were discovered, thus clearing up the 'mystery' of the missing patrol.

The Battle of the Tenaru

On 13 August, the Japanese High Command ordered Lieutenant General Haruyoshi Hyakutake's Seventeenth Army at Rabaul to retake Guadalcanal. The naval commander for this operation was to be Rear Admiral Raizo Tanaka. With no clear intelligence picture of the American forces on Guadalcanal, Hyakutake decided to retake it with 6,000 troops from the 7th Division's 28th Infantry Regiment and the Yokosuka Special Naval Landing Force. These units would be followed by the 35th Brigade.

The spearpoint of the effort would be made by the reinforced 2nd Battalion of the 28th Infantry Regiment, led by Colonel Kiyono Ichiki. Ichiki and an advance element of 900 of his troops were taken to Guadalcanal and landed at Taivu Point on the night of 18 August 1942. At the same time 500 troops of the Yokosuka Fifth Special Landing Force went ashore to the west at Kokumbona.

These landings were the first run of what would be nicknamed the 'Tokyo Express' by the Marines. It was basically a shuttle run organized by Admiral Tanaka. Composed of cruisers, destroyers and transports, it shuttled troops and supplies at night from Rabaul to Guadalcanal. The route they took down the Solomons chain was nicknamed the 'Slot'.

After landing at Taivu, Colonel Ichiki established his headquarters, sent out scouting parties and awaited the arrival of the remainder of his regiment. Once he had the rest of his troops and accurate intelligence on the Americans he would attack. The intelligence picture Ichiki had was that a raiding party of Americans was cowering in a defensive perimeter around the airfield. Ichiki's plan was to march to the former Japanese construction camp east of the Tenaru, establish it as his headquarters and then move against the Americans. After learning that his scouting party had been destroyed by the Marine patrol on 19 August, Ichiki changed his plans. Fearing he had lost the element of surprise he decided to march westwards with the troops he had to hand. His knowledge of the terrain east of the Tenaru was incomplete, but he did not expect to encounter any Americans east of the airfield.

On the night of 20/21 August, Marine listening posts on the east bank of Alligator Creek, (then believed to be the Tenaru River) detected the movement of a large body of Japanese troops. The listening posts had no sooner withdrawn than a severely wounded native, Jacob Vouza, a sergeant in the native police contingent, stumbled into the Marine lines and, before collapsing, imparted the news that the Japanese were going to attack. Vouza had been captured, tortured and bayoneted by the Japanese in an attempt to gain information on the

▲*Colonel Kiyono Ichiki was the leader of the 900-man Japanese force that attacked the Marines at 'Alligator Creek'. Contrary to popular belief, he did not commit suicide after burning his regimental* colours after the aborted attack: last seen he was rallying his men as they attacked the Marines. More than likely he was killed attempting to cross the sand spit. (USMC)

▲*Sergeant Jacob Vouza of the Solomon Islands police force was on his way to his village at Roroni when he was captured by the Japanese. After finding an American flag on Vouza, the Japanese* tortured him to obtain information on the Americans. Bayoneted and left for dead, Vouza managed to make it to the Marine lines to warn them of Ichiki's impending attack. (USMC)

Americans. Left for dead, he had managed to make his way to the Marine lines. (Honoured by the Allies for his heroism, Vonza was later knighted and died in 1984 at the age of 92; his statue is the centrepiece of a memorial unveiled on 7 August 1992 on Guadalcanal.)

No sooner had Vouza arrived than the first Japanese, who were marching in formation, ran into a single strand of barbed wire placed across the sand bar at the mouth of the creek. This temporarily disorganized the leading elements of Ichiki's force, who were not expecting to run into any defensive positions so far east.

The ensuing battle that erupted, which would later be referred to erroneously as the Battle of the Tenaru, was fierce and savage. Using human wave tactics, the Japanese attempted to crush Lieutenant Colonel Edwin A. Pollock's 2nd Battalion, 1st Marines, which was defending the area.

Unable to dislodge the Marines, who were now using heavy machine-gun fire and canister fire from two 37mm anti-tank weapons to decimate his troops, Ichiki sent part of his force south along the east bank to cross the creek upstream in an attempt to outflank the Marines. This attempt failed. He then sent a company out through the surf in an attempt to break through from the north. This attempt also failed. The last anyone saw of Colonel Ichiki he was moving forward towards the sand bar, where he was undoubtedly killed.

Mount Austen

Henderson Field

Ilu River

▲This picture shows the east bank of 'Alligator Creek' (referred to as the Ilu River). Ichiki launched his attack from the east across the sand bar. The Marines occupied the west bank and stopped Ichiki's attack. Henderson Field, Ichiki's objective, is seen in the background. (US Navy)

▶ This is the sand bar at the mouth of 'Alligator Creek' where Colonel Ichiki attempted to cross. In the confusion of the battle, the creek was misidentified as the Tenaru River, and the battle fought there has always borne the name 'Battle of the Tenaru'. This position is from the Marine side looking east towards the direction of the Japanese attack. (USMC 54891)

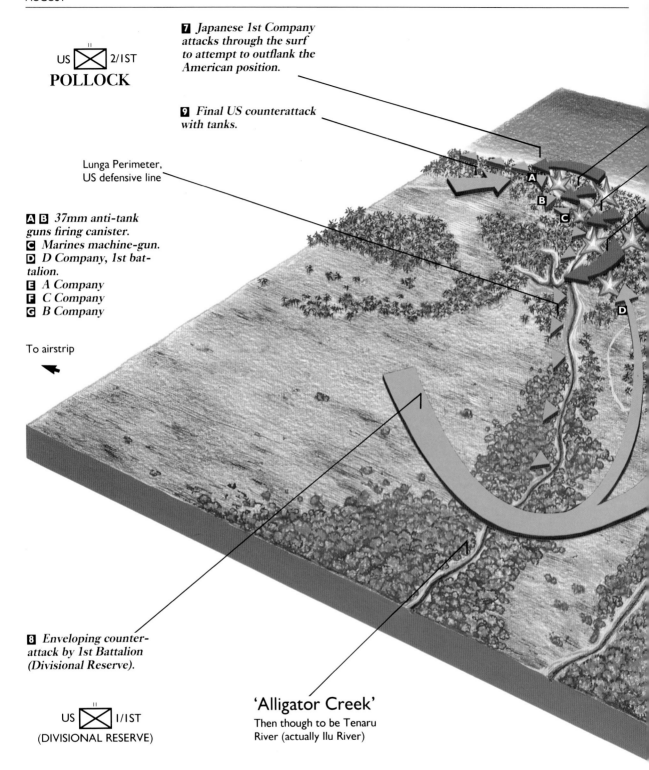

US ⊠ 2/IST
POLLOCK

7 *Japanese 1st Company attacks through the surf to attempt to outflank the American position.*

9 *Final US counterattack with tanks.*

Lunga Perimeter,
US defensive line

A B *37mm anti-tank guns firing canister.*
C *Marines machine-gun.*
D *D Company, 1st battalion.*
E *A Company*
F *C Company*
G *B Company*

To airstrip

8 *Enveloping counterattack by 1st Battalion (Divisional Reserve).*

US ⊠ I/IST
(DIVISIONAL RESERVE)

'Alligator Creek'
Then though to be Tenaru River (actually Ilu River)

BATTLE OF THE TENARU

20–21 August 1942

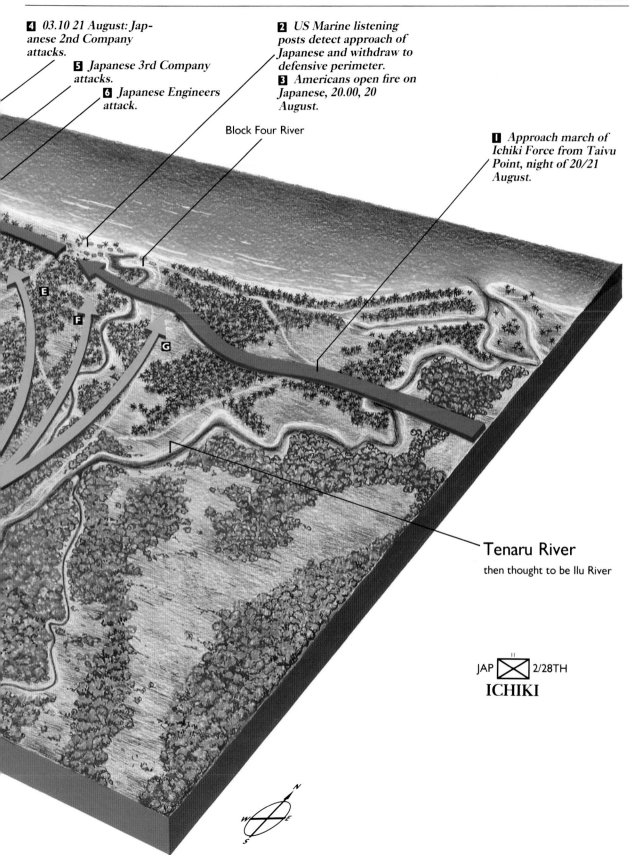

4 *03.10 21 August: Japanese 2nd Company attacks.*

5 *Japanese 3rd Company attacks.*

6 *Japanese Engineers attack.*

Block Four River

2 *US Marine listening posts detect approach of Japanese and withdraw to defensive perimeter.*
3 *Americans open fire on Japanese, 20.00, 20 August.*

1 *Approach march of Ichiki Force from Taivu Point, night of 20/21 August.*

E

F

G

Tenaru River

then thought to be Ilu River

JAP ⊠ 2/28TH
ICHIKI

◀This Marine tank and its crew were part of the enveloping force that destroyed Ichiki's troops after crossing over the creek at its mouth. The canister fire from the 37mm cannon and the machine-gun fire from the tanks' 30-calibre light machine-guns wreaked havoc on the Japanese. (USMC 50560)

◀The aftermath of the Battle of the Tenaru clearly indicates the determination of the Japanese attackers. The dead Japanese in the foreground had actually penetrated to the west bank of the creek before they were stopped by the defending Marines. The Marines in the background are walking through the area to survey the aftermath of the battle. (National Archives 80-G-M077

◀Japanese soldiers of the Ichiki detachment lie dead on the beach after they were shot trying to outflank the Marines. This group moved through the surf and attempted to attack from the north. (USMC)

The fight continued throughout the night. In the battle, one machine-gun team distinguished itself by its overt acts of bravery. The weapon was deployed near the mouth of the river and was exacting a heavy toll on the Japanese attackers. In an attempt to silence the gun, the Japanese killed the gunner, Private Johnny Rivers, but not before his finger froze on the trigger and 200 more rounds were fired. Private Albert Schmid took over the gun; and Corporal Leroy Diamond helped him spot targets until he was wounded. Schmid continued to fire at the Japanese until a grenade landed in front of him. The resulting explosion and fragmentation blinded Schmid; however, he attempted to continue fighting the Japanese. For their action, both Schmid and Diamond would receive the Navy Cross, the Navy-Marine Corps' second highest award for bravery.

In the morning the Marines were still holding. It was then decided to conduct a double envelopment to eliminate Ichiki's force. Supported by light tanks, artillery and newly arrived fighter planes, the 1st Battalion, 1st Marine Regiment, which had been held as Division reserve, outflanked Ichiki's force and destroyed it. Of the original 900 Japanese troops, 800 were dead or dying on the sand bar and in the surrounding jungle. The cost to the Marines was light: 34 killed and 75 wounded.

▲ This bridge, constructed after the Battle of the Tenaru, gives an indication of the terrain the Marines who enveloped Ichiki had to move through. It was undoubtedly terrain like this that caused Ichiki to launch his attack over the sand bar rather than attempt a flanking movement. (USMC 50465)

The Battle of the Eastern Solomons

While the issue on land was being decided the Japanese assembled a major naval task force under Admirals Tanaka and Mikawa. At the same time an American naval task force under Admiral Fletcher which was operating south-east of the lower Solomons in what it believed to be a safe area, became engaged in the Battle of the Eastern Solomons.

Unaware of what had happened to Ichiki, the Japanese had planned on reinforcing him with a larger secondary force of about 1,500 troops. This force departed on 19 August in four transports screened by four destroyers. They were to land on Guadalcanal on 24 August. To support the transports and operations ashore the Japanese dispatched two naval task forces composed of five aircraft carriers, four battleships, sixteen cruisers and thirty destroyers.

Three American carrier groups, comprising three aircraft carriers, one battleship, six cruisers and eighteen destroyers, were operating about a hundred miles south-east of Guadalcanal. Somehow, an erroneous intelligence report on 23 August indicated that the large Japanese force, believed to be in the area, was returning to the Japanese base at Truk Island. Operating on this mistaken belief, one of the carrier groups centred around *Wasp* departed from the group to refuel.

This left two carrier groups formed around *Enterprise* and *Saratoga*. Shortly after the *Wasp* group departed, patrol planes discovered the Japanese transport group 350 miles from Guadalcanal. The next day, 24 August, American carrier planes discovered the Japanese forces, and at the same time Japanese carrier planes discovered the American forces.

In the ensuing air-to-ship, air-to-air battle, the smaller American force turned back a larger Japanese force. The Japanese were able to land 1,500 troops and bombard Henderson Field; but they were not able to intervene in the ground fighting. Also, they were no longer able to control the air space over Guadalcanal. The Japanese lost the carrier *Ryujo*, one destroyer, one light cruiser and ninety aircraft, with one seaplane carrier and a destroyer damaged. Shortly after the battle the

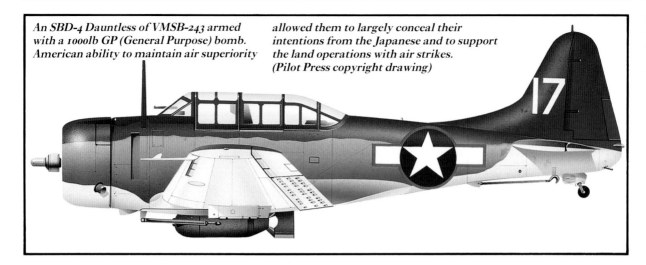

An SBD-4 Dauntless of VMSB-243 armed with a 1000lb GP (General Purpose) bomb. American ability to maintain air superiority allowed them to largely conceal their intentions from the Japanese and to support the land operations with air strikes. (Pilot Press copyright drawing)

American naval force départed. The Americans had sustained damage to one aircraft carrier, *Enterprise*, and had lost twenty planes. Far more serious losses followed. On 31 August, the aircraft carrier *Saratoga*, patrolling west of the Santa Cruz Islands, was torpedoed. The aircraft carrier *Wasp*, on patrol south-east of the Solomons, was torpedoed and sunk on 15 September. The battleship *North Carolina* was also torpedoed at the same time by a torpedo launched from the same spread that hit *Wasp*. The waters in this region were known, thereafter, as 'Torpedo Junction'. With one carrier sunk and two damaged, *Hornet* was the only American aircraft carrier in the South Pacific.

The Second Battle of the Matanikau

The last action during the month of August was a land battle. A second action was planned by the 5th Marines and was designed to place the 1st Battalion, 5th Marines, ashore west of Point Cruz. The mission of this battalion remains unclear: the battalion commander was given verbal orders and did not disclose them in their entirety to his staff.

The battalion landed unopposed at 0730 on 27 August. Because of the narrowness of the coast in that region and thick jungle terrain, the movement of the battalion was slowed and channelized. Steep ridges overlooked the battalion's route of march, and covering troops had to be placed on them to secure the flanks. But within a short time it became apparent that the security force could not keep pace with the main body. All contact between

the two groups was physical, owing to an absence of squad-type radios. The terrain eventually wore down the covering force, necessitating relief. Once this was accomplished, the battalion continued to a point along the coast where the coral ridges narrowed the coastal plain down to 200 yards wide. Here the Japanese opened fire from concealed, dug-in positions.

The leading company began to take casualties as it attempted to deploy. A second company was ordered to make a flanking movement towards the north-east as the endangered company made an assault from the west. This attack was supported by weapons from a third company. But the terrain and climate proved too much for such a manoeuvre, and the attack bogged down. Realizing that he could not dislodge the Japanese defenders from their strongpoint, and that further unsupported attacks would cause unnecessary deaths, the battalion commander requested permission to withdraw. The regimental commander, Colonel Hunt, relieved the battalion commander, placing the executive officer in charge.

Colonel Hunt then went down to the battle area and began to supervise the operation directly. He dictated that the battalion would remain in the field, and that the Japanese would continue to be attacked until defeated. The attack was launched the next morning – and met no opposition. The Japanese had withdrawn during the night. The battalion moved by coastal road to Matanikau village, where it was picked up by boat and taken back to the Lunga Perimeter.

SEPTEMBER

While the ground fighting was going on, important strategic developments were taking place. A Marine air wing was beginning to establish itself at Henderson Field. On 3 September 1942, the 1st Marine Aircraft Wing, under Brigadier General Roy S. Geiger, arrived. Geiger and his staff immediately reported to General Vandegrift and established a cooperative rapport that was to remain continuous throughout the campaign.

The conditions for air operations out of Henderson Field were as primitive as they could possibly be. However, like their fellow Marines in the Division, the Wing was soon to adapt to the conditions on the ground and to take control of the air war. In fact, with the arrival of the Wing, the tide in the air would eventually be turned against the Japanese pilots.

The Tasimboko Raid

After the Tenaru battle there were no major engagements until mid-September. However, there were reports from natives at the end of August that two to three hundred Japanese were fortifying the village of Tasimboko, about eight miles east of Lunga Point. In early September, the natives reported there were now several thousand

▶ The pagoda-like structure set on a small hill overlooking Henderson Field became the operations centre for the airfield. It was equipped with a ground-to-air radio system that allowed the pagoda to contact planes on station and vector them towards incoming Japanese aircraft. (USMC 50032)

▶ As the Marines began to improve their existing environment, the Pagoda was also improved and made into a usable shelter. A radio tunnel network was dug into the hill under the Pagoda so that operations could be shifted there in case of air raid or bombardment. Eventually the structure was torn down when General Vandegrift concluded that the Japanese were using it as an aiming point to shell and bomb the airfield. (USMC 51812).

Japanese occupying that area. These reports were dismissed by Marine intelligence, but as a precautionary measure it was decided that an amphibious raid should be made against what was believed to be a small Japanese garrison force.

The Marines selected for the raid were from the 1st Raider Battalion and the 1st Parachute Battalion, who had recently been brought over from Tulagi. These two units had been formed into a composite battalion as a result of combat losses and were placed under the command of Lieutenant Colonel Merrit A. Edson. To conduct the raid they would sail on destroyer transports from the Lunga area to a point east of Tasimboko. Due to a shipping shortage, the Raiders would be landed first and the ships would return for the Parachutists.

The Raiders landed at dawn 8 September, followed shortly afterwards by the Parachutists. As they moved west they met minimal resistance until

▲ Major General Kawaguchi (seated, centre) with his staff officers. The picture was probably taken in the Philippines. Kawaguchi landed near Tasimbogo from destroyers on 6 September. Two days later he was attacked by Raiders and Parachutists as he made his way into the jungle. He was to meet the Marines again on 'Bloody Ridge'. Kawaguchi was defeated and his brigade destroyed. (National Archives)

they approached Tasimboko, when resistance sharply increased. The Japanese troops, estimated at 1,000, were well armed and equipped. They were also supported by field artillery firing at point-blank range. In order to continue the attack, Edson set in motion an enveloping movement from the south. Using the Parachutists as rear and flank security, the Raiders initiated the attack and eventually, with air support from Henderson Field, the Japanese were forced from the village.

After occupying the village the attacking Marines discovered thousands of life jackets and enough supplies to feed as many troops as there were life jackets. What they did not know was that the Japanese they had just fought were the rear party of the 35th Infantry Regiment (or Kawaguchi Brigade, as it was referred to). Totalling more than 3,000 Japanese commanded by Major General Kiyotaki Kawaguchi, it had arrived between 29 August and 1 September.

Two events saved the smaller Marine force from being destroyed by the larger Japanese force. First was the fact that Kawaguchi had already formed his command to move south-west through the jungle. His intention was to move undetected to the south of Henderson Field and then launch an attack north from the jungle. Second, an American resupply convoy en route to Lunga Point was passing by the area. The Japanese incorrectly concluded that the convoy was reinforcing the Marine attacking force and a full-scale landing was being made. Kawaguchi and Edson would meet again, less than a week later, on a grassy ridge overlooking Henderson Field.

The Battle of 'Bloody Ridge'

After Tasimboko it was decided to put the Raiders and Parachutists in a reserve position. They were to occupy a defensive position on a series of grassy ridges south of Henderson Field, near the Division command post.

Patrols and native scouts that frequented the area south of Henderson Field began to encounter increasing Japanese opposition. Small artillery pieces were often located at various sites within range of the Marine perimeter, and on 10 September native scouts reported that the Japanese were cutting a trail from the east and were about five miles from the Perimeter. All these indicators pointed to the fact that a major Japanese offensive was in the making.

On 12 September, the Raiders attempted to patrol south of their position and encountered unexpected Japanese resistance. To add emphasis to the Japanese presence in the area, the ridge positions were bombed in a daily air raid. Unable to advance, they consolidated their positions on the southernmost knoll of the ridge complex. This would be the start of a crucial battle that would be called the Battle of 'Bloody Ridge' – a decided turning point in the campaign.

To defend the area, Edson positioned his composite battalion of Raiders and Parachutists in a linear defence along the southernmost ridge and in the surrounding jungle. The western flank was

▶ *General Vandegrift's tent near 'Bloody Ridge'. Because of the frequent shelling of Henderson Field, General Vandegrift moved his command post out to a quieter area in early September. He then had the Raiders moved on to the ridge near his position to cover the southern end of the perimeter. It was thought that this area was a quiet sector and would not see much action. Immediately after the battle, Vandegrift relocated his command post back to the Henderson Field area. (USMC 50489)*

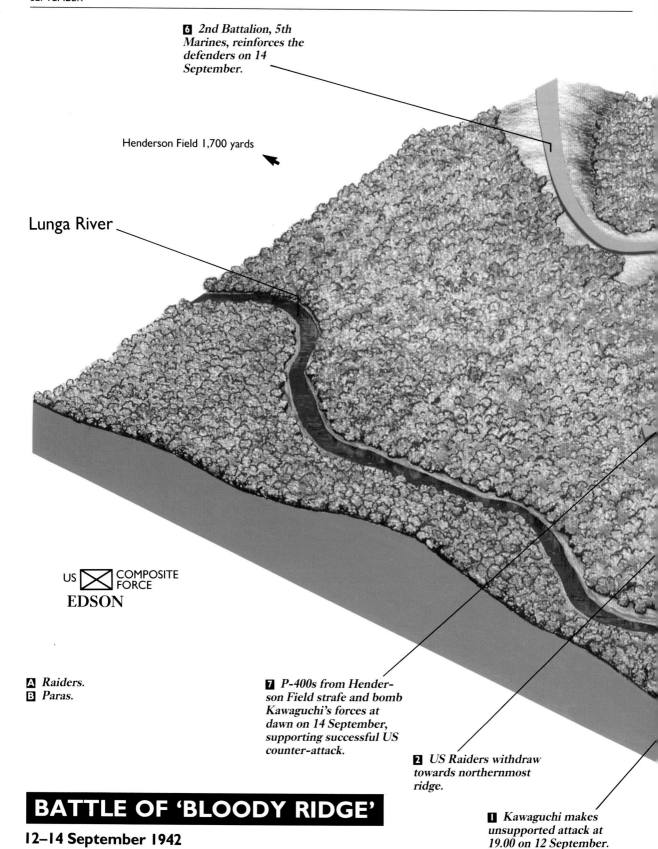

6 *2nd Battalion, 5th Marines, reinforces the defenders on 14 September.*

Henderson Field 1,700 yards

Lunga River

US ⊠ COMPOSITE FORCE
EDSON

A *Raiders.*
B *Paras.*

7 *P-400s from Henderson Field strafe and bomb Kawaguchi's forces at dawn on 14 September, supporting successful US counter-attack.*

2 *US Raiders withdraw towards northernmost ridge.*

BATTLE OF 'BLOODY RIDGE'

12–14 September 1942

1 *Kawaguchi makes unsupported attack at 19.00 on 12 September.*

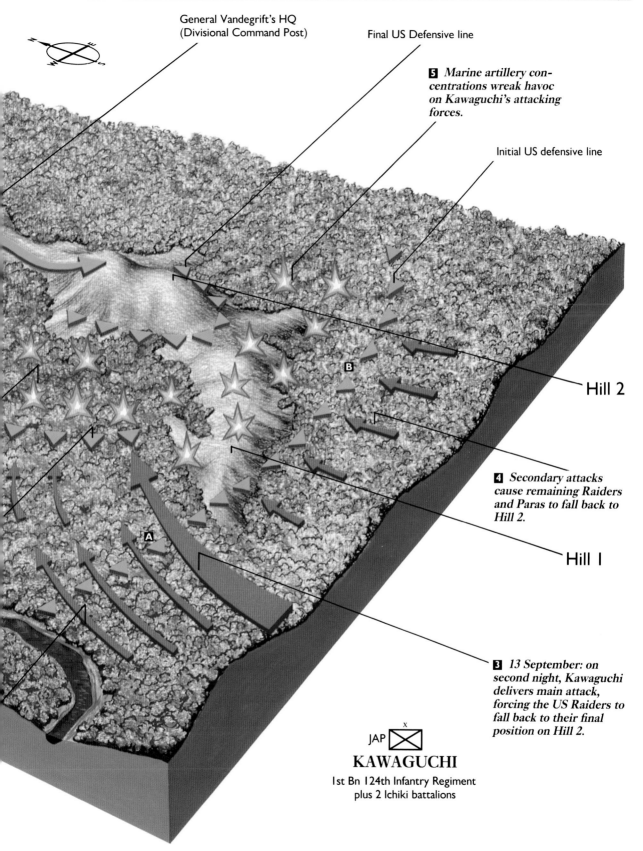

General Vandegrift's HQ
(Divisional Command Post)

Final US Defensive line

5 *Marine artillery concentrations wreak havoc
on Kawaguchi's attacking
forces.*

Initial US defensive line

Hill 2

4 *Secondary attacks
cause remaining Raiders
and Paras to fall back to
Hill 2.*

Hill 1

3 *13 September: on
second night, Kawaguchi
delivers main attack,
forcing the US Raiders to
fall back to their final
position on Hill 2.*

A

B

JAP $\boxtimes^{x}$

KAWAGUCHI

1st Bn 124th Infantry Regiment
plus 2 Ichiki battalions

▲ This is a view of the southernmost portion of 'Bloody Ridge'. It was here that Kawaguchi struck the Marines repeatedly from the thick jungle seen to the south. The Marines held a linear defensive position that stretched off to the left of this photograph. In the determined attacks, the Marines were pushed back north towards the airfield. (USMC 54970)

▼The thick jungle is clearly evident in this picture. Here we see a Marine scanning it for signs of Japanese movement. Should any activity be detected, it can be forwarded on the field telephone seen immediately behind the Marine. This photograph was taken on top of 'Bloody Ridge', and Mount Austen can be seen in the right background. (USMC 61547)

▲The southern ridge line. This picture shows a connecting trench to a covered machine-gun position located on the military crest of the forward slope. The thick jungle is present in the foreground. It was from the jungle that the Japanese attack came. Mount Austen looms on the horizon. (USMC 53094)

▼Edson's final position was the northernmost ridge seen in the background. Had it fallen on the night of 13/14 September there would have been nothing to stop the Japanese from advancing to Henderson Field. This picture was taken from the southern ridge looking north. (USMC 5000)

Conditions on Guadalcanal were equally appalling for Japanese and Americans alike. The Japanese lost around 9000 men from disease and starvation during the campaign. (Shirley Mallinson)

anchored on the Lunga River. The attack began that evening with shelling from Japanese warships, followed by repeated probings of the Marine lines from the jungle to the south. Later that night the numerically superior Kawaguchi Brigade repeatedly struck the Marines. The attack was preceded by a 20-minute naval bombardment, followed by a flare fired just forward of the Marine lines. As the flare faded away, Kawaguchi ordered his troops to initiate their attack. Powerful thrusts were directed from the west primarily against the companies that occupied the jungle terrain flanking the ridge. The Raiders were pushed back, and at times there was danger of some of the flanking companies being cut off.

The next day, 13 September, Edson attempted to use his reserve companies to dislodge the Japanese who had established a western salient into his position. This daylight attack did not meet with success, so Edson ordered his Marines to prepare and improve existing positions while waiting for the inevitable night attack. Throughout the day Japanese planes attacked the Lunga Perimeter, sometimes bombing the ridge.

The second night, Kawaguchi struck with two infantry battalions. He succeeded in driving the Marines back to the northernmost knoll of the ridge. From this final position the Marines held back the Japanese onslaught. Kawaguchi struck twelve times, each attack being preceded by rocket flares. The fighting was fierce, each side sensing the importance of the terrain feature they were holding or fighting for. Kawaguchi knew that he would have to overwhelm the Raiders and Parachutists if his attack on Henderson field were to succeed; Edson knew that at this stage of the battle his troops were no longer just fighting to save Henderson Field – they were fighting to save their very lives.

The flares fired by Kawaguchi's troops served as a signal for his troops to attack and also indicated the direction of attack, which made an excellent reference point for Marine artillery fire. With their guns firing direct support at close range, the defending Marines were able to hold.

At dawn on 14 September, planes from Henderson Field and the 2nd Battalion, 5th Marines supported the Raiders and Parachutists in driving

▲ This picture was taken near the aid station on 'Bloody Ridge'. Had this last northern ridge fallen, the Japanese would have been able to advance down the dirt road in the rear of the picture to Henderson Field. The closeness of the jungle to this ridge and its seemingly impenetrable nature caused the Marines to think the Japanese would not attack the perimeter from this southerly direction. (USMC 50003)

▼ This is the road that leads from 'Bloody Ridge' to the airport. In this picture it is very easy to see why the defence of 'Bloody Ridge' was so critical. Once the Japanese advanced to the open plain in the foreground, they would have seized the airfield and driven a deadly wedge between the Marine forces. Had the Japanese succeeded, there is some doubt whether they could have been ejected. (USMC 52059)

the remainder of Kawaguchi's forces into the jungle. Kawaguchi had been defeated; the majority of his troops were either dead or dying in the jungle or on the slopes of the ridge that overlooked Henderson Field.

In the Battle of 'Bloody Ridge', the Marines had achieved a significant victory over a superior Japanese force and undoubtedly saved Henderson Field from capture. The Marines lost 31 killed, 103 wounded and nine missing; the Japanese lost more than 600 killed. For his heroic defence on 'Bloody Ridge', Edson, along with one of his company commanders, Major Kenneth D. Bailey, would receive the Congressional Medal of Honor.

While Kawaguchi was attacking at 'Bloody Ridge', a second unit of his force, about two companies, attacked The 3rd Battalion 1st Marines at 'Alligator Creek'. A fight developed that lasted through the night but the Marines repulsed it decisively. A third attack, probably led by Colonel Oka's command, struck the 3rd Battalion, 5th Marines from the west. This attack was also repulsed.

September Matanikau Action

With all the Japanese attacks repulsed, General Vandegrift decided to expand the Marine perimeter. Bolstered by the addition of the 7th Marines, recently transported from Samoa, Vandegrift tasked them with clearing the Japanese from the Matanikau area. The action was planned initially to be accomplished in two separate phases. A reconnaissance in force this time by the 1st Battalion, 7th Marines, was to be conducted from 23-26 September in the area between Mount Austen and Kokumbona. On 27 September, the 1st Raiders Battalion was to conduct an attack at the mouth of the Matanikau River with the objective of pushing through to Kokumbona and establishing a patrol base there.

The 1st Battalion, Seventh Marines, under the command of Lieutenant Colonel Lewis B. 'Chesty' Puller, set out for the Mount Austen area on 23 September. During that day, no contact with the Japanese was made. Late in the evening of the following day, however, the battalion made contact

with a strong Japanese force near Mount Austen. In the ensuing action, which was broken off at nightfall, the battalion sustained seven killed and 25 wounded. Puller's Marines planned to continue the attack the next day, but requested to evacuate all their wounded before attacking again. General Vandegrift, fearing that Puller had made contact with a strong Japanese force, sent the 2nd Battalion, 5th Marines, to reinforce him. With the increase in forces, Puller was able to detach two of his companies to escort the wounded back to the Marine lines.

The combined force then continued its advance to clear the east bank of the Mantanikau. As it approached the river mouth on 26 September, the combined force was taken under fire by the Japanese from the west bank and the controlling western ridges. The 2nd Battalion, 5th Marines succeeded in making its way to the mouth of the river, but could not force a crossing. It was decided to have Puller's Marines and the 2nd Battalion, 5th Marines hold and engage the Japanese at the mouth of the river.

The 1st Raider Battalion, meanwhile, had set out from the Perimeter to accomplish its portion of the overall mission. However, developments at the Matanikau River caused their plan of operation to be altered. The Raiders would move up the east bank of the river, cross at a spot where that river forked about 2,000 yards upstream, and strike the Japanese from the right rear. The action began early on 27 September 1942 with the Raiders, now under Lieutenant Colonel Sam Griffith (Edson having been promoted and given command of the 5th Marines), moving up to their intended crossing point. As it moved into position, the unit discovered that a sizable enemy force had crossed the river and had taken up strong positions on the east bank.

Fighting soon erupted and Griffith was wounded. His new executive officer, Major Bailey (who had won the Medal of Honor on 'Bloody Ridge') was killed. The concentrated fire of the Japanese from the front flanks succeeded not only in stopping the assault but in preventing the Raiders deploying. From this point on, the American operation degenerated. A message from the Raiders was interpreted incorrectly at Division headquarters, and it was erroneously inferred that the Raiders had successfully crossed the river.

In order to assist them, it was decided to send out the two companies from Puller's battalion in a shore-to-shore landing. Their mission was to cut off any retreating Japanese and assist the units fighting at the Matanikau. Naval gunfire support would be provided on this portion of the operation by the destroyer *Ballard*. The landing was to be made in two waves west of Point Cruz but did not receive the requested fire support from the destroyer, the result of an earlier air raid that disrupted fire support communications. Fortunately the landing was unopposed.

The first opposition came in the form of mortar bombs, which fell on the Marines just as they reached the ridges 500 yards south of the landing beach. One of the first bombs to fall killed Major Otho L. Rogers, the battalion executive officer, who was commanding this phase of the operation. To make matters worse, a strong enemy column was observed coming from the Matanikau River, and this began to engage the Marines. Now all three Marine forces were in combat with the Japanese but unable to support each other.

The most serious threat was directed at the force that had landed west of Point Cruz. It was in danger of being surrounded. Unfortunately, radio equipment had not been brought ashore, and the Division command post was not aware of what was happening. This situation was quickly rectified when the Marines spelled out the word 'HELP' with their T-shirts. The message was spotted by a dive-bomber pilot, Lieutenant Dale M. Leslie, who radioed a message to the 5th Marines.

Puller, who had been with the Matanikau force, now realized how serious the situation was and left the Matanikau area to rescue his isolated companies. Securing permission to take a small flotilla of landing craft up the coast, Puller set out on the rescue mission. En route, he came across the destroyer, *Ballard*, which he hailed down and boarded. This small task force then continued towards the beleaguered Marines.

When *Ballard* showed up on station, its fire direction centre could not communicate with the Marines on shore, so fire support was not immediately available. In order to signal to the ship, Sergeant Robert D. Raysbrook, exposed himself to Japanese fire. Standing up on the ridge, Raysbrook

▶ *This is the terrain on the east bank of the Matanikau that Lieutenant Colonel Puller's Marines operated in as they swept north to clear the east bank in late September 1942. The Matanikau River can be seen through the trees slightly left of centre. (USMC 116749)*

Guadalcanal represented the first use in a combat zone of the LVT-1 (Landing Vehicle Tracked), popularly known as the 'Alligator'.

The amtracs of the 1st and 2nd Amphibian Tractor Battalions provided logistical support for the landings. (Terry Hadler)

began semaphoring fire directions to *Ballard*. (For his heroism, he was to be awarded the Navy Cross, as well as a comparable award by Great Britain.) As the Marines withdrew from the ridge, under the cover of naval gunfire, Platoon Sergeant Anthony P. Malinowski, Jr., single-handedly covered their withdrawal with a Browning Automatic Rifle until he was killed, an action that earned him a Navy Cross.

Once the Marines reached the beach, they set up a hasty defence and waited for the approaching landing craft. Japanese fire from Point Cruz to the east and Kokumbona to the west then began to hit the approaching landing craft, causing casualties.

Lieutenant Leslie, who had remained in the air over the area in his dive-bomber, flew low over the landing craft and strafed Japanese positions on the beach. Also in this action, a Coast Guard Signalman 1st Class, Douglas Munro, manning a machine-gun on one of the landing craft, began to engage the Japanese. For his heroic lifesaving actions under fire, he became the only Coast Guardsman to win the Medal of Honor.

The companies were finally evacuated at a cost of 24 killed and 23 wounded. The Japanese force the Marines came into contact with was estimated to be 1,800 strong and had lost 60 killed and 100 wounded. Once the withdrawal was accomplished, the Marines along the Matanikau also pulled back to the Perimeter, leaving the Japanese still in control of the region and ending the ground fighting for the month of September.

The naval actions during the month were limited to the nightly attempts to interdict the 'Tokyo Express'.

▶ *In early October the Japanese, using long range artillery, began to bombard Henderson Field. Weapons such as this 105mm artillery piece, with its battery headquarters located near White River west of Point Cruz, disrupted airfield operation. The Marine attack in the Matanika area in early October struck the Japanese just as they were preparing to launch an attack. The purpose for the Japanese attack was to secure the east bank of the Matanikau for firing positions for these types of artillery pieces. The Marines referred to the Japanese artillery as 'Pistol Pete'. (USMC)*

OCTOBER

Early in October a Marine Raider patrol reported a Japanese build up in the east, near Gurabusu and Koilotumaria, two native villages lying between Lunga and Aola. The Americans concluded that the Japanese in the area were possibly planning another attack from the east. To counter this suspected attack it was decided to bring the 1st Battalion, 2nd Marines, over from Tulagi and to make a shore to shore landing. The target date for the landing was 9 October. The crossing was made in Higgins boats towed by larger landing craft. The operation was marred when one of the Higgins boats' bow assembly pulled loose during tow. The boat sank immediately, drowning 18 Marines and sailors. Subsequent rescue operations delayed the landing and caused operational plans to be changed.

Koilotumaria was attacked first on 10 October and no opposition was met. However, the Marines did discover positions for more than 200 Japanese in the area. At Gurabusu, which was attacked two hours later, some opposition was met and over-come. The Japanese lost 30 killed and the Marines lost one killed and one wounded. A large amount of supplies were captured and destroyed, but the main Japanese force was not located. All indications pointed to the fact that the Japanese forces in the area had moved south into the jungle and would possibly link up with existing Japanese forces on Guadalcanal.

October Matanikau Battle

October was a busy month for both sides. The Americans wanted to drive the Japanese from their Matanikau stronghold, and intelligence reports indicated that the Japanese were massing in the region for another all-out attack. To add credence to these reports, recently landed Japanese artillery, nicknamed 'Pistol Pete', was beginning to range in on Henderson Field, interrupting airfield operations.

General Vandegrift initiated a plan of attack that called for the 5th Marines (minus one

battalion) to conduct a spoiling attack at the mouth of the Matanikau River, which would focus Japanese attention on that area; meanwhile the 7th Marines, (minus one battalion), reinforced by the 3rd Battalion, 2nd Marines, would cross the river upstream, then turn north to clear the area on the west bank. The operation would be supported by artillery and from the air. The objective of the attack was to establish a line far enough to the west to prohibit Japanese artillery from firing at Henderson Field.

The Japanese had prepared a similar plan. The 4th Infantry Regiment, under Colonel Tadamasu Nakaguma, was to seize positions east of the Matanikau River. By doing this the Japanese would be able to establish better positions for their artillery while denying the Marines their Matanikau line.

Fortunately for the Marines, they put their plan into action first. The battle lasted from 7 to 9 October; the plan of attack roughly followed the previous month's aborted attack in the Matanikau region. The plan called for the 5th Marines to set up positions on the east bank of the Matanikau running south from the mouth by 1,800 yards. The main force, composed of the 3rd Battalion, 2nd

◀ *The terrain the Marines moved through in the Matanikau region was hardly passable. Often the point elements had to blaze a trail through tangled terrain, and progress was extremely limited. In this picture, a machine-gun crew struggles to get its ammunition cart up a slight slope. Working like this in the heat and humidity sapped the endurance of the Marines. (USMC A 702876)*

Marines, plus a scout-sniper group commanded by Colonel William J. Whaling, and the 7th Marines would cross the Matanikau at its upstream fork and move northwards. It would then cross the high ground south of Matanikau village and assault the village. The attack formation would have Whaling's group secure the high ground overlooking the west bank. The 7th Marines would operate on the high ground just to the west of Whaling and seize the high ground south-west of Point Cruz, cutting off any retreating Japanese. 8 October was the date set for the operation.

On 7 October the advance began. By noon, the 3rd Battalion, 5th Marines, had made contact with a company sized Japanese unit east of the river and a short distance inland from the river's mouth. The Marines began to drive the Japanese back and contained a large number of them on the east bank. The Japanese then launched several strong counterattacks, all of which were beaten back.

Next day the Raiders were fed into the lines to reinforce the 3rd Battalion, 5th Marines. That night, the Japanese attacked again: at 1830 there was one final attack the brunt of which was taken by the Raiders. Heavy hand-to-hand fighting took place, but in the end the Raiders won. They lost 12 killed and 22 wounded; the Japanese lost 60 killed.

The main attack, which was held back until 9 October because of torrential rain, was now launched. The Whaling group crossed the river quickly, occupied the high ground west of the river and pushed north along the west bank. The 7th Marines followed and were equally successful.

The 1st Battalion, 7th Marines, led by Lieutenant Colonel Puller was operating at the most westerly point of the operation when it came across a large concentration of Japanese from the 4th Infantry Regiment camped in a deep ravine. Calling for artillery support and using all available mortars and weapons, Puller's battalion poured a deadly fire upon the Japanese trapped in the ravine, a process of elimination that continued until ammunition was exhausted. In the fighting the Marines killed more than 700 Japanese with a cost to themselves of 65 killed and 125 wounded. They withdraw from the area when word of an impending counter-offensive was received.

The Japanese Counter-Offensive

The Japanese, who had been planning a full scale counter-offensive since August, had completed new preparations by October. Their first attempts by the Ichiki and Kawaguchi Brigades had met with failure, essentially because they had underestimated the troop strength of the Americans and had sent forces that were numerically insufficient. The October counter-offensive directed by General Hyakutake, who commanded the 17th Army, called for elaborate plans to recapture Guadalcanal. In a joint Army-Navy operation, two army divisions, the 2nd (Sendai) and the 38th, were used to augment 17th Army units. All existing Japanese units on Guadalcanal would also be used in this all-out effort.

The Battle of Cape Esperance

This major counter-offensive was to be launched on three fronts. The first phase began at sea, with the Battle of Cape Esperance. In this battle the opposing naval forces made contact near Savo Island. The Americans under Rear Admiral Norman Scott took up a north–south position against the Japanese force that was moving at a right-angle towards it. Admiral Scott then executed a classic crossing the 'T' manoeuvre, the main batteries of the American ships being brought to bear on the Japanese ships, which were travelling in a line-ahead formation that restricted their return fire. As a result of this engagement the Japanese were forced to retire. On each side a destroyer was lost and a cruiser damaged. It was not a major victory, but the naval balance of power was starting to shift towards the Americans.

The Battle For Henderson Field

The victory at Cape Esperance was short lived. On 13 October 1942, the Japanese struck Henderson Field with an intense aerial bombardment, causing damage so severe that the airfield could be used only for emergency landings. No sooner had the last Japanese aircraft departed than Japanese 150mm howitzers located near Kokumbona opened fire. The Marines did not have an effective

The Matanikau Offensive of 7-9 October 1942

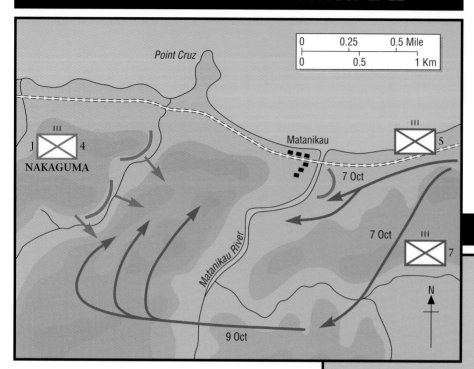

▶ *Damage wreaked on Henderson Field by battleships in mid-October. The constant bombardment by the Japanese, coupled with aerial bombing, virtually closed down the field to all but emergency operations. With the field virtually knocked out, the Japanese believed they could take Guadalcanal with ease. (USMC 61548)*

The Battle for

counter-battery weapon with which to engage the Japanese. The attack continued throughout the day. Shortly before midnight – in a night that would be remembered as the 'Night of the Battleships' – two Japanese battleships, *Haruna* and *Kongo*, began a systematic bombardment of Henderson Field. When they retired, bombers hit the airfield again. By the afternoon of 14 October, Henderson Field was completely out of action. Air operations were shifted over to a rough grassy runway to the south-east; but on this strip, Fighter Strip No 1, only minimal operations could be carried out.

On 15 October, five Japanese transports covered by their screening warships began to unload troops and supplies at Tassafaronga Point, ten miles to the west. The Americans managed to put up a few planes and, coupled with American Army bombers from Espirito Santo in the New Hebrides, managed to sink one transport and set two on fire. The Japanese were forced to retire, but not before they had landed between 3,000 and 4,000 troops and 80 per cent of their cargo.

With the arrival of the last of his troops, General Hyakutake was confident of success.

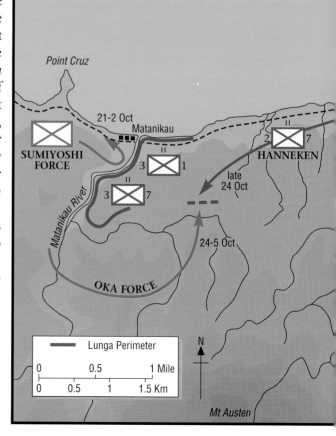

Henderson Field, 23-5 October 1942

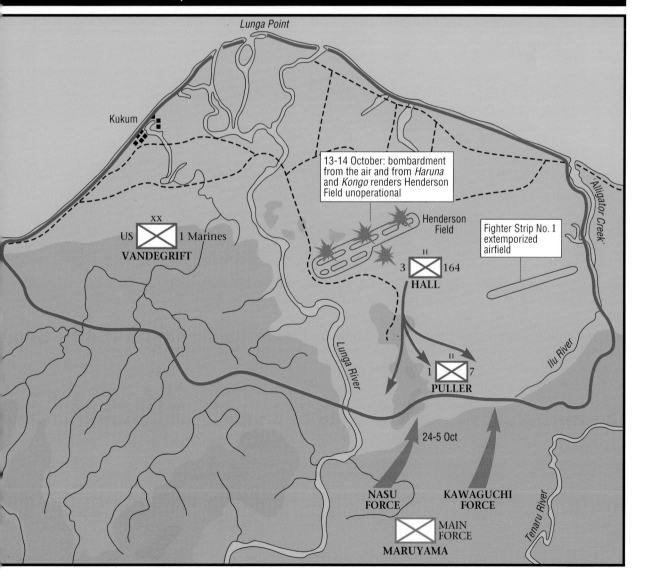

13-14 October: bombardment from the air and from *Haruna* and *Kongo* renders Henderson Field unoperational

Fighter Strip No. 1 extemporized airfield

Indeed, so confident were the Japanese that they had drawn up a surrender plan, which entailed General Vandegrift, along with his staff officers and interpreters, advancing along the north coast road. They would carry one American flag and a white surrender flag. The surrender would take place at the mouth of the Matanikau River. Once the surrender was accomplished, the code name, 'Banzai', would be signalled to herald the success.

The plan of attack was to be four-pronged. Lieutenant General Maruyama was to lead the main force and attack from the south, near 'Bloody Ridge'; Major General Kawaguchi's force would attack from the south-east between, 'Alligator Creek' and 'Bloody Ridge'; Major General Nasu would attack from the south-west, between the Lunga River and 'Bloody Ridge'. The second prong, under Major General Sumiyoshi, was to attack from the west with tank support and cross the Matanikau River. The third prong, under Colonel Oka, was to cross the Matanikau River a mile upstream and move north against the Marines occupying a series of ridges east of the river. The fourth prong called for an amphibious assault at Koli Point; in the event this was cancelled when the Japanese believed American resistance was about to collapse.

The attack was to commence on 22 October; however, movement through the jungle caused unexpected delays – delays that upset a very elaborately coordinated attack schedule. The route of march selected by General Maruyama, called the 'Maruyama Trail', led through some of the

▲ With Henderson Field virtually out of commission, operations were shifted to a muddy fighter strip located north-east of Henderson. Here, planes could take off and land, making a few sorties a day until Henderson was operational. In this photograph a group of F4F-4s are readied for take off from Fighter Strip No 1. (USMC 52801)

thickest jungle on Guadalcanal. Having no engineering equipment, the Japanese were forced to hack through the jungle with hand tools. All supplies had to be manpacked, and the artillery pieces were the first to be left along the tortuous trail that made its way up and down the steep slopes south of Mount Austen. In a single file column that inched along, Maruyama was unable to maintain his schedule: by 22 October he had to postpone his attack to the 23rd; on the 23rd, he postponed it to the 24th.

Meanwhile General Sumiyoshi, who was out of communication with Maruyama, began his attack on the afternoon of 21 October. The attack started with increased artillery fire directed against the 3rd Battalion, 1st Marines, holding the east bank of the Matanikau River. Immediately after the artillery fired, a strong patrol accompanied by nine tanks attempted to cross the sand bar. They were driven back with the loss of one tank.

The following day was quiet until 1800. Then the Japanese attacked again. Once again artillery bombarded the Marines, and tanks, followed by a massive troop attack, struck the Marine lines. The Marines were ready. Artillery from ten batteries of

the 11th Marines and a concentration of anti-tank weaponry waited for the Japanese. The concentrated fire of the supporting arms wreaked havoc with the Japanese attack. The massed Marine artillery fire virtually annihilated Sumiyoshi's troops and destroyed three of his tanks in an assembly area; nine others were destroyed by anti-tank weapons and were left burning on the sand bar. Sumiyoshi had been defeated; the Marines had held the western sector.

The following night, 24 October, in the middle of a blinding rain storm, Maruyama's forces launched their attack against the 1st Battalion, 7th Marines, commanded by Lieutenant Colonel Puller. The attack began about 2130 in the evening when a Marine listening post opened fire on the advance elements of the Japanese 29th Infantry Regiment and retreated. Their movement was shielded by a blinding rain storm. The Japanese, under Maruyama, had finally hacked their way through the jungle to the south of the Marines and were launching their attack. They had crossed the upper reaches of the Lunga River and were now just south of 'Bloody Ridge'. To support their attacks they had nothing more than machine-guns; all the artillery and mortars had been abandoned

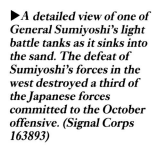

▲ *Lieutenant General Masao Maruyama, Commanding General of the Second (Sendai) Division, attacked the Marine perimeter from the south in October. Maruyama's troops, using hand tools, cut a trail through the torturous jungle but were not unable to maintain the planned attack timetable. The result was an uncoordinated attack that was defeated. (USMC)*

▶ *A detailed view of one of General Sumiyoshi's light battle tanks as it sinks into the sand. The defeat of Sumiyoshi's forces in the west destroyed a third of the Japanese forces committed to the October offensive. (Signal Corps 163893)*

along the 'Maryuama Trail'. Maryuama had hoped for bright moonlight to orientate his troops, but the clouds and rain made the night black. The clash with the outpost was unavoidable and tipped off the Americans. The front lines were quiet for about two hours until suddenly the 29th Infantry attacked Puller's battalion east of 'Bloody Ridge'.

Simultaneous with Maryuama's attack was Colonel Oka's attack on the south-western side of the Marine perimeter. Marine planners at Division headquarters correctly assessed that Maryuama's attack was the main effort and immediately ordered the 7th Marines reserve force (3rd Battalion, 164th Infantry) to reinforce Puller. The battalion, under Lieutenant Colonel Robert K. Hall, had only recently arrived on Guadalcanal, and were in bivouac south of Henderson Field, about a mile from Puller. With rain falling heavily, and with poor visibility, Hall's battalion marched out to link up with Puller. The Marines continued to hold, and Hall's battalion was guided into their position. The two battalions did not defend separate sectors but were intermingled along the front lines. The Japanese resolutely attacked during the night, but every charge was beaten back by the Marines and soldiers.

The following day, 25 October, became known as 'Dugout Sunday'. The Japanese continually shelled and bombed Henderson Field in one of the heaviest concentrations to date. The Marines reorganized their lines and waited for the night, which would bring on the inevitable Japanese attacks. Maruyama struck the Marines as he had the previous night. His 16th and 29th Infantry Regiments attacked savagely along the southern portion of 'Bloody Ridge'. Again the Marines and soldiers, supported by Marine 37mm anti-tank weapons firing canister rounds, repulsed the final assault.

One Marine who distinguished himself throughout this action was Platoon Sergeant 'Manila John' Basilone, who, operating in imminent danger and constantly exposing himself to hostile fire, kept the machine-guns in his section of the front lines operating under almost impossible conditions. For his constant feats of heroism in this action he was to be awarded the Congressional Medal of Honor.

At dawn Maruyama withdrew, leaving more than 1,500 of his troops dead in front of the Marine lines. Among the dead were General Nasu and Colonels Furumiya and Hiroyasu (commanding the 29th and 16th Regiments, respectively).

Also on 25 October, Colonel Oka's forces attacked the 2nd Battalion, 7th Marines on the ridges east of the Matanikau River. In a fierce night battle, Oka's forces also met with defeat. The battle began shortly after the 2nd Battalion, 7th Marines, under Lieutenant Colonel Herman Hanneken, had been quickly moved into position on a ridge line near the Matanikau. They were positioned there to deny the Japanese an avenue of approach in case they should attempt to outflank the 3rd Battalion, 7th Marines, and 3rd Battalion, 1st Marines, who were holding the Matanikau River line. Hanneken's battalion was in an exposed position: there was no continuous line, and the battalion did not tie in with the others. It occupied a position on a ridge formed by two hills whose long axis ran generally east–east, and was occupied by the Marines some time about 1830 on 24 October.

The battle began on the evening of 25 October 1942. During the night, numerous attempts at infiltration were made by Colonel Oka's troops, who had been observed crossing Mount Austen's foothills the day before. Three separate attacks were made on the east flank at 2130, and at 2300 a battalion sized unit attacked. All these attacks were beaten back.

At 0300, under pressure of an overwhelming attack, the Marines on the eastern portion of the ridge, were pushed off, with the exception of one machine-gun team. Those on the western portion of the ridge fought back strongly, and before the Japanese could consolidate their hold a counter-attack was launched, led by the battalion executive officer, Major Odell M. Conoley. Forming a composite group of Marines from the headquarters section, Conoley drove the Japanese back off the ridge.

Also during this action, a platoon sergeant by the name of Mitchell Paige won the Congressional Medal of Honor for holding the Japanese at bay as they overran the eastern portion of the ridge. By holding his position against seemingly insur-

General Sumiyoshi's attack across the Matinakau was supported by several Type 97 Chi-ha medium tanks of the 1st Independent Tank Company, which was formed from veteran crews of the 4th Company, 2nd Tank Regiment. (Steven J. Zaloga)

mountable odds. Paige was able to disrupt the Japanese and prevent them from outflanking the Marine positions. In a further heroic action, Paige led a group of Marines in an attack that broke the back of the final Japanese assault. In that attack, Paige cradled a .30 calibre water-cooled machine-gun in his arms as he ran forward firing it into the Japanese.

These unsuccessful Japanese attacks marked the end of their October counter-offensive. It would also be the high water mark for the Japanese in the campaign. Other battles, many just as fierce, were yet to be fought, but October would be the decisive month on land.

▶ *Conditions were so bad on Guadalcanal in October that General Vandegrift directed Lieutenant Colonel Twining, the Assistant Operations Officer, to prepare a secret withdrawal plan. The plan was set up to enable the Marines to withdraw from the Lunga area, fight a delaying action to the east and conduct guerrilla warfare from the hills to the south. Fortunately, the plan was never implemented. This picture shows Lieutenant Colonel Twining, in the foreground, at his desk in the operations section. (USMC 52548)*

The Battle of Santa Cruz

At sea, October ended with the Battle of the Santa Cruz Islands. In that battle, a strong Japanese force that had been manoeuvring in the area was attacked by a naval task force under Rear Admiral Thomas C. Kinkaid. The ensuing battle was a series of air-to-ship and air-to-air actions in which the Americans lost an aircraft carrier and a destroyer, while another aircraft carrier, a battleship, a cruiser and a destroyer were damaged. The Japanese lost no ships while sustaining damage to three aircraft carriers and two destroyers; but their forces departed the area.

▼ *Henderson Field from the air. This picture taken in November shows the progress made on the airfield by the Americans. The main runway, which was improved by adding Martson steel matting and crushed coral, is evident. Also, taxi-ways to facilitate take-offs and landings have been added. In the middle background lie the foreboding grass covered slopes of Mount Austen, which was still in Japanese hands. (USMC 171864)*

▶ *Admiral Halsey, who took over as commander of the South Pacific Area from Admiral Ghormley, is visited by Admiral Nimitz, Commander in Chief Pacific. (National Archives)*

NOVEMBER

November was a month of change in the campaign. The South Pacific Area received a new commander: Admiral Ghormley was relieved and Admiral William F. 'Bull' Halsey took command. Although Halsey officially assumed command on 20 October, he was not able to visit Guadalcanal until 8 November; but with Halsey came the much needed troops and supplies to maintain the American presence in the area.

The Naval Battle For Guadalcanal

The month was characterized by heavy naval actions. The Japanese organized four naval task forces for their November operations. Two bombardment forces were to shell Henderson Field; a third was to transport the 38th Division and its equipment to Guadalcanal; a fourth would be in general support.

The American naval forces under Halsey's command were organized into two task forces. One was led by Admiral Turner and the other by Admiral Kinkaid. These forces, although limited, had the task of reinforcing and resupplying Guadalcanal as well as stopping the Japanese from taking it over.

Admiral Kinkaid, who had the majority of warships, would cover Admiral Turner's amphibious force of warships and transports. Turner's force was subdivided into three groups: the first, led by Admiral Scott, would carry reinforcements to Guadalcanal; the second, led by Admiral Callaghan, would screen the third group. Admiral Turner would assume direct command of the third group, which was composed primarily of transports and carried critically needed supplies and reinforcements for Guadalcanal.

The groups arrived at the island and began resupply operations at 0530 on 12 November. At 1035 American aircraft reported a large Japanese naval force that included battleships sailing towards Guadalcanal. By late afternoon Turner had unloaded 90 per cent of his cargo and withdrew from the area, leaving Callaghan and Scott's forces to engage the Japanese.

The Japanese force, which had been spotted, consisted of the battleships *Hiei* and *Kirishima*, one light cruiser and fourteen destroyers. Their orders were to neutralize the airfields on Guadalcanal. Once the airfield had been put out of operation the Japanese could safely transport their troops to the island. The Japanese ships carried high-explosive shells for bombardment instead of armour piercing ammunition – which would later prove a blessing for the Americans once the two forces engaged. High-explosive shells reduced the effectiveness of the Japanese 14-inch guns, as the shells could not always penetrate the armour plate on the American cruisers.

In what would be called the First Battle for Guadalcanal, Admiral Callaghan led his outmatched cruiser force against the Japanese battleship force that was to bombard Henderson Field. The main action began at night near Savo Island. Callaghan's radar located the Japanese ships first. The vanguards of the opposing forces intermingled and the American column penetrated the Japanese formation; then a wild, confused mêlée began. The Japanese illuminated the American cruiser force and opened fire. The outnumbered Americans returned fire from all directions and the engagement degenerated into individual ship-to-ship actions. In the confusion both sides fired on their own ships. When the battle was over, Admirals Callaghan and Scott were dead, but the Japanese had been turned back. Not one Japanese shell had struck Guadalcanal. Of the thirteen American ships involved, twelve had been either sunk or damaged, while the Japanese had lost a battleship and two destroyers, with damage to four cruisers.

The November 1942 Battles on Guadalcanal

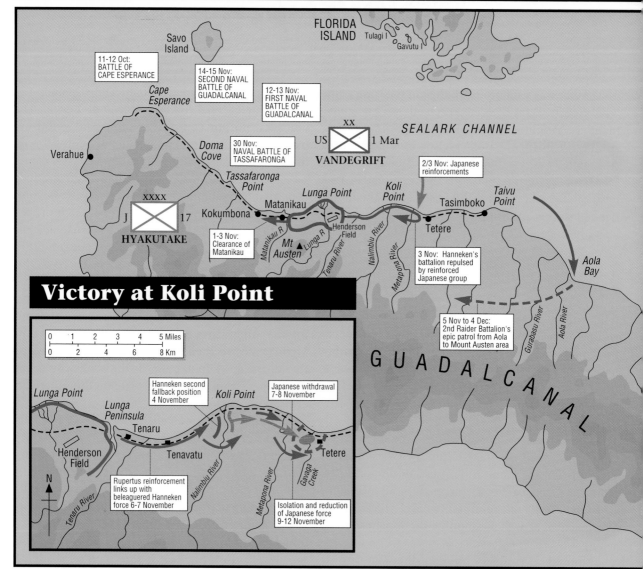

On 13 November, the Japanese attempted to reinforce Guadalcanal with a naval task force that included eleven transports. They were caught in the light the following day by both carrier and land based aircraft. Seven of the transports were sunk, and the four survivors continued toward Guadalcanal. Next day, they were discovered beached at Tassafaronga Point, there to be destroyed in short order by American aircraft, long range artillery and naval gunfire. Equally important as the destruction of the transports was the turning back of their screening force, which was to have bombarded Henderson Field.

November Matanikau Action

On land the situation was also improving. The 5th Marines spearheaded a western attack that cleared the Japanese out of the Matanikau area. Two other regiments, 2nd Marines less its 3rd Battalion but reinforced by the Army's 1st Battalion, 164th Infantry, continued the advance, stopping just short of Kokumbona.

This western plan of attack was essentially the same as all previous attacks in the Matanikau region. The 5th Marines supported by units of the

▲ *Prior to the 1 November attacks in the Matanikau region, Colonel Edson, now commanding the 5th Marine Regiment, speaks to his officers. Edson is seen here giving them a basic outline of upcoming events and future operations in the area. This setting is a captured Japanese building east of the Lunga River. (USMC)*

Division's Special Weapons Battalion, would attack west on a 1,500 yard frontage with two battalions abreast. The main attack was to be made along the high ground south of the coast. The 2nd Marines, who had recently arrived from Tulagi and were considered fresh, would follow up by advancing along the coastal plan. In order to protect the southern or inland flank, the 3rd Battalion, 7th Marines, would operate in force in that area. As a prelude to the attack, the 1st Engineer Battalion succeeded in erecting three makeshift bridges across the river.

The attack, which was preceded by an intense artillery and naval bombardment and supported by air strikes, began on schedule at 0700 on 1 November. The leading elements of the 5th Marines crossed the bridges and fanned out, moving into the hills overlooking the coast. There was no concentrated resistance in the area, and the advance continued into the early afternoon, with the 2nd Battalion, 5th Marines, advancing along the high ground to the west. As they pushed forward they met no determined resistance, but they soon lost contact with the 1st Battalion, 5th Marines, who were advancing west along the coast to the north.

As the 1st Battalion, 5th Marines, were making their advance they began to run into very stiff resistance from Japanese troops dug into a steep ravine located to the south. During the remainder of the day, the Americans maintained position facing the Japanese and were reinforced by the 3rd Battalion, 5th Marines.

Next day, 2 November, the two battalions began flanking movements that eventually boxed in the Japanese. Late in the afternoon, in a separate action, two companies from the 3rd Battalion, 5th Marines, ran into heavy opposition from a strong Japanese force concentrated between the coastal road and the beach. One of the companies, Company I, led by Captain Erskine Wells, launched the only documented bayonet charge of the campaign and routed the enemy.

In order to destroy the Japanese in the ravine, Marine half-tracks mounting 75mm guns were called up, but the terrain in the ravine was too rough for them to be deployed. The final phase of the attack was initiated at 0800 on the 3rd: the 2nd Battalion, 5th Marines, continued to attack the

◀Marines from the 5th Marines move up toward the Matanikau for the 1 November push. This attack would establish a Marine presence once and for all on the west bank of the Matanikau. The attack would take the Marines as far as the White River, which was to the west of Point Cruz. (USMC 51335)

◀This bridge was one of three constructed by the 1st Engineer Battalion to support the 1 November Marine attack. The bridges were constructed on the night of 31 October. Made out of fuel drum floats and other bridging materials, they were assembled and positioned quickly. The Marines crossing the bridge are part of the reserve force from the 2nd Battalion, 2nd Marine Regiment. (USMC 51337)

Japanese in the ravine until they were destroyed, the 1st Battalion, 164th Infantry, then assisting the Marines in mopping up bypassed pockets of resistance. The Japanese lost 239 killed during this action.

Action At Koli Point

On the opposite side of the Perimeter, the 7th Marines and the remainder of the 164th Infantry made an eastern push that drove the Japanese from the Koli Point area. This action was undertaken by the 2nd Battalion, 7th Marines, led by Lieutenant Colonel Herman H. Hanneken. The battalion was trucked east from the Tenaru River on 1 November; next morning they began a forced march that took them by nightfall to a position along the beach east of the Metapona River, where they dug in.

That night, the Japanese succeeded in landing an infantry battalion in the area, their mission being to make contact with surviving Japanese and explore the possibility of establishing an airfield in the region. Torrential rain began to fall, and this put the Marines' radios out of action, so Hanneken had no way to alert his superiors at the Lunga Perimeter of the Japanese landing in the area.

The battle began at daybreak the next day, 3 November, when a Japanese patrol blundered into the Marine lines. Initially the Japanese did not respond aggressively, but once they had recovered their composure they began to bombard Hanneken's battalion with heavy and accurate artillery fire.

With his communications still inoperable and having no supporting arms at his disposal, Hanneken fought a withdrawing action. He took up a position on the other side of the Metapona River, which was to his rear. Despite the fact that this move had to be made in full view of the attacking Japanese it was successfully executed, and a new defensive line was established. But before the situation could be stabilized a small force of Japanese, which had been landed the previous night, struck Hanneken from the rear. About that time, communications were briefly re-established by the Marines, and word was sent back about their predicament to the Division command post.

There were three events occupying their attention: the attack west of the Matanikau by 5th Marines, Hanneken's predicament, and the landing of a Marine reconnaissance force at Aola for airfield survey. To relieve the pressure on Hanneken, General Vandegrift reinforced him with the 1st Battalion, 7th Marines, plus the command element of the 7th Marines, and sent in an air strike. This, however, went horribly wrong, the aircraft bombing and strafing Hanneken's Battalion in error.

Meanwhile Hanneken had not been idle. He launched an attack against the Japanese force to his rear then fell back again to establish a position west of the Nalimbu River. With the assistance of Marine artillery and naval gunfire, Hanneken held. He then established a small beachhead, which was used to land the command element of 7th Marine Regiment, along with the 1st Battalion, 7th Marines, under Puller.

On 4 November, both battalions began an eastward advance under the cover of artillery and naval gunfire. Their action was reinforced by the Army's 164th Infantry (minus its 1st Battalion). Overall command of the operation was placed under General Rupertus, the Assistant Division Commander, 1st Marine Division.

On 6-7 November, after a difficult movement through the jungle, the 164th Regiment linked up with the Marines. The combined forces then advanced eastward. No resistance was met as the Japanese took up a position east of the Metapona River to permit their main force to escape.

By 9 November, the combined American forces had located the Japanese once again and began to surround them. Over the next few days all Japanese attempts to break out were foiled, and the Marines and soldiers, supported by artillery, began to reduce the pocket. By 12 November, they had completed their mission. In this final eastern action, the Americans had lost 40 killed and 120 wounded; the Japanese lost more than 450 killed.

The Aola Operation

In order to cut off any Japanese forces that managed to escape, General Vandegrift asked Admiral Turner to release operational control of

This US Army Private attaches an M1905 bayonet to his M1 Garand rifle. In the latter stages of the campaign, including the battle for the Gifu, the Army provided the bulk of the forces, although a large portion of the 2nd Marine Division was still present. (Shirley Mallinson)

the 2nd Raider Battalion, which Turner had been holding in reserve for another operation. They were landed at Aola to conduct an epic long range patrol from that region to the Mount Austen area. The patrol started out on 5 November. Their main mission was to patrol the Mount Austen area aggressively, destroying any long range artillery that they could locate; in addition, they were to locate and patrol suspected trails leading from the south over Mount Austen and any trails leading from Mount Austen to Kokumbona. Cargo planes from Henderson Field would make periodic supply runs to resupply them. Over the next thirty days the Raiders destroyed numerous artillery pieces and killed 488 Japanese at the cost of 16 killed and 18 wounded, but they were unable to locate any of the suspected trail systems and entered the Lunga Perimeter on 4 December.

The Second Naval Battle For Guadalcanal

After reorganizing their naval forces, the Japanese began to prepare for another reinforcing naval operation. In this Second Naval Battle for Guadalcanal, Admiral Halsey directed Rear Admiral Willis A. 'Ching' Lee to take his battleships, *Washington* and *South Dakota*, and four destroyers to intercept the Japanese. The two forces made contact and in a sharp naval engagement the Japanese were turned back.

The Battle of Tassafaronga

The last naval action in November was the Battle of Tassafaronga. Attempting to resupply the Japanese forces, a 'Tokyo Express' destroyer force was organized for a fast run. Supplies sealed in waterproof drums would be dropped off the destroyers as they ran parallel to the Japanese lines, it being left to the tide to then wash the drums ashore. In the event only a third of the supplies actually reached the Japanese troops and Admiral Tanaka was intercepted by an American task force commanded by Rear Admiral Carleton H. Wright. In the ensuing battle, in which each side lost a destroyer, the Japanese were again turned back. With the close of the month of November, the Japanese no longer enjoyed control of the waters surrounding Guadalcanal.

▲The men of the 2nd Raider Battalion landed at Aola Bay in early November 1942. Part of their mission was to cut off any Japanese stragglers in the area and patrol west to Mount Austen. Here, part of the 2nd Raider Battalion (also known as Carlson's Raiders) assisted by Solomon Islanders crosses an open grassy plain in the Koli Point region. (USMC 51729)

▼The 2nd Raider Battalion continued west until it reached Mount Austen. The battalion was to search for a trail from the south to the summit of Mount Austen. It was also to look for a connecting trail leading to Kokumbona. Here members of the Raider Battalion begin to move up the foothills into the Mount Austen area. (USMC 51728)

THE ARMY TAKES OVER

December saw some definitive changes in the campaign. The Lunga Perimeter was not much larger than it had been in the early days, but there were now enough troops to take decisive offensive action. The American Army was ashore in force, and was led by Major General Patch, who had the AMERICAL Division under his command. This was a unique division in that it had been formed entirely outside the United States, its name being a contracted form of 'America' and 'New Caledonia'.

With Admiral Halsey in overall command, the bleak days were ending. Troops and equipment were pouring into Guadalcanal, and some of the worst-hit Marine units had been relieved and given a much needed rest. Meanwhile the new Army P-38 fighter aircraft was making its début in the area, and B-17 bombers were now based at Henderson Field. And with the tide of war turning it was decided to relieve General Vandegrift's 1st Marine Division. On 9 December, after more than four months of protracted combat, the Marines were pulled out. Sick, tired, dirty and exhausted, they were glad to leave their island purgatory. Command of the ground forces was now turned over to General Patch of the Army, who was left with an experienced cadre of troops, for he still had a major portion of the 2nd Marine Division in his command. This gave him a well balanced force, elements of that division having been on Guadalcanal from the first days. There were also experienced Army and National Guard units ashore.

Intelligence reports indicated that 25,000 Japanese were still on the island – in comparison with 40,000 Americans. However, the exact disposition of the Japanese forces was not known, although it was generally assumed that they were in the Mount Austen and Kokumbona area, and were still being resupplied by the 'Tokyo Express'.

The American objective selected for December was Mount Austen. General Vandegrift had originally planned to capture and incorporate it into the Lunga Perimeter but had changed his plans because of its distance and the limitations of his manpower. Nevertheless, the Army planners deemed Henderson Field would never be secure unless Mount Austen were captured, and it would also need to be secured if the Matanikau region were to be brought completely under American control. A key terrain feature in the fighting, Mount Austen is not a single hill mass, but a spur of Guadalcanal's main mountain range. Jutting northward, it dominates the area between the Matanikau and Lunga Rivers. Its 1,514-foot summit is about six miles south-west of Henderson Field and would afford a commanding view of the airfield. Rather than a single peak, it is a series of jungle ridges, a dense rain forest covering the top and waist-high grass over much of the foothills.

It was in this foreboding terrain that Colonel Oka set up his defensive position – a line around Mount Austen's slopes. His force comprised the 124th and 128th Infantry and the 10th Mountain Artillery Regiments.

For the American soldiers who would have to fight there, Mount Austen was a jungle nightmare. Supplies had to be manpacked up the steep slopes and casualties evacuated back the same way. There were no trails – they would come later, eventually being widened to accommodate jeeps, which could assist with resupply and evacuation. But by then the battle would have shifted and the process started all over again.

The fighting was fierce, and the Japanese were well dug in. The attack, which began on 17 December 1942, was not over until 23 January 1943. American soldiers of the 132nd Infantry, which bore the brunt of the fighting, were engaged in a series of battles along the northern ridges. Attacking from east to west, they were eventually halted by the strongest Japanese position, the Gifu,

▶ *Conditions on Guadalcanal were certainly not luxurious, and shelter was a combination of what could be found. This picture shows a bomb-proof dugout in front of a lean-to. Note the ample use of captured Japanese rice bags. (USMC 61519)*

which was commanded by Major Takeyoso Inagaki of the 2nd Battalion, 228th Infantry Regiment.

Named after a prefecture in Honshu, Japan, the Gifu was on the western slope of Mount Austen. The strongest part was a horseshoe shaped line, which ran just below the summit. In a series of interconnecting and mutually supporting pillboxes, the Japanese were able to put up an effective resist to the Americans. Initially, the Gifu was difficult to pinpoint. Its north-west boundary was known to the soldiers of the 132nd Infantry only after they had stumbled into the carefully prepared Japanese fields of fire. For days the extent of the position was unknown, and it seemed impossible to outflank until a patrol moving to the south-west through almost impenetrable jungle was able to fix its south-western edge.

By this time, however, hard hit by fatigue and illness and after 22 days of intense jungle warfare, the soldiers of the 132nd Infantry were incapable of further offensive action. (They had lost 112 killed, 268 wounded and three missing; the Japanese had lost about 450 killed.) So, with the 132nd Infantry ringing in the Gifu, the month of December ended. On 4 January 1943, soldiers of the 2nd Battalion, 35th Infantry relieved them, and with the arrival of these fresh troops a new offensive could be mounted.

The January Offensive

With the start of the New Year, General Patch, now commanding XIV Corps, (Americal Division, 25th Infantry Division, 43rd Infantry Division and 2nd Marine Division), resolved to bring matters to a close and drive the Japanese from Guadalcanal: in a series of quick offensive actions, he decided to drive westwards and crush Japanese resistance between Point Cruz and Kokumbona.

The 25th Infantry Division, under the command of Major General J. Lawton Collins, was to sweep the hills overlooking the coast. At the same time, the 2nd Marine Division, commanded by Brigadier General Alphonse De Carre, the Assistant Division Commander, would sweep the coastal area. The 25th Infantry Division, minus the 35th Infantry, in a four day operation cleared out a stubborn Japanese strongpoint west of the Matanikau River in a series of hills known as the 'Galloping Horse', as it bore a resemblance to one from the air. With the clearing of these hills the southern flank was secure for the 2nd Marine Division to attack along the coast.

The 2nd Marine Division, holding a line at Point Cruz, remained in place for the first three days of the 25th Infantry Division's southern operation. On the fourth day, 12 January, it launched a supported offensive against the Japan-

THE JANUARY OFFENSIVE

Clearing the slopes of Mount Austen and the Matanikau sector

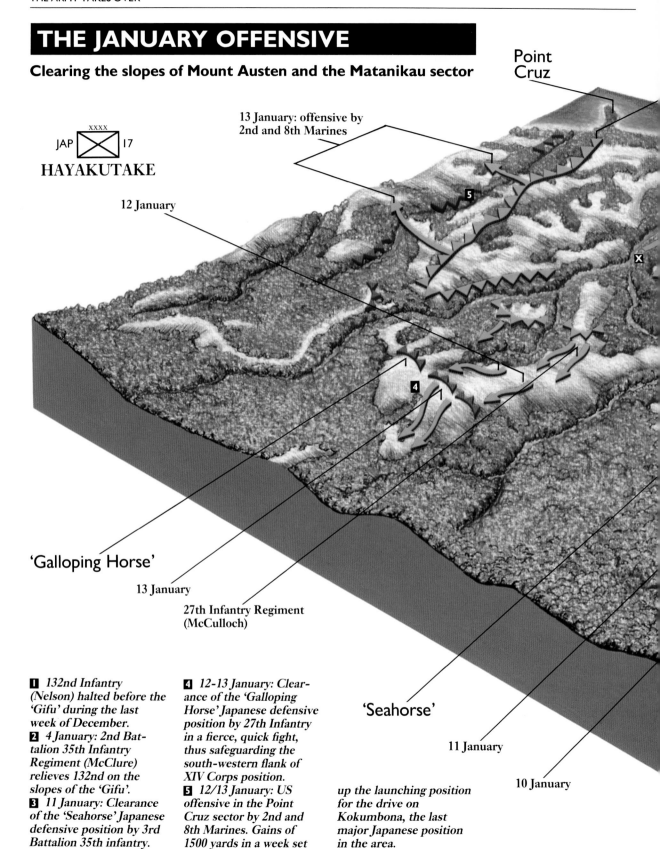

Point Cruz

13 January: offensive by
2nd and 8th Marines

```
        xxxx
JAP  [ X ] 17
HAYAKUTAKE
```

12 January

'Galloping Horse'

13 January

27th Infantry Regiment
(McCulloch)

'Seahorse'

11 January

10 January

1 *132nd Infantry (Nelson) halted before the 'Gifu' during the last week of December.*
2 *4 January: 2nd Battalion 35th Infantry Regiment (McClure) relieves 132nd on the slopes of the 'Gifu'.*
3 *11 January: Clearance of the 'Seahorse' Japanese defensive position by 3rd Battalion 35th infantry.*

4 *12-13 January: Clearance of the 'Galloping Horse' Japanese defensive position by 27th Infantry in a fierce, quick fight, thus safeguarding the south-western flank of XIV Corps position.*
5 *12/13 January: US offensive in the Point Cruz sector by 2nd and 8th Marines. Gains of 1500 yards in a week set*

up the launching position for the drive on Kokumbona, the last major Japanese position in the area.

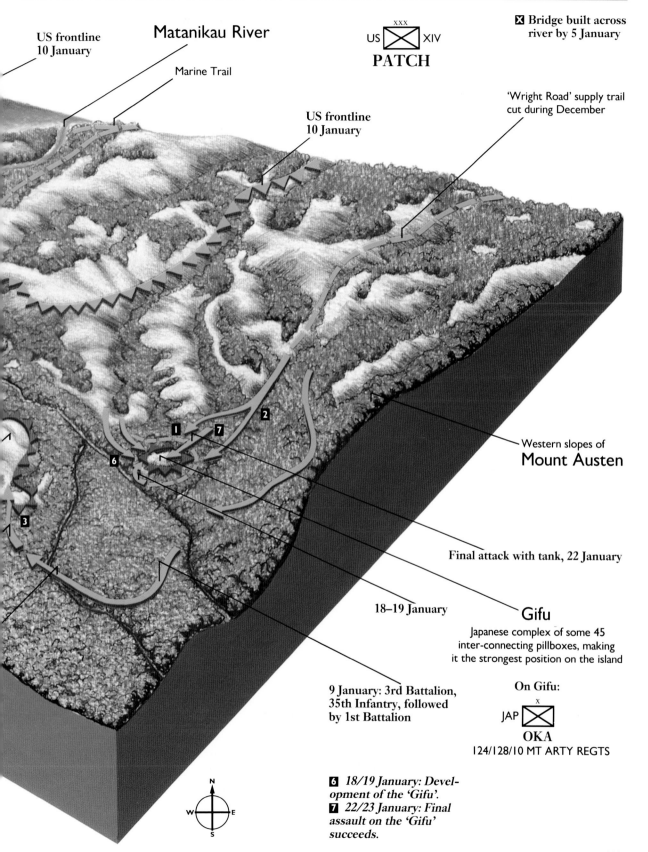

US frontline 10 January

Matanikau River

Marine Trail

US frontline 10 January

US ⟨XXX⟩ XIV
PATCH

X Bridge built across river by 5 January

'Wright Road' supply trail cut during December

Western slopes of **Mount Austen**

Final attack with tank, 22 January

18–19 January

Gifu
Japanese complex of some 45 inter-connecting pillboxes, making it the strongest position on the island

9 January: 3rd Battalion, 35th Infantry, followed by 1st Battalion

On Gifu:

JAP ⟨X⟩
OKA
124/128/10 MT ARTY REGTS

6 *18/19 January: Development of the 'Gifu'.*
7 *22/23 January: Final assault on the 'Gifu' succeeds.*

N / W–E / S

ese 2nd (Sendai) Division holding the Point Cruz sector. In a one week period the Marines advanced more than 1,500 yards to a position from which a Kokumbona offensive could be launched. In the process they killed an estimated 650 Japanese.

While these gains were being made, the 35th Infantry was engaged in heavy fighting at the Gifu, on Mount Austen, and in the hilly jungle area to the south-west centring on a feature known as the 'Seahorse', from its resemblance in an aerial photograph. In a difficult one day battle the 3rd Battalion, 35th Infantry, seized the 'Seahorse', effectively encircling the Gifu.

Reduction of The Gifu

With the 'Seahorse' thus secured, the difficult task of reducing the Gifu fell to the 2nd Battalion, 35th Infantry. The battle lasted two weeks and was fought against Japanese who were determined to fight to the death. Early in the battle it was realized that tank support would be essential, but none was made available until the end of the operation. Advances were usually made in 100 yard increments. So well were the Japanese concealed that it was often difficult to locate their main line of resistance. Time and time again companies moved up only to be pushed back.

The double envelopment attack was launched on 18-19 January. Gradually resistance began to slacken, and on 22-23 January, three Marine tanks with Army crews were sent to assist in the fighting. Two of them broke down en route; the third pressed on.

In a hellish battle in the jungle, the lone tank supported by sixteen infantrymen penetrated to the heart of the Gifu and then began a systematic destruction of pillboxes and Japanese soldiers. By the night of 22/23 January, the Gifu was quiet. Later that night, the Japanese under Major Inagaki launched an attack to the north-east, but by then the outcome was inevitable, and after a short fight Inagaki and his soldiers were all killed. The reduction of the Gifu had cost the Americans 64 killed and 42 wounded; the Japanese had lost more than 500 killed. Resistance east of the Matanikau River ceased.

With the capture of 'Galloping Horse', the 'Seahorse' and the Gifu, the 25th Infantry Division was able to clear the remaining hills on the southern flank and begin the drive to Kokumbona. In a final two day offensive that ended on 24 January 1943, Kokumbona was captured by the 27th Infantry and the Japanese were driven out of the region. At the end of January, the final task facing XIV Corps was that of pursuing and destroying the Japanese before they could dig in or escape.

◀ *In December 1942, the 2nd Marine Division, as part of General Patch's XIV Corps, made a bold push into the Point Cruz area. This is a forward observation team positioned on a hill overlooking Point Cruz, which is jutting off into the background of this picture. (USMC 53451)*

▶ *As the 2nd Marine Division began its drive toward Kokumbona, it ran into periodic pockets of Japanese resistance. Here Marines carry off one of their wounded, as a 37mm anti-tank gun crew take cover behind their gun and jeep. (USMC 53449)*

▼ Below left: *A Japanese anti-aircraft gun captured in the drive to Kokumbona. Kokumbona was an important Japanese base camp. It was a trail junction and sat in an ideal, covered bay in which supplies could easily be landed. Its capture was a heavy blow to the Japanese who were now starting to retreat to the west. (USMC 53428)*

▼ Below right: *As the 2nd Marine Division began to pursue the retreating Japanese along the coast, they erected bridges by 'field expedient' means. These Marines are crossing the Bonegi River on crude log bridges. (USMC 53424)*

THE FINAL PHASE

By the first week of February 1943, Admiral Halsey had been led to expect the Japanese to make another full scale offensive – all intelligence reports pointed to an all-out Japanese effort in the region. But American intelligence had been deceived by the Japanese. After repeated failed offensives, the Japanese had decided to withdraw. To deceive the Americans, and to give the impression that they were preparing for a major offensive, they increased their activities in the area while in reality preparing to evacuate their remaining troops from Doma Cove in the Cape Esperance area. To cover this withdrawal, the Japanese placed 600 troops ashore near Cape Esperance on 14 January, and an additional force landed for a short time in the Russell Islands just to the northwest of Guadalcanal. The Japanese plan called for night withdrawal by destroyer transport, but in the event this was not possible. Barges were to be used to transport the troops to the Russells, where they would be picked up and then taken north.

The Final Push

XIV Corps reached the Poha River on 25 January. Now the campaign began to enter its final stage. A field order was issued directing a combined Army Marine Division (CAM) to attack west on 26 January at 0630; the 6th Marines would move along the northern or beach flank while the 182nd Infantry advanced along the southern, more hilly flank. The 147th Infantry would be in Division reserve, while the American and 25th Division's artillery, along with 2nd Marine Air Wing, would provide direct support for the operation.

The CAM Division's attack began on 26 January and advanced 1,000 yards beyond the Pona River. The Division continued its advance the next day to the Nueha River, where it consolidated its positions.

On 29 January 1943, General Patch detached the 147th Infantry from the CAM Division and reinforced them with artillery from 2nd Battalion, 10th Marines, and 97th Field Artillery Battalion. This composite force was placed under Brigadier General Alphonse De Carre, the Assistant Division Commander, 2nd Marine Division, and was tasked with pursuing the Japanese.

On 30 January at 0700, the 147th Infantry advanced westwards. The supported advance was slowed down by determined Japanese resistance at the Bonegi River. The attack continued the next day, assisted by artillery support. The plan of attack called for the 1st and 2nd Battalions to force a crossing along the coast while the 3rd Battalion would cross inland and capture the ridges to the south, but determined Japanese resistance stalled the coastal advance.

On 1 February 1943, Brigadier General Sebree, Commanding General of the American Division, took command of the operation. The attack continued, but so did Japanese resistance, which effectively stopped the Americans. Then on 2 February the Japanese pulled back. It was estimated that 700-800 Japanese had been in the area. Between 3 and 5 February, the Americans advanced west to the Umasani River, meeting no organized resistance.

By early February, General Patch was convinced that the Japanese were no longer going to mount a new offensive. He considered that they were probably planning a withdrawal from Guadalcanal – which he wanted to prevent.

XIV Corps staff had completed plans to land a reinforced battalion on the south-west coast; their mission would be to advance to Cape Esperance and attack the Japanese from the rear, cutting off their escape route. The attack would be led by the 2nd Battalion, 132nd Infantry Regiment under Colonel Alexander M. George. Further consider-

Victory on Guadalcanal, January to February 1943

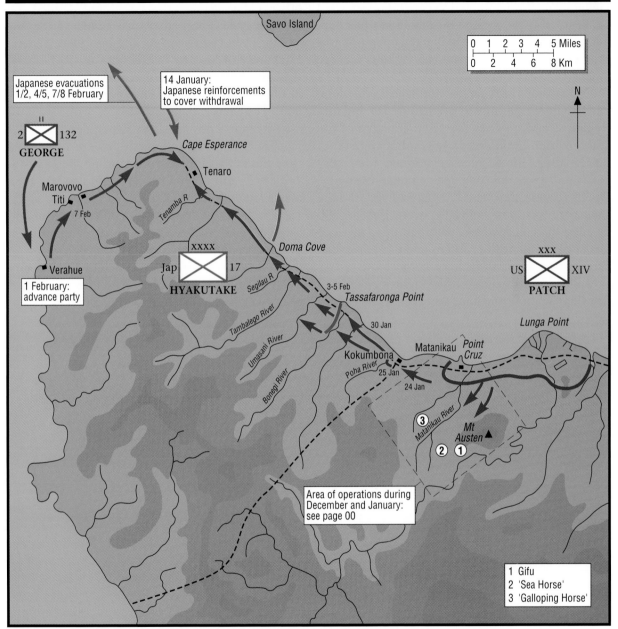

Japanese evacuations
1/2, 4/5, 7/8 February

14 January:
Japanese reinforcements
to cover withdrawal

2 ‖ 132
GEORGE

Savo Island

Cape Esperance

Tenaro

Marovovo
Titi

7 Feb

Tenamba R.

Verahue

1 February:
advance party

XXXX
Jap [ ] 17
HYAKUTAKE

Segilau R.

Doma Cove

3-5 Feb
Tassafaronga Point

30 Jan

Tambalego River

Umasani River

Bonegi River

Kokumbona

Poha River

25 Jan

24 Jan

③

②①

Matanikau

Point Cruz

Matanikau River

Mt Austen ▲

Lunga Point

XXX
US [ ] XIV
PATCH

Area of operations during
December and January:
see page 00

1 Gifu
2 'Sea Horse'
3 'Galloping Horse'

0 1 2 3 4 5 Miles
0 2 4 6 8 Km

N

ation led to the conclusion that the reinforced battalion might not be sufficiently strong enough to land should there be heavy Japanese opposition, so a small reconnaissance force would land first and set up an advanced post at Titi to determine the strength of the Japanese. This was accomplished in a shore to shore landing on 1 February. Once ashore, the force made effective an reconnaissance of the entire area and recommended that

the battalion be landed at Verahue then move toward Titi.

On 2 February Colonel George's battalion began its advance. Two days later it linked up with the reconnaissance force at Titi, then continued its advance. By 7 February it had reached Marovovo where it settled in for the night.

The movement to Marovovo had been somewhat constrained by a lack of accurate information about the Japanese in the area, and during the day Colonel George had been wounded in the leg. General Patch, who wanted the operation speeded up, sent Colonel Gavan to the battalion's position; but once there he concluded that the operation was progressing satisfactorily and had Colonel George evacuated by boat.

Meanwhile, back at the north coast, General Patch relieved the under-strength 147th Infantry Regiment and ordered the 161st Infantry of the 25th Division (Reinforced), to continue pursuit of the Japanese. Both forces continued their respective advances, meeting only minimal resistance. On 9 February, they met at Tenaro village, and the campaign was now officially over. But 13,000 Japanese had escaped Guadalcanal: the American pincer plan, although excellent in conception, had been executed too slowly.

Indeed, the Japanese had fought a calculated delaying action throughout the final phase, which had begun on 12 January when the Japanese high command issued orders for the withdrawal. Staff officers boarded a destroyer and landed on Guadalcanal. There they proceeded to Seventeenth Army Headquarters and informed General Hyakutake of his new instructions on 15 January. Explaining this new plan to his troops as a change in disposition due to an upcoming future operation, Hyakutake then ordered a withdrawal of Seventeenth Army to Cape Esperance on 22-23 January 1943. The rescuing destroyers made three runs and evacuated the troops during the nights of 1/2, 4/5 and 7/8 February; they were then evacuated to Buin and Rabaul.

The Japanese in the end had been skilful and cunning. Nevertheless the essential significance of the campaign was unchanged. The first phase of the Solomons campaign was concluded as a victory for the Americans, and the first major step had been taken in the reduction of Rabaul.

EPILOGUE

Guadalcanal provided an archetype for jungle and naval warfare in the Pacific. A hard fought campaign that shattered the myth of Japanese invincibility, it was certainly a campaign played out daily in the American press. For months it was a touch and go operation, and there was a national sigh of relief when the Japanese finally withdrew.

From the campaign a seasoned fighting force was created. Veterans came back to teach new replacement troops or stayed on to bolster the ranks of the newly formed units that would carry on the fighting. Most important, the campaign validated the theories and practice of amphibious warfare that had been taught at the Marine Corps schools at Quantico, Virginia, in the late 1920s and 1930s. The concept, though not unique, was certainly not well received in certain military circles – mainly because of memories of the failed attempt at Gallipoli, on the coast of Turkey, in the First World War.

The important gain for the Americans was Guadalcanal itself. It would be developed into one of the largest advanced naval and air bases in the region and would be a springboard for future amphibious operations in the region. And by holding it the Americans had kept open the lines of communication with Australia.

The cost of the campaign had not been prohibitive for the Americans. Total Army and Marine losses were 1,600 killed and 4,700 wounded. The Japanese lost considerably more: 25,400 from all services. Naval losses were more even with each side losing about 25 major warships.

◀ *Once the island was secured, it became a staging area for operations up in the northern Solomons. Henderson Field became an important air base for the region. In this picture the original fighter strip has been improved and expanded into a larger bomber strip with taxiways and hard stands. (USMC 108690)*

▶ *This is Fighter Strip No 2, located west of the Lunga River. It was constructed to alleviate aircraft congestion at the Henderson Field complex. It was from this fighter strip, that the P-38 fighter planes that shot down Admiral Yamamoto on 18 April 1943 took off. (Signal Corps 171861)*

THE BATTLEFIELD TODAY

Guadalcanal has taken many modern steps forward since the Second World War, though it retains many of its past links. It is no longer the remote country it once was but has become a new, emerging nation that is enjoying self-rule.

The most noticeable political change since the war is that the seat of government has moved from Tulagi. It is now located in Honiara, the new capital city on Guadalcanal. Honiara stretches roughly from the Matanikau River west beyond Point Cruz, an area where some of the heaviest fighting occurred.

From the Fiji Islands, Guadalcanal is only a short aircraft flight to Henderson Airport (not the original, but very close to its site). After leaving the aircraft one of the first sights you see as you look west is Mount Austen. With its dominating height, it is not hard to determine why it played such a critical role in the campaign.

The primary area of interest to the historian will, of course, be the battlefields. When touring the battlefields, it is best to rent a four-wheel drive vehicle and hire a local guide. This saves time, money and a lot of frustration. The landing beaches, Alligator Creek, Henderson Field, and 'Bloody Ridge' are all in close proximity and can easily be seen in a day. Mount Austen and the Gifu, although farther away, make for a pleasant drive and tour. From Mount Austen, you get more of a Japanese perspective of the campaign. Some of the other battlefields, such as 'Galloping Horse' and the 'Seahorse', are some distance inland and require proper acclimatization and physical endurance to get to. They are best not tackled alone. An easy way to see them and other remote sites is by charter helicopter.

For the scuba diver, the offshore waters have a variety of ships and planes to dive on. The major warships are down in water too deep to dive safely, but the transports beached and sunk in the November battle are all accessible.

Other areas of interest are Tulagi, Gavutu and Tanambogo. These areas are not often visited and it is wise to coordinate travel and lodging beforehand. There is an abundance of historical wrecks in the area, and these are accessible only by small boat. Most notable is *Kikutsuki*, a Japanese destroyer sunk by pilots from *Yorktown* on 4 May 1942 during a raid made as part of the Battle of the Coral Sea. Later the 34th SeaBees raised the ship, utilizing it as a floating dry dock.

For more detailed information contact the Guadalcanal Tourist Authority, Honiara, Solomon Islands.

CHRONOLOGY

3 May 1942: The 3rd Kure Special Naval Landing Force invades and captures Tulagi, the seat of British Government in the Solomon Islands. They also capture Gavutu, the headquarters for Lever Brothers.

4 May: American carrier planes from *Yorktown* and *Enterprise* make a raid on shipping in Tulagi Harbour, as part of the Battle of the Coral Sea.

8 May: Japanese forces are defeated in the Battle of the Coral Sea. The Japanese invasion forces bound for New Guinea are turned back.

3-4 June: The Americans achieve a strategic victory in the Battle of Midway Island.

8 June: General MacArthur suggests to General Marshall (Army Chief of Staff) that an offensive be taken with New Britain, New Ireland and New Guinea as the objective. MacArthur would be in command.

12 June: General Marshall meets with Admiral King (Chief of Naval Operations) and attempts to foster MacArthur's plan.

14 June: Advance elements of the US 1st Marine Division land in Wellington, New Zealand. They are not expected to see combat until after January.

25 June: Admiral King, after studying the Army plan, rejects it as too ambitious and suggests that the Solomon Islands and Santa Cruz Island be taken first, then New Britain, New Ireland and New Guinea. Admiral Nimitz would be in command.

26 June: General Marshall and Admiral King cannot come to agreement on an offensive plan. King, fearing delays, orders Admiral Nimitz to begin planning to retake the Solomon Islands. Nimitz alerts Vice Admiral Ghormley.

26 June: Admiral Ghormley calls General Vandegrift, the Commanding General of 1st Marine Division to Auckland to announce to him that his division will lead an amphibious assault in the Solomon Islands on 1 August.

29 June to 2 July: General Marshall and Admiral King continue to debate the strategic plan and its commander.

2 July: General Marshall and Admiral King reach an agreement and sign the 'Joint Directive for Offensive Operations in the Southwest Pacific Area Agreed on by the United States Chief of Staff'.

6 July: The Japanese send a survey party to Guadalcanal to select the site for an airfield on the north coast plain. A site is selected near Lunga Point and construction begins. Mid-August is the estimated completion date.

7 July: Vice Admiral Ghormley is selected to command the Guadalcanal–Tulagi amphibious invasion.

11 July: The remainder of the 1st Marine Division reinforced arrives in Wellington, New Zealand.

22 July: The amphibious force sails from New Zealand for the Solomons. The invasion date has been postponed to 7 August.

28-31 July: An amphibious rehearsal is conducted at Koro in a remote area of the Fiji Islands.

7 August: The amphibious force conducts an assault on Guadalcanal, Tulagi, Gavutu and surrounding islands. Tulagi and Gavutu are opposed landings; Guadalcanal is not.

8 August: The Japanese airfield is seized and named Henderson Field in honour of a Marine pilot killed at Midway.

9 August: The Battle for Savo Island. A Japanese naval force under Admiral Mikawa surprises an American naval force near Savo Island. The Americans lose four cruisers sunk and one damaged. The Japanese depart the area with damage to one destroyer. The overall result is that the American Navy departs area, leaving Marines on shore unsupported.

19 August: First Battle of the Matanikau. Battalion sized operation. One company proceeds west along the coast to fix the Japanese at mouth of the river while a second company lands to the west to cut off retreating Japanese. A third company launches the main attack from jungle to the south.

21 August: Battle of the Tenaru. 900 Japanese under Colonel Ichiki attack 2nd Battalion, 1st Marines, at 'Alligator Creek'. In the ensuing action, Colonel Ichiki and his troops are defeated.

24 August: Battle of the Eastern Solomons. A Japanese attempt to reinforce Guadalcanal and block American interdiction of their naval forces. It is not a decisive naval battle, but the Japanese are pulled back.

8 September: Tasimboko Raid. Raiders and Parachutists strike the rear party of the Kawaguchi Brigade, destroying the Japanese supplies. The Marine force narrowly averts destruction by the timely arrival of supply ships mistaken by the Japanese as a reinforcing invasion force.

12-14 September: The Battle of 'Bloody Ridge'. The Japanese under Major General Kawaguchi initiate a three-pronged attack to retake Henderson Field. The attacks are disjointed and unsuccessful. The main attack is launched from the jungle south of a series of ridges south of Henderson Field; the two other attacks strike the Lunga Perimeter from the east and west.

23 September to 9 October: General Vandegrift initiates three operations to expand the Lunga Perimeter by attempting to push the Japanese from Matinkau; but the Japanese hold on the area proves too strong.

11 October: Battle of Cape Esperance. Mutual attempts to land reinforcements lead to a naval clash near Savo Island. The American Navy crosses the 'T' on the Japanese. The naval balance of power begins to shift toward the Americans.

23-26 October: Battle for Henderson Field. Major Japanese air-land-sea offensive. A three-pronged attack is planned, but attacks are not coordinated and are unsupported. The Japanese are defeated.

26 October: Battle of the Santa Cruz Islands. A Japanese victory by naval forces supporting the land operation.

12-13 November: First Naval Battle of Guadalcanal. An American cruiser force intercepts a Japanese battleship force. In the ensuing battle, Admirals Scott and Callaghan are killed, but the Japanese are turned back.

14-15 November: Second Naval Battle for Guadalcanal. American battleships turn back a Japanese naval force.

1-4 November: American western offensive. Elements of the 1st Marines cross the Matankau and push past Point Cruz.

2-3 November: American eastern offensive. Elements of the 7th Marines push the Japanese out of the Koli Point area.

5 November to 4 December: 2nd Raider Battalion ('Carlson's Raiders') conducts a historic patrol from Aola to Mount Austen.

30 November: Battle for Tassafaronga. A Japanese destroyer force dropping off supplies is driven away by American forces.

9 December: 1st Marine Division is relieved and sails from Guadalcanal.

15 December 1942 to 26 January 1943: The American Army engages in a bitter fight to drive the Japanese from the Mount Austen area.

13-17 January: The 2nd Marine Division launches an offensive that pushes the Japanese from the Point Cruz area.

22-3 January: The westward push continues and the Japanese are driven out of Kokumbona area.

1-8 February: The Japanese withdraw from Doma Cove on destroyers.

9 February 1943: Guadalcanal is secured by the Americans.

A GUIDE TO FURTHER READING

There is no single definitive book on the Guadalcanal campaign, although there are many claims to that effect. To assist the serious student of the campaign, many primary source books are listed below. This list in itself is not a complete one, but it covers the major works.

Coggins, Jack. *The Campaign for Guadalcanal*. New York, Doubleday and Company, 1972.

Craven, Wesley Frank and Cates, James Lea (eds). *The Pacific: Guadalcanal to Saipan. August 1942 to July 1944 – The Army Air Forces in World War II*, vol. 4. Chicago, University of Chicago Press, 1950. pp. 37-60.

Frank, Richard B. *Guadalcanal: The Definitive Account of the Land Battle*. Random House, New York, 1990, VII–800.

Ferguson, Robert Lawrence. *Guadalcanal, Island of Fire; Reflections of the 347th Fighter Group*. Tab Books, Blue Ridge Summit, 1987. VII–256.

Guadalcanal: Island Ordeal, Ballantine Books, Inc., New York 1971.

Guadalcanal Remembered. Doddimead & Company, New York 1982. V-332.

Hammel, Eric. *Guadalcanal: Starvation Island*. Crown Publishers, Inc, New York. V-478.

Hammel, Eric. *Guadalcanal, The Carrier Battles*. Crown Publishers, Inc., New York. V-505.

— *Guadalcanal, Decision at Sea*. Crown Publishers, Inc., New York. V-480.

Hough, Frank O., Lt Col USMCR, and Ludwig, Verle E., Maj USMC, and Shaw, Henry I., Jr. *Pearl Harbor to Guadalcanal – History of US Marine Corps Operations in World War II*, vol. 1. Washington, Historical Branch, G-3 Division, Headquarters, US Marine Corps, 1958. pp. 235-74.

Hoyt, Edwin P. *Guadalcanal*. Military Heritage Press, 1988. 1-322.

Isley, Jeter A. and Crowl, Philip A. *The US Marines and Amphibious War*. Princeton, Princeton University Press, 1951. pp. 72-165.

Johnston, Richard W. *Follow Me! The Story of the Second Marine Division in World War II*. New York, Random House, 1948. pp. 24-81.

Kilpatrick, C. W. *The Naval Night Battles in the Solomons*. Exposition Press of Florida, Inc., Pompano Beach, 1986. 1-170.

Leckie, Robert. *Challenge for the Pacific*. Doubleday and Company, Inc., New York, 1965. VII-372.

Edward, Lee Robert. *Victory at Guadalcanal*. Presidio Press, Novato, 1981. V-260.

McMillan, George. *The Old Breed: A History of the First Marine Division in World War II*. Washington, Infantry Journal Press, 1949. pp. 25–142.

Merillat, Herbert C., Capt USMCR. *The Island: A History of the Marines on Guadalcanal*. Houghton Mifflin Company, Boston 1944. VII-283.

Miller, John, Jr. *Guadalcanal: The First Offensive – The War in the Pacific – United States Army in World War II*. Washington, Historical Division, Department of the Army, 1949. xviii-413.

Morison, Samuel Eliot. *The Struggle for Guadalcanal – History of United States Naval Operations in World War II*. vol. v. Boston: Little, Brown and Company, 1950. xxii, 389 pp.

Sherrod, Robert. *History of Marine Corps Aviation in World War II*. Washington, Combat Forces Press, 1952. pp. 65-129.

Stone, John Scott. *Iron Bottom Bay*. Stone Enterprises, Pivarr, Texas, 1985. 1-384.

Tregreskis, Richard. *Guadalcanal Diary*. Random House, New York, 1943. 1-263.

Zimmerman, John L., Maj USMCR. *The Guadalcanal Campaign*. Washington, Historical Division, Headquarters, US Marine Corps, 1949. vi-189.

INDEX